FROM VIRTUE TO VICE

Food, Nutrition, and Culture

Series Editors: Rachel Black, Boston University
Leslie Carlin, University of Toronto

Published by Berghahn Books in Association with the Society for the Anthropology of Food and Nutrition (SAFN).

While eating is a biological necessity, the production, distribution, preparation, and consumption of food are all deeply culturally inscribed activities. Taking an anthropological perspective, this book series provides a forum for thought-provoking work on the bio-cultural, cultural, and social aspects of human nutrition and food habits. The books in this series present timely food-related scholarship intended for researchers, academics, students, and those involved in food policy.

Volume 1
GREEK WHISKY
The Localization of a Global Commodity
Tryfon Bampilis

Volume 2
RECONSTRUCTING OBESITY
The Meaning of Measures and the Measure of Meanings
Edited by Megan B. McCullough and Jessica A. Hardin

Volume 3
RE-ORIENTING CUISINE
East Asian Foodways in the Twenty-First Century
Edited by Kwang Ok Kim

Volume 4
FROM VIRTUE TO VICE
Negotiating Anorexia
Richard A. O'Connor and Penny Van Esterik

From Virtue to Vice

Negotiating Anorexia

Richard A. O'Connor and Penny Van Esterik

berghahn
NEW YORK · OXFORD
www.berghahnbooks.com

Published in 2015 by
Berghahn Books
www.berghahnbooks.com

© 2015 Richard A. O'Connor and Penny Van Esterik

All rights reserved.
Except for the quotation of short passages for the purposes
of criticism and review, no part of this book may be reproduced
in any form or by any means, electronic or mechanical,
including photocopying, recording, or any information
storage and retrieval system now known or to be invented,
without written permission of the publisher.

Library of Congress Cataloging-in-Publication Data

From virtue to vice : negotiating anorexia / by Richard A. O'Connor and Penny Van Esterik.
 p. ; cm. — (Food, nutrition, and culture ; volume 4)
Includes bibliographical references.
ISBN 978-1-78238-455-7 (hardback) — ISBN 978-1-78238-456-4 (ebook)
 I. Van Esterik, Penny, author. II. Title. III. Series: Food, nutrition, and culture ; v. 4.
 [DNLM: 1. Anorexia Nervosa—psychology—Personal Narratives.
 2. Anorexia Nervosa—etiology—Personal Narratives. WM 175]
 RC552.A5
 616.85'262—dc23
                            2014033557

British Library Cataloguing in Publication Data

A catalogue record for this book is available from the British Library.

Printed on acid-free paper.
ISBN: 978-1-78238-455-7 hardback
ISBN: 978-1-78238-456-4 ebook

To our daughters and our interviewees, who gave so generously of their time, wisdom, and experience.

Contents

Acknowledgments — ix

Introduction. Negotiating Anorexia — 1

Section I. The Disease: An Activity Disorder

Chapter 1. The Person: Working with Interviews — 17

Chapter 2. Medicine: Reworking Cartesian Knowledge — 29

Chapter 3. The Stories: Respecting Diversity — 38

Chapter 4. Bioculturalism: Seeing Holistically and Historically — 54

Chapter 5. Bodily Bent: The Individual's Constitution — 67

Chapter 6. The Activity: How Ascetic Doing Takes Over — 88

Chapter 7. The Core: Elementary Anorexia — 110

Section II. The Life Cycle: A Developmental Disorder

Chapter 8. Youth: How Adolescence Invites Anorexia — 121

Chapter 9. Coming of Age: Meeting an Imagined Real World — 134

Section III. Modern Traditions: Cultural Paths into Anorexia

Chapter 10. Virtuous Eating: A Modern Morality — 155

Chapter 11. The Conflicted Body: Sympathy and Control as
  Competing Virtues   167

Chapter 12. The Attractive Person: A Modern Appearance Ethic   176

Section IV. Recovery: Finding Balance

Chapter 13. Getting Out: Undoing Anorexia   189

Chapter 14. Staying Out: Redoing Life   205

Conclusion   214

References   219

Index   235

Acknowledgments

Anorexia hijacked our careers. We both had other plans. But when anorexia came crashing into Richard's life, he fought back with the tools of his trade. Then Penny joined him as co-conspirator. This horror, we declared, cannot stand. That gave us a project with a purpose.

We all seek purpose, but not everyone has the privilege to pursue it. We have been graced by supportive families and generous colleagues. Our research began when Amorn and Carolyn O'Connor thought that understanding our family crisis might help others. Since then their unfailing support has inspired our work. Amorn's two brothers contributed their academic expertise: as a philosopher and editor, John sharpened our arguments; and as a neuroscientist, Daniel kept biomedicine salient. We have also benefited from Chandra Van Esterik's support and John Van Esterik's critical skills and close involvement.

Many colleagues have graciously heard us out and contributed their expertise. We are particularly indebted to Gustaaf Houtman, Leif Jonsson, Deb McGrath, Donna Murdock, Jim Peterman, Woody Register, Jim Scott, Jerry Sullivan, and Nikki Tannenbaum. Leeat Granek's interviewing talents enriched our Toronto cases, and we thank Dagmar Gundersen for typing up interviews. Early in our work, Anne Becker, a major figure in eating disorder research, graciously welcomed our fledgling efforts. We are also deeply indebted to the insights of Rebecca Lester and Megan Warin, which have advanced our work. So too have a series of research grants from the University of the South as well as the encouragement of its students.

We have dedicated our book to our daughters as well as our interviewees. The volunteers who generously and courageously told us their stories gave us a gift we now pass on to readers.

Introduction
Negotiating Anorexia

To this day, I really don't know why, all of a sudden, I decided to have these weird eating patterns and not eat at all. Exercise so much. I think that I was just a perfectionist, just wanting to make my body even more perfect. But the thing is, a skeleton as a body really isn't perfect. So I don't know exactly what my train of thinking was.

Anorexia mystified Becca. The usual explanations did not work: she had no weight to lose ("*people would always tell me how skinny I was*"), no festering trauma, no troubled psyche. An upbeat person ("*I'm very energetic and very bubbly*"), she had a strong family ("*really loving and supportive parents*") and got along splendidly at school. A top athlete, she made excellent grades and had good friends. Life was going great. Then anorexia struck. Neither Becca nor her family nor her therapists knew why.

While a clinician would rightly diagnose atypical anorexia nervosa, Becca's case is not unusual. Many cases defy the type. Indeed, perhaps most do because the diagnostic criteria are insensitive to cultural differences (A. Becker 2007), indifferent to adolescent development (Lester 2011), compromised by comorbidities (Rosling et al. 2011: 309), and inadequate for research (Agras et al. 2004: 518). Yet the real problem is not an ill-conceived type. It is trying to type a moving target. Anorexia is a fluid *relationship* with us, its interlocutors, not a stable object in nature we can mark, measure, and conquer. What medicine struggles to do—pinpoint a single disease in nature—takes the wrong road.

We began interviewing the recovered like Becca, confident that anthropology knew the right road. Medicine, we thought, was missing anorexia's cultural logic. Now we question anthropology too. Its confidence in culture is misplaced: anorexia is a practice, not a culture; an activity, not a symbol; an accident, not a statement. What interpretive anthropology struggles to do—weave anorexia into culture's web of meaning—takes yet another wrong road.

Negotiating Anorexia

The right road engages anorexia as it is. That path opens when we give up pigeonholing to negotiate with what we encounter. That give-and-take is not new—it is how skilled clinicians engage difficult diseases (Lester 2007: 382; Luhrmann 2000), and how some cure anorexia even though medicine has no cure (Clinton 2010). These individual successes reveal an institutional failure: why does medicine not adopt what these successful practitioners do? Such an approach made other diseases curable. Why not anorexia? Lesser hurdles aside, the real impediment is epistemological: the negotiating that can cure anorexia undoes the subject/object divide. That Cartesian distinction—separating subjective opinion from objective fact—anchors biomedicine. It is how modern medicine trusts what it knows and justifies what it does. That is not easy to negotiate.

In organizing its efforts, medicine readily sees disease as a discrete object separate from the patient as a curable subject. How well that division works varies: it is at its best against an invading organism, like a parasite or bacteria; it gets befuddled by cancer, an affliction where the patient's defenses cannot distinguish a healthy cell (self or subject) from a cancerous one (other or object); and it is defeated by mental illnesses like anorexia that interweave person (self) and pathology (other).

Anorexia's self/other ambiguity throws medicine into an ethical and therapeutic minefield. Were the disease an invader, like an infection, doctor and patient would join forces. Yet anorexia is a civil war. The aggressor is the sufferer's will, a tyrant that starves her body. Treatment cannot excise her will like a tumor and get a healthy person back. Worse, intervening can feed a will fed on opposition. Here, where curing-by-conquest medicine fails, negotiating beats warring.

Negotiating adapts to an ecological truth: humans are immersed interactively in nature, so we cannot change our doings and surroundings without also changing ourselves. An anorexic person[1] tries to deny that truth. Aiming to change only her body, she accidentally changes her very being. Treatment faces the same truth. Both sufferer and caregiver get caught up in what Bateson (2000: 313, 315) would call "an unusually disastrous variant" of Cartesian dualism. When one part of an "internally interactive system" tries to assert a "unilateral control over the remainder," its victories die quickly.

Negotiating Disciplines

Negotiating also adapts to the intellectual truth that disciplines divide up knowledge and proselytize for their piece. That cuts up anorexia, making one syndrome many—an emaciated patient to a physician, brain circuitry to a neuroscientist, socioeconomic correlates to an epidemiologist, lived morality to a philosopher, freelance asceticism to an anthropologist. Who has it right? That is the wrong question. It is better to keep all this useful knowledge in play. To do that we recognize anorexia's multiplicity and, by negotiating disciplinary differences, consider what biomedicine, the clinic and anthropology each has to offer.

What Biomedicine Offers. By dividing spirit from matter, Descartes made the mother distinction that now breeds endless others: mind vs. body, religion vs. science, subject vs. object, nurture vs. nature, culture vs. biology—and many, many more. And each of these world-halving distinctions creates its own lesser world (e.g., biology as a discrete realm) that itself gets divided again and again (e.g., biology into botany and molecular biology). Following that logic, biomedicine breaks any disease apart, expecting to find its cause amid the pieces. That misses anorexia fourfold.

First, breaking up anorexia's mind-with-body oneness makes the disease mental *or* physical, nurture *or* nature, culture *or* biology—or some mix of these supposedly separable entities. Yet anorexia is a biocultural hybrid that is inherently inseparable along mind/body lines. To be sure, the disease is divisible—later we will describe how activity and constitution function as parts—but biomedicine force-fits it into Cartesian dualism. Like a frog halved with a meat cleaver, its pieces do not add up, and they hide how the organism actually works.

Second, life's surface spawns anorexia, but modern medicine posits underlying causes. That puts Plato's rationalism over Aristotle's empiricism, the clinician's logic over the sufferer's experience, and anorexia's true nature *behind* appearances. We disagree. The anorexic's practices and feelings create anorexia. It is the offspring of a conspicuous activity, not a symptom of some deeper hidden disorder.

Third, while anorexia arises through the relation of its parts, medical specialization presumes one or another separate part is causal. So the cause is mental or nutritional or genetic or hormonal. Here relentless reductionism breaks anorexia's whole into ever-smaller pieces, confident that the pathology is one bad piece or another. Yet that is like separating hydrogen from oxygen to study water—what you are studying vanishes. As a whole, anorexia is greater than the sum of its parts.

Fourth, while moral sentiments drive anorexia, modern medicine divorces health from morality. That is a point of secular pride. In this ontology, where humans become amoral pragmatists, exposing the anorexic's self-serving motives (beauty, power, attention, resisting adulthood) explains or even cures the disease. Yet this misunderstands not just the sufferer but our species. Humans evolved out of group life, so our healthy functioning gives us a moral sensibility that we can neither fully control nor easily explain. When medicine posits amoral motives instead, it makes anorexia's roots and resilience incomprehensible.

The logics we have just described—dualism, rationalism, reductionism, secularism—distort anorexia. A purist might thus dismiss this medical knowledge as inherently flawed. But that would be a waste. Knowing the flaw, we can make allowances to salvage findings. That is what clinicians do every day.

What the Clinic Offers. A single profession, modern medicine leads one life in healing and another in research. Ideally the two are complements, or research serves the clinic. In practice, however, the two pull in different directions: where research fragments to analyze, the clinic connects to treat; researchers seek universals while healers address variety; and whereas the lab's one truth is replicable, the clinic's bottom line is whatever cures.

With anorexia the lab often follows its logic rather than the clinic's needs. Ever more specialized, today's research gets farther and farther from the clinic's real people. Take a top journal and try to find a three-dimensional sufferer, someone with values and agency, family and friends. Instead you find systematic depersonalization. The person vanishes into indices and averages. Lost too are clinical successes that lack controls. Take the work of Louis Mogul. A practicing clinician, his 1980 article connected anorexia to asceticism and adolescence just as we have. In 2001, when O'Connor spoke to eating disorder clinicians where Mogul once practiced, no one had even heard of him. His clinical breakthrough—approaching anorexics as ascetics—had vanished. Apparently adolescence and asceticism were too big and nebulous for the lab. Here research fails to engage anorexia as it is, as the clinic does every day.

What Anthropology Offers. Anthropology prides itself on engaging reality as it is. Seeing wholes in life, the field studies them naturalistically. Culture, the whole that distinguishes the discipline, is just one among many. Here, as a theory, holism posits life's interconnectedness. Instead of isolating elements as lab logic does, it insists on "seeing any characteristic in terms of others" (Durrenberger 1996: 367). Take the strict dieting called restricting. Our informants wove that practice into cultural notions of virtue, achieving, progress, and propriety. In their lives restricting was being good. How ironic then, that outsiders would suppose it was *looking* good! Of course that is how reductionism distorts: by isolating anorexia, stripping away the context that explains it, the disease becomes an inkblot open to any interpretation. To avoid such grievous errors, anthropologists apply holism religiously. It is proper procedure, a method to use everywhere rather than just a theory to apply selectively.

Necessary and useful as holism is, anthropology overuses it. Because holism virtually "defines anthropology as a discipline" (Durrenberger 1996: 367), professionals find the interconnectedness in every case. Sometimes that works (e.g., holism shows anorexia's restricting has wider moral meanings); other times it does not (e.g., as an activity the syndrome stands alone and is not cultural). To analyze anorexia incisively, we therefore apply holism selectively rather than categorically.

In this study the critical whole is the person. To get at that reality we interviewed recovered anorexics to get their insider perspective. Taking a person-centered approach, we studied life-cycle, social, and cultural impacts holistically and treated conventional biomedical knowledge discursively, using it to fill in the larger holistic picture.

Reworking Descartes. Despite their different methods, biomedicine, the clinic, and anthropology get at related truths. So medicine's lab research and anthropology's fieldwork are often compatible. Only when one method's hardliners exclude other ways can we not learn from each other.

Had medicine never isolated anorexia, we would know too little to even begin this book. But since isolating has found no cure, now we should try contextualizing. To that end we rework Cartesian evidence freely, seeing what the facts can say about the biocultural realities the context suggests. So while we analyze our interviews naturalistically, seeking operant wholes, we relate those findings to biomedical knowledge. We might devote a book to how biomedicine distorts anorexia, but that will not cure anyone. What is needed instead—or at least what anthropology can offer—is to use biomedical knowledge constructively rather than just deconstructing its claims.

Context and Emergence

Anthropology offers the clinic and biomedicine a rich sense of life's interconnectedness. That holistic sensibility, the fruit of culture-crossing fieldwork, may not suit all maladies, but it is vital for studying anorexia. Here, to use holism incisively, we distinguish context from emergence. We have just said restricting (a behavior) is closely connected to virtue and achieving (cultural notions). If these traits and restricting are simply *associated*, leaving their differences unresolved and other connections intact, then here holism adds only context. Yet should these traits coalesce into a coherent lifestyle—if the truly virtuous and achieving must restrict eating—then these traits and behavior *integrate* with each other and thereby separate from their erstwhile surroundings. That closure creates a new, lesser whole that stands apart from its once wider web. That is emergence.

The Principle of Emergence. Characterized as "the whole is greater than the sum of its parts," emergence is when otherwise discrete elements (parts) integrate into a system (the whole) that takes on a character all its own. Emergence recognizes how life organizes itself in complex systems within systems, a truth that ecology stresses. Called by various names,[2] ordinary thought uses emergence no less than science does. Take the popular notion of personality. That idea says a person has a distinctive enduring style (a personality—the whole) quite apart from ever-changing events (the parts) that make up a life. That explains how the same event (e.g., death of a parent) can cripple one person, empower another, leave yet a third unmoved, and so on. So an event's impact (how it functions in the person's life) depends on the emergent nature of the whole (the personality), not the universal nature of that part (all deaths are troubling). That upends reductionism: what happens (the response to death) cannot be reduced to the part (the death itself) because its impact depends on the emergent whole (the personality).

Anorexia as Emergent. Emergence makes anorexia out of willful starving. Someone who once ate freely begins to feel hunger as weakness and fasting as strength until starving feels virtuous and rewarding.[3] Once those associations form, then like any brain pathway, they grow quicker and surer with use. An ascetic practice (the whole) thereby comes to generate the thoughts and feelings (the parts) that make the practice increasingly compelling and eventually inescapable. Once that loop closes, little else matters. Loved ones' pleas, medical interventions, and even one's own hesitations and bodily needs are all outside the loop, irrelevant to the system.

Once closed, this deadly loop is exceedingly hard to break. How does a mere arrangement of parts overcome all manner of interventions? Were anorexia an invading organism, the answer would be obvious—it is fighting for its life. Indeed, that captures how vigorously and ingeniously the syndrome resists intrusions. Yet the disease is neither literally alive nor actually alien. Whence then such remarkable powers? There are reductive and emergent answers. The reductive ones posit some prior biological, psychological, or cultural dysfunction behind the starving; then, only curing that underlying problem will stop the disease. The emergent answer says the cause is *in* what is immediately apparent: sustained starving reorganizes the person bioculturally into a starver. There need be no deeper problem.

Were it a contest, the emergent answer would win on two principles. One is "first do no harm": in presuming a hidden pathology it cannot specify, the reductive answer unleashes suspicions that harm sufferers and their families (e.g., Vander Ven and Vander Ven 2003; Way 1995). The other principle is Occam's razor: reductionism's long, tenuous causal chain supposes unknown links to distant causes in an unknowable past, whereas for emergence the causal chain is short and clear, invoking direct links to immediate causes in a known present. All else equal, that makes emergence better science than reductionism (O'Connor and Van Esterik 2008).

Yet all else is not equal. Our evidence supports emergence strongly. Every interviewee kept an ascetic practice. That common denominator quite plausibly turned them into ascetics—you become what you do. Where there were deeper problems, no one attributed recovery to their resolution. Indeed, nothing we heard suggests underlying biological, psychological, or cultural causes overpowered the person.

Clinical experience also supports emergence. Reductionism assumes a simple mechanical system with linear response, which would make anorexia easy to treat: if the syndrome is nothing but the sum of its parts, removing the right element should cure the disease. Yet endless efforts have manipulated anorexia's every imaginable aspect, all to no avail. That failure is diagnostic. So too, small inputs (e.g., dieting) can produce large results (the syndrome, an entirely new way of life) while big inputs (major interventions like hospitalization) can have little or no result (e.g., many relapse after release), pointing to the workings of a complex non-linear system (Martin 1994). As an emergent whole it has great autonomy and resilience.

An Activity Disorder

What pulls a person's parts into an anorexic whole? Anorexia taps the human capacity to get lost in a challenging activity. Here, the syndrome develops an inner gravity, pulling the actor in an ever-expanding involvement. Bit by bit, the ascetic practice rises to meet ever-greater challenges (e.g., cut another hundred calories, run a mile more) until starving becomes "not a 'state of mind' . . . but rather a state of the body" (Bourdieu 1990: 68). Then the person goes wherever the activity takes her. Leaving family, friends, and reason behind, she withdraws to an island of inner involvement where spirit (one's self, will, identity) gets entangled in matter (one's body, the food one does and does not eat), creating a biocultural hybrid that takes on a life of its own. Because that life develops out of starving and exercising as activities, we call anorexia an activity disorder.

While the activity creates the disease, two other realities converge to make that happen. One is local virtue: anorexics-to-be reorient their lives through an act of moral willing (Mattingly 2010) that exaggerates surrounding moral discourses (achieving, control, healthy eating).[4] The other converging reality is the person's constitution: while growing up, people who later develop anorexia show remarkable capacities for sympathy, self-denial, and achieving. Taken together, these three realities—activity, virtue, and constitution—interact to spawn a fourth reality, anorexia. What typically pushes the three together is adolescence.

A Developmental Disorder

Though many cultures orchestrate how children become adults, modernity makes adolescent growth a do-it-yourself project. Anorexia is one way it gets done wrong.[5]

Anorexia as Misdirected Development. Ideally adolescence builds on the past to open the future. To quote Erikson (1964: 91), there should be "a progressive continuity between that which [the young person] has come to be during . . . childhood and that which he promises to become . . . between that which he conceives himself to be and that which he perceives others to see in him and to expect of him." That is how adolescence expands outward, opening doors. Anorexia goes the opposite way: life collapses into a narrow goal-directed domain (restricted eating, intensive training, obsessively healthy living) where the person overdoes the regulatory virtues (self-denial, self-control, perfectionism) that success requires. Our interviewees were successful children, suggesting their well-developed regulatory strength. Adolescence then exaggerates this controlling. Like a coup, one moralistic faction seizes the person and tyrannizes the rest with its puritanical control and virtue.

What causes the coup? Anorexics grow up as conspicuously good children (Bruch 1962: 192). Then, when youth culture invites wrongdoing, moralistic over-controlling would seem to *defend* a virtuous self against temptation—at least, that is what the Cartesian individual/society opposition supposes. Yet the same behavior might as readily follow from an individual/society synergy where anorexia *expresses* who you are by the values you live (discipline, self-denial, willpower, toughness, individuality, relentless effort). Here anorexia would be a mechanism of identity rather than defense.

Is anorexia defensive or expressive? In theory defense withdraws in weakness from surroundings that the expressive engages in strength. In practice all real cases are mixed and ambiguous (the anorexic withdraws *and* engages, is weak *and* strong). Judging by the clinical literature, where troubles abound (sexual abuse, parental death, dysfunctional parenting, etc.), anorexia is defensive: controlling eating rescues an out-of-control life. Although that fits a few cases in our sample, we more often found expressive anorexia: our interviewees were asserting their identity and values as youth do. That positions anorexia in adolescent development gone wrong.

Modernity's Misdirecting Developments. Whereas defensive anorexia might occur in any place or day, expressive anorexia has distinctively modern roots. In the late nineteenth century, as rapid social change eroded customs that once organized everyday life, choice expanded rapidly. In that openness two movements arose that now invite eating disorders. One is sports: some cases in our sample develop directly out of athletics, and every one exemplifies the achieving, toughness, and relentless effort that contemporary sports inculcate. The other movement, virtuous eating, counters declining customs with stricter eating and bodily control. In this "compensatory control," restrained eating takes on "independent moral functions, denoting good character" and makes dieting "a moral statement at a time when more conventional statements have less meaning" (Stearns 1997: 64, 247).

Is this moralistic eating some cult? Now widespread, virtuous eating typifies the upper middle class and is so well established that Giordano (2005: 8–9) can attribute eating disorders to "the consistent expression of values that have ancient roots in Western culture." As such these "are not the *symptom of an underlying mental disorder.* . . . They are . . . ordinary morality, which is just being *taken seriously.*"

Repositioning Anorexia

Explaining anorexia by its surroundings challenges three schools supposing darker, deeper or wider causes. One school posits a prior trauma. Early on that trauma was distinctive—malignant mothering, a cold father, sexual abuse—but evidence kept overturning specifics; by now any trauma will do. When someone like Becca objects, insisting her prior life was happy, she gets told she is "in denial." We believe Becca: our evidence roots anorexia in a present practice, not prior trauma.

A second school makes anorexia a woman's disease. That forgets male anorexics, perhaps one in three (Woodside et al. 2001), and dismisses cases that originate in athletics, healthy eating or self-improvement—all gender-neutral practices. True, anorexia strikes more women than men, but then its gateway practices involve women more than men. Here anorexia is no more a woman's disease than the gender ratio reversed (Keyes et al. 2008: 25) makes alcoholism a man's disease. What is gendered is the entry, not the disease.

A third approach, biomedicine, now attributes anorexia to a "multifactoral" convergence of causes (A. Becker et al. 2004; Collier and Treasure 2004). That captures an important truth, for a host of factors do combine to make anorexia. But what we have found, emergence, says differing parts (e.g., different personalities, opposite motives, various events, disparate social situations) can make the same anorexic whole. What is decisive is the activity, not the ingredients. In looking outside the activity, factor analysis overlooks the internal gravity that makes the disease.

Negotiating Knowledge and Theory

Opening with Becca's type-defying case highlighted how current thinking fails to address anorexia as it is. That failure, we argue, is ultimately epistemological: contemporary Cartesian dualism hides the ways the disease works. As anorexia will not change to suit us, our epistemology must change to suit it.

A Holistic Epistemology. For Descartes, knowledge begins by separating mind from body. By setting humans apart from nature, that dualism makes us subjects who can see and study the world as an object. For Bateson (2000) that separateness is illusory. Humans are always in the world. In fact, that immersion is how we can know life empirically even as we live it ecologically. In that oneness, where mind and body constitute each other, humans are historically contingent biocultural wholes, hybrids that arise from and then interact with their surroundings. That is true for a single person or our entire species, a small group or a vast civilization. At any level, humans move in nature as it moves in us. Bateson discerned this all-embracing ecology decades ago, Goldschmidt (2006) recently applied it to nurture, and we now apply it to anorexia.

How do we get from this sweeping epistemology to anorexia's particularities? Theory builds bridges. In theorizing we have no stake in any particular theory. All we care about is making sense of three bodies of evidence. Our primary body is what our interviewees said and did. Our secondary ones are the biomedical literature and the following anthropological findings:

- Contemporary eating can evoke pride, shame, guilt, or anxiety in a distinctively modern moral discourse (Counihan 1999; Mintz 1993) that invites eating disorders.
- Culture-of-thinness explanations fail in the field. Any dieting done for looks pales beside anorexics' religious meanings and moral motives (Banks 1992, 1996, 1997; Lester 1999; O'Connor 2000). These enact local scripts (Gooldin 2008; Lester 2007; Pike and Borovoy 2004), not media manipulations.
- An anorexic practice does not enact the wider culture directly but creates its own micro-worlds out of embodied experience (Gooldin 2008; Shohet 2007; Warin 2010) and Foucauldian technologies of self (Lester 1997).
- Studying anorexia ethnographically questions misplaced medicalization (O'Connor and Van Esterik 2008) and shows how clinical settings can reproduce the disorder they aim to cure (Gremillion 2003; Lester 2007; Shohet 2007) or create new relationships that stabilize the disease (Warin 2005, 2006).

In applying these and other findings we are empirical pragmatists: as empiricists we anchor anorexia in an observable activity and its concrete consequences; and as pragmatists we act like Lévi-Strauss's (1966) bricoleur, a French handyman who makes do with whatever is at hand to fashion something workable. Here, culling evidence widely, we negotiate theory pragmatically.

Pragmatic Theorizing. Like other complex diseases, anorexia gives ambiguous evidence. As a relationship with researchers that changes as their queries do, the syndrome is too fluid and various for any single explanation. That puts theorizing at a crossroads. Is one explanation better than many? Is our goal epistemological consistency or empirical engagement? To balance the two we work within a biocultural epistemology while shifting theory and method as anorexia's particulars do.

Meaning as Hermeneutics: In today's anthropology, culture as meaning neatly captures anorexia's moral impetus and its projects of virtuous self-improvement (dieting, training, healthy eating, bodily control). It does not, however, explain the pathology. As we will see, anorexia's cause is an activity, *not* culture; what unfolds is accidental, not symbolic; and the pathology's engine is experience, not meaning.

Experience as Phenomenology: Anorexia develops out of what anorexics experience. To get at this reality we built on the phenomenology of Bourdieu, Merleau-Ponty and Csordas. Bourdieu (1990) captured how starving, like any serious practice, follows its own internal logic. From Merleau-Ponty (1964) we learned how anorexia's sympathies and mis-development can have ontogenetic origins. And Csordas's (1994: vii) cultural phenomenology, by "synthesizing the immediacy of embodied experience with the multiplicity of cultural meaning," showed how adolescence, eating, the body, and appearance are all discourses that energize anorexia.

History as Bioculturalism: Hermeneutics unlocks meaning as phenomenology does experience, but neither theory can account for anorexia's persistence. Bioculturalism does. It theorizes how the symbolic and the physiological join synergistically to create a hybrid that then lives on. Like any emergent whole, it persists by adapting to changing conditions. Indeed, once established, the disorder makes the meanings and experiences that keep it going. That is the horror—ending what began the disorder need not end the affliction.

Cross-Activity Comparison: Our pragmatic theorizing risks cherry-picking. While hermeneutics, phenomenology, and bioculturalism each has its own rigor, moving between the three allows us to pick and choose what we explain. Are we choosing what fits our argument and ignoring the rest? After all, by saying that anorexia is an activity disorder and misdirected development, we make general claims about activities and development. Can we test these holistically? In anthropology comparing cultures usually does that cross-checking, but that will not work if anorexia's context is an activity, not a culture. What rigor demands, then, is comparing activities.

Compare three activities—monasticism, elite athletics and breastfeeding. All irreversibly change the person, altering one's very being as anorexia does. Like anorexia, each is a clearly bounded, well-focused, demanding activity that, when pursued wholeheartedly, remakes the person in its image. How? All create their own tight little world within the larger looser one, pulling the person away from existing persona and into a new way of life. Here monasticism and elite athletics share anorexia's unbending asceticism. Monk, top athlete or anorexic—all three live by strict regimens that grow to organize every moment of every day. All three also find that just working to get better tightens rules and kills compromises. Then, when the regimen demands more than the body should bear, a devotee pushes through pain to be a better person morally (monks) or competitively (athletes) or both (anorexics).

Breastfeeding is the odd activity out. It is as commonplace as the others are exceptional, as life-affirming as they are life-denying. Yet breastfeeding enacts developmental change just as our interviewees' mis-development does. In both cases that change is a life-cycle transition that our era no longer celebrates or even facilitates. Worse, modernity has shattered customs that once enabled breastfeeding and socialized eating. Worse still, that loss has opened both activities to the over-controlling and endless perfectionism that incites anorexia and impedes breastfeeding (O'Connor and Van Esterik 2012). Our companion volume, *The Dance of Nurture: Embodying Infant Feeding*, further unpacks the biocultural processes that make breastfeeding life-giving and anorexia life-taking.

The Plan of the Book

Where biomedicine isolates anorexia and thereby narrows it, our project contextualizes and thereby widens it. Section I studies the disease in itself. It explores how quite various motives initiate the disease, which then follows its own inner logic. Over time, restricted eating and excessive exercise bootstrap the actor into anorexia as a self-sustaining disease. Section II then looks at how adolescence and coming of age evoke an anorexic response. That response taps traditions of virtuous eating, bodily discipline, and appearance that Section III explores as the anorexic's ascetic response to modern life. In Section IV the recovered tell us how they escaped anorexia and stay healthy.

Notes

1. Some prefer "anorexic person" to "anorexic," distinguishing the person from the disease. We use the longer phrasing occasionally as a reminder that we are talking about whole people who happen to be anorexic. Why not drop the dubious term altogether? Our project would suffer. Imperfect as it is, anorexic is clear and succinct. It eliminates a distinction that does not always matter to advance an argument that does.
2. Our term, emergence, comes from biology. The principle goes by Gestalt in psychology and metaphysical holism in philosophy. It is fundamental to hermeneutics, systems theory, chaos theory, and anthropology's holism.
3. In studying Ethiopian hermits, Bushell (1995: 554, 560) found that after the initial discomfort, fasting can lead to "disappearance of the pain, discomfort, and dysphoria of hunger, and their replacement with feelings of well-being, tranquility, and even euphoria." Apparently ascetic practice reprograms the person's drive/reward architecture, uncoupling "the (most probably endogenous opioid-mediated) experience of reward from the object of reward." Not eating then produces the rewarding experience once gained from eating.

4. Mattingly's phrase captures how self-improvement projects can end up as anorexia. Moral willing would seem to exercise a somatic mode of attention (Csordas 1993) and, with success, progressively reshape one's identity (Holland and Eisenhart 1990).
5. A. Becker et al. (2004: 82) saw "strong evidence" for psycho-developmental factors in anorexia's etiology. Collier and Treasure (2004) saw developmental and biological explanations displacing social and cultural ones.

SECTION

I

The Disease
An Activity Disorder

Modern medicine isolates disease. Can we isolate anorexia? Yes and no. Anorexia is not a stable object that can be fixed in space and time. Yet as a pattern that persists, changing doggedly as the sufferer does, anorexia has continuity over space and time. By tracing that integrity within and across cases, we can isolate anorexia conceptually if not physically.

Section I isolates anorexia's core. Using different bodies of evidence, each chapter rigorously pursues a different angle. One by one these angles converge on a single conclusion: anorexia begins in an ascetic activity (dieting, exercising, healthy eating) that takes on a biocultural life (an integrity) of its own. The activity thereby swallows the actor, leaving no one to stop or even control the ascetic practices. Anorexia need have no deeper or darker cause.

CHAPTER 1

The Person
Working with Interviews

How did the person disappear from anorexia? In the 1870s, when Gull and Lasègue first isolated the disease, the patient held center stage; and in the 1960s, when Bruch began the body image era, case studies were common. But they are not today—not in top journals, anyway. As research specializes, indices displace individuals, and correlations replace context. Articles apply tests built on other tests built on samples built to generalize, getting ever farther from the whole that makes a person.

Our study puts the person back in anorexia. In this chapter, working outward from how one person remembers anorexia, we develop five "frames for knowing" that respect yet go beyond the individual's story. What results—five bodies of knowledge—studies anorexia holistically and rigorously yet pluralistically.

Seeking the Anorexic's Perspective

When we began our research, biomedicine rarely studied how sufferers experienced anorexia.[1] Interviews, we knew, could fill a glaring gap. Yet could we get the anorexic's perspective? Working with practicing anorexics was neither practical (anorexics are notoriously secretive) nor ethical (we are not clinicians). Interviewing the recovered was the best we could do. Was it good enough? We went ahead with trepidation.[2]

We taped and transcribed in-depth interviews with twenty-two recovered anorexics, fifteen in Tennessee and seven in Toronto.[3] In our Tennessee set, all but one were current or former students at a small, selective liberal arts college in rural Tennessee (Sewanee: The University of the South), and all but two grew up in the southern United States. The Toronto set, all Canadians, were recruited through a large cosmopolitan university (York University), and their families ranged from long established to recently immigrated. All interviewees were uncompensated volunteers who graciously gave their time to advance our research.

Interviews began by saying, in effect, "Anorexia is poorly understood. We need your help to solves its mysteries." Everyone embraced that challenge. We solicited this as "your story" and asked to hear it "as if you were telling a friend." Lasting one hour to over two, interviews began with background queries, next heard each story as a whole, and then asked follow-up questions to recover what the narrative lost, slighted or hid.

Approached as seasoned experts, our informants spoke freely from experience, using "narrative as a reflexive, generative, and flexible mode of thinking" (Garro 2000: 77). Sometimes they came across as reporters just getting the facts right, other times as guides explaining local ways to an outsider, and still other times as fellow detectives sharing clues to what happened. Most openly welcomed the opportunity to tell their story, and everyone appeared to appreciate having a sympathetic, knowledgeable listener to hear it all. Tentative at the start, sessions took on a cathartic character.

Interviewees remembered anorexia's landscape well but found its mentality elusive. So Francesca initially has "*a hard time getting back into the mindset*," but once she does, "*it definitely brings me right back to that place.*" Practices were clearer than beliefs. We expected to get inside an insidious cult. What we heard instead sounded more like an addictive sport. Interviewees spoke like retired Olympians, now putting their playing days in perspective. That past, a lapsed practice, was well remembered and readily described. Not so the mindset. What we heard was quite conventional. Any distinctive beliefs were either lost or never mattered much.

We discovered that the recovered have insights that the anorexic's perspective precludes. Worried that recovery had distorted the past, we initially thought we would have to factor out how the recovered now saw their illness. Yet they taught us three larger lessons. First, the morbid *beliefs* we struggled to reconstruct did not explain anything new. Anyone familiar with dieting or training already knew what our interviewees recalled. Second, the recovered knew the *practices* that had once constituted their anorexia. Here we needed to factor their viewpoint in, not out. Third, anorexia was two diseases in one. Center stage struts the syndrome clinicians battle directly, an ontological reality we might call "the disease of the moment." Backstage hides another affliction, an ontogenetic reality we shall call "mis-development." The latter, a missing piece of anorexia's puzzle, is a life-course reality where the recovered can tutor us all.

Remembering Anorexia

Our interviews centered around each person's story. These will be told one by one over several chapters. Composed in recovery, these narratives typically incorporate therapy's lessons, largely work within cultural as well as popular expectations, and tailor the experience to fit what illness stories can and should say (A.

Frank 1995; Wikan 2000). Such stories give clues to what happened, but they cannot resurrect the past. What they can do—and do quite well—is capture the actor's agency while putting anorexia in life-course perspective. We begin with O'Connor's daughter, whose anorexia began early in adolescence and was completely cured by her sixteenth birthday. Interviewed at nineteen by Van Esterik, this is Amorn's story in her own words.[4]

> Let me begin by saying how it started. I did gymnastics at the age of three to eleven, then quit for middle school. That was a very vulnerable time in my life. I think it is for everyone. Gymnastics was all I'd really known. I tried different sports to fill the gap, but nothing really—I wasn't particularly good at any one of them. I guess I wanted to be good like I was at gymnastics. Gymnastics was my identity, how people knew me. It's how I identified myself and then all of sudden that wasn't there at a very crucial, critical age. So there was an emptiness, a great big void inside. In school there was a lot of low self-esteem provoked by my peers. I think all that came together. That time in my life—beginning to go through adolescence—all of a sudden my body started to change and it felt really uncomfortable.
>
> That summer I started restricting. It's not like one day I just said, "I'm going to go on a diet." I never called it a diet. I just started restricting my food and then it became a cycle. It started with being obsessed with fat calories and that went on for a while and then I didn't want to eat sweets and then it just eventually was no longer about the food at all. It was more about control I was exerting over myself. That's how it started.
>
> I started to restrict my lunches, eating things that felt simple, like just cereal or toast instead of the entrées. An entrée you don't know what's in it. Eating simple foods lessens that pressure. Then eventually I ended up not going to lunch at all. I'd make up excuses that I was going to the library, that I'd already eaten lunch. So I began to lie to my friends. What I'd do is, I'd go hide in the library and study. I became a very good student that year. That was ninth grade.
>
> I realized I could get away with not eating breakfast before school. Then I was like, "Well, I set that standard" and then I'd try not eating a lunch and then I could get away with that. So the only meal I'd eat would be dinner and it went on and on like that. It was kind of self-denial: what can I get away with, like denying myself the most of, I guess. Denial and weakness for goals. The weaker I could make myself, the better I felt. So the fewer meals I ate, the weaker I'd get. The goal wasn't the pounds. When I'd see that I weighed ninety-nine pounds, I'd be like, "Oh, I wonder if I can get down to ninety-five" but it wasn't the weight, the pounds.
>
> I stopped hanging out with friends altogether. My life was just waking up and going to school. I'd just look forward to being able to go home—no connection with my friends, although they were worried about me and always asking concerned questions. But I just tried to hide as much as I could and not make myself available—that was a connection to a life I was trying to deny or give up. The more that

I could just be in my own little world, the more I felt I could control what I wanted to control. I definitely became this very withdrawn person. I didn't know who I was. I lied to all my friends. Lied to my family about having eaten. Things like that. My life became very secretive and very isolated.

In the beginning I felt powerful. Then once it took over I just felt completely out of control and helpless. I don't know that I chose, "Well, anorexia is going to replace gymnastics," but looking back on my life, anorexia is what replaced that. It became my identity. It became how I related to the world, even in a non-existent kind of way. It became how I knew myself and a way to succeed in something.

First Frame: The Story in Itself

A generation ago medicine slighted personal stories. A story like Amorn's was too subjective, merely anecdotal, superficial. Medicine sought deeper causes, dismissing details to get at the underlying disease. That attitude lives on, but now many clinicians value stories (Coles 1989). So too do social scientists. Humans, we suppose, spin webs of meaning. Her story does double duty: it is at once a sweeping metaphor that captures life's weblike coherence, and a specific tool to open its inner logic.

For us a story is a frame for knowing. Instead of seeing *through* a story reductively, our method sees *with* stories (as a lens or perspective) or *within* them (as a meaningful context). Each story stands on its own—it is that person's view of his or her illness and is thus complete. We grant that stories can hide other truths, but for our purposes whatever is missing, mistaken, or hidden is just part of a pattern that we understand holistically rather than reductively.

Amorn's story puts anorexia in life-cycle perspective. She attributes her illness to adolescence. She says that once, and her story's details say it repeatedly: its themes (identity, peers) are adolescent hotspots, her actions (testing limits as self-discovery) typify adolescence, and her chosen path (making self and body into a project) is how many teens mature. We happen to agree with her and found adolescence in every story we heard, but the larger point is less that conclusion than her coherence. She might have given us scattered ideas lacking theme or closure. What we got instead—a clear coherence that came freely—justifies taking stories seriously. Our other interviews were much the same.

Second Frame: The Setting as Structure

One by one these stories put anorexia in the actor's hands. Are they right? Many structural explanations disagree. Bordo (1997), for example, says anorexia is "the crystallization of a culture" that abuses women. Is structure then a better explanation than agency? That particular structural explanation is not better—it is theoretically naive, methodologically flawed, empirically unfounded, historically incoherent.[5] Yet our interviews do suggest a local structure/agency interplay. Here, acting as "pattern finder" rather than "pattern maker" (Spence 1982: 293), we found four biocultural complexes.

- ***Lifeworld:*** When Amorn describes *"a great big void inside"* and then *"the weaker I could make myself the better I felt,"* she recalls her life-world before and then within anorexia. Like a snapshot, each is a subjective, actor-centered view of the person's social and cultural surroundings. It is in this larger setting that anorexia gets its moral impetus as achieving, self-improvement, discipline, willpower, or control—all virtues in their lifeworld.
- ***Life cycle:*** When Amorn remembers, *"That was a very vulnerable time in my life,"* she takes a life-cycle perspective (cf. Erikson 1971). Where lifeworld takes a moment's snapshot, lifecycle plays a feature-length film. Hindsight that puts Amorn's anorexia in life-cycle perspective cannot replace knowing how she felt at the time. We need both.
- ***Constitution:*** A gymnast growing up, Amorn built body and self—her constitution—around her sport's physical toughness, mental courage, and work ethic. In our usage constitution is biography, character, habit, and body all rolled into one. Early in life, as mind and body interact and interweave, a unique constitution arises. The result, a hybrid of biology and culture, begins epigenetically and progressively takes on a momentum that gives us our distinctive dispositions. So none come cold to anorexia. All arrive constitutionally disposed for or against the disease.
- ***The Activity:*** Amorn started restricting only to have that activity take control (*"it took over"*). As she set standards, met them, and then raised the bar, her involvement grew (Holland and Eisenhart 1990). It *"became a cycle,"* redefining who she was (anorexia *"became my identity"*). In effect, she got caught up in restricting's inner logic, just as a sport or career can become all-absorbing. Once an activity takes hold, prior motives fade (it was *"no longer about the food"*). Then the activity—in this instance anorexia—creates all the thoughts, feelings, and motives (e.g., *"control"*) it needs to sustain itself. That loop swallows the actor in the activity.

These four complexes are influential but not determining. Although their combined structural weight looks overwhelming, actors can and indeed must play one against another. For example, getting into an activity takes one out of the surrounding lifeworld. So whether agency is sought or not, the actor must choose. Given how anorexia activates these irreconcilable structures, the syndrome itself is irreducibly plural.

Third Frame: The Set of Stories

Amorn's story stands on its own, but we must also weigh her words against similar stories. This is our third frame—the set of interviews. It builds on the others: our first frame (the story) respects each interviewee as a separate expert; the second frame (the setting) factors in structural influences; and now this frame sifts the collective wisdom of twenty-two separate witnesses, each with firsthand experience. Here, in seeking commonalities, we distinguish three sorts of knowledge: stand-alone facts, the insider's perspective, and an anthropological picture.

Stand-Alone Facts. While one person's memory could distort anorexia. However, when separate observers agree, or their versions cluster in types, their individual observations carry collective authority as stand-alone facts.

Speaking separately, our informants describe eight features (chapter 6). Arising mid-course (after restricting and exercising intensify but before the syndrome exerts a life-threatening grip) our informants' experiences were exhilaration (a visceral thrill at starving), discipline (a life-ordering food/exercise regimen), isolation (turning inward, becoming mentally self-absorbed, physically distant, and socially detached), feedback (weighing and mirror-gazing to gauge results), goading (motivational techniques), consolidation (as tastes and attitudes change), deception (secrecy's meaning and power), and surrender (controlling yields to helplessness).[6]

The Insider's Perspective. Taking each story in its own terms (the first frame), we can now realistically identify three commonalities. First, all interviewees highlight their agency. Anything but passive victims, everyone stresses actively pursuing ascetic practices. Amorn illustrates this clearly. She decides her fate. Although her identity dilemma is structural (a consequence of social and cultural forces she neither controls nor fully grasps), that is no more than background. Center stage goes to how *she* addresses *her* difficulties and calculates *her* restricting. All our stories highlight the interviewee's conscious agency.

Second, our interviewees dispute anorexia's conventional explanations. Some do it flatly; others counter clichés methodically. Take Amorn: her tale centers on identity, not beauty; it begins with healthy eating (cutting fat), not weight-loss dieting; she sees her emaciated body, not a distorted body image; her motives are consciously calculated (that is the game of it), not unconscious; her efforts wrestle with adolescent angst, not childhood trauma; and her aims are local (how friends see her, success at sports) or developmental (testing herself, pushing limits), not media-manufactured. Quietly yet insistently she challenges how outsiders twist anorexia.

Third, no one explains or even pauses over anorexia's takeover. Again Amorn illustrates. Describing her controlling and intentions quite clearly, she neither explains nor even mentions how control slips from her hands. Crucial as that is, it gets just three words ("*it took over*") that explain nothing. It is a stunning reversal: she pursues a meaningful course (improving herself, taking control of her life) until, unexpectedly, anorexia comes out of nowhere to seize control inexplicably. Though the scenario begins culturally (e.g., she explores alternatives, works on identity, asserts control—all as her culture would have her do), it ends incoherently. Her meaningful pursuits collapse, ending in opposites (e.g., she loses her social identity and control of her life). All our stories have this curious absence—the decisive event slips by unnoticed.

These three commonalities paint a single picture: acutely aware of their agency, no one knows how they lose it; and though they know conventional explanations are wrong, they have nothing better to say. Anorexia, it would seem, exploits blind spots: outsiders cannot see what insiders experience, and insiders cannot see the coup that takes their agency.

The Anthropologist's Picture. Taken together, the interviews support four generalizations. The first concerns unity of practice. Everyone discovers similar technologies of self (Foucault 1990: 10, 31; Lester 1997) that remake the person's acts, thoughts, and feelings around self-denial. Techniques that begin as means to an end (losing weight, getting in shape, healthy eating) become ends in themselves.

Second, there is diversity of person and case. Our twenty-two stories show great variety in motivation (e.g., dropping out vs. standing out), character (from sociable to shy, effusive to reflective), passions (ballet, wrestling, running, art), social status (from school leader to social nobody), family (from intact to broken, supportive to detached), social situation (e.g., newcomer in a large school vs. same small class for eight years), sophistication (The Royal Ballet in Winnipeg vs. wrestling in rural Georgia), cultural background (from Russian immigrant to native Alabaman), and socioeconomic status (from foraging in Toronto to New York City's old-money elite). In sum, all sorts of people in all sorts of settings can get ensnared in the same techniques for all sorts of reasons. This diversity reveals that the loose links in anorexia's causal chain are person and case (many varieties could fill the bill), whereas the practice is a tight, precise link (only certain techniques work).

Third, anorexia involves adolescence, which is almost always the age of onset and the developmental stakes. For our informants, anorexia asserts autonomy, explores the self, and establishes an identity—all part and parcel of how youth grow into adults.

Fourth, anorexia taps deep moral roots. The syndrome's implicit values (control, self-denial, physical toughness, moral persistence) dovetail with how interviewee constitutions and lifeworlds embrace self-improvement. Here three powerful cultural currents converge: relentless achieving (pushing oneself academically, athletically, artistically), expressive individualism (adopting a lifestyle that expresses one's individuality; see Bellah et al. 1985), and virtuous living (whereby disciplined eating and a thin body mark the good person; see Stearns 1999). In perhaps all but two cases, this combination inspired the moral willing (Mattingly 2010) that led to anorexia.[7]

Together, these generalizations move anorexia out of the psyche and into a practice. That solves an old mystery: why has endless looking found no underlying pathology? Anorexia's cause, a practice, hides in plain sight. Yet solving that mystery opens another: how does a practice become a pathology? Our fourth frame, asceticism, answers that.

Fourth Frame: Asceticism

How does restricting turn pathological? In twenty-two independent accounts, no one explains that change. Yet their separate stories show one striking commonality: an ascetic practice.

Asceticism's Character. An ascetic chooses and keeps a regimen that denies creature comforts. Having a regimen is critical, as erratic acts of self-denial are not transformative. Choice is also critical, as involuntary starving is not asceticism. Celibacy, seclusion, poverty, toil, and vigil are all ascetic austerities that, like fasting, sacrifice physical or social comforts to make you a better person.

Asceticism's ends vary widely but produce striking similarities. Across ages and traditions, practitioners report a religious high of purity, power, and transcendence. Adepts show "intense concentration" in honing "simplicity and hardness" (Hardman 1924: 2). Making their body "the abode of ascetic practice," they cultivate an ascetic self "characterised by will, by agency and by resistance" (Flood 2004: 59) whose "distinctive goal" is "the alert, methodical control of one's own pattern of life and behavior" (Weber 1964: 168).

Asceticism follows various traditions. In the West asceticism goes back to the Greeks' *askesis*, an athlete's disciplined training. That word subsequently came to cover the extreme austerities of early Christian hermits, training as spiritual athletes, as well as the more domesticated monastic orders that developed later. For centuries monks and nuns were society's ascetic specialists, sacrificing for the good of all. Then the Reformation sent those ascetic ideals out into everyday life. Its injunction, find God's purpose in your work, lives on (Weber 1958). Often secularized, disciplined work and achieving redeem many modern lives.

Are Anorexics Ascetics? Can the asceticism that makes postulants into monks turn adolescents into anorexics? Four separate bodies of evidence say it does. One is our interviews. Every interviewee lived ascetically long before anorexia, developing self-denial in sports, dance, art, or school. Then, once starving began, they felt the same transcendent high of purity and bodily mastery that religious ascetics celebrate.

A second body of evidence comes from clinicians and academics. Many professionals stress anorexia's religious or moral energy: Banks (1997: 233) characterizes it as asceticism "encoded in religion," Garrett (1998) describes a "distorted spirituality," and other experts repeatedly find religious, moral, or simply ascetic motives.[8] Our informants rejected overtly religious explanations because for them, religion was beliefs, not actions. But they lived an incarnate religiosity nonetheless.

Asceticism's Dark Side. A third body of evidence is the scholarship on monasticism. For monastic authorities, one of asceticism's "palpable errors" (Allegre 1955: 254) is the extremism whereby self-denial is "liable to extravagance and excess" (James 2002: 280). Indeed, monks can overdo austerities, "only too often" becoming "unbalanced" (Mitchell and the Carisbrooke Dominicans 1955: ix) and imagining that "flesh is bad and needs mortification" (Bolster and de Lange 2002: 10). Is that how strict dieting morphs into body-hating anorexia? Human asceticism has a "seductive nature" (Cognet 1955: 52), an inner pull that takes some ascetics too far.[9] The anorexic, it would seem, is a sorcerer's apprentice, a talented amateur who stumbles on a risky secret: the human body can slip into an ascetic whirlpool that exhilarates unto death.[10] Virtuous living, monasticism shows, can turn pathological.

A fourth body of evidence comes from World War II research on starving. In one large, well-controlled experiment, volunteers ate regularly for three months, starved for six, and then got normal rations for another three (Keys and Laboratory of Physiological Hygiene 1950). Extensive testing established each volunteer's physical and psychological normalcy. Yet once starving began, anorexic-like abnormalities appeared (Garner 1997: 153–161) and persisted after regular rations resumed. It took thirty-three weeks for everyone to regain a normal appetite, and even then some unexpectedly took up food-related careers (e.g., cook, farmer).

Fifth Frame: Clinical Inference

In medicine clinical inference generalizes within a case. Anthropology, Geertz (1973: 26) observes, does the same to study culture. Each field "begins with a set of . . . signifiers"—"symptoms" for medicine, "symbolic acts" for anthropology—and "place[s] them within an intelligible frame" to "ferret out the unapparent import of things." For us, one "unapparent import" of starving is how that part (a signifier) fits into the whole of asceticism (an "intelligible frame") as a morally driven activity.

Two clinicians offer complementary insights. One, Lewis Mogul (1980), found his patients' asceticism controlled instinctual drives, compensated for feeling powerless, and expressed a "wish for aesthetic and moral transcendence."

Our interviewees readily voiced the latter, saying starving was exhilarating and strangely fulfilling, and displayed youth's moral questing and adventurous excess. In saying the adolescent "goes in for extremes—total commitments and total repudiations," Erikson (1971: 257–259) might as well be describing anorexics.

Anorexics, Hilde Bruch (1962: 192) tells us, were distinctively virtuous children. A pioneer in anorexia's modern diagnosis, she describes her patients as "outstandingly good and quiet children, obedient, clean, eager to please, helpful at home, precociously dependable, and excelling in school work." Indeed, until recently clinicians highlighted how anorexia strikes classically good girls in good families. Likewise, we found that conspicuous virtue pegs our sample perfectly. To Bruch this people-pleasing shows weakness, a failure to develop autonomy. We read the evidence differently: consistently pleasing others takes social smarts and intuitive skill. After all, even well-intentioned kids stumble over adults' contradictory expectations. Success in navigating those interpersonal rapids suggests anorexics grew up socially and morally precocious. That would explain the reason and manner of their agreeableness as children as well as their adolescent crisis. Imagine a virtuous, caring sense of self that hits adolescence. Suddenly, meanness rules middle school and growing up requires rebellion. Taking refuge in food and exercise rituals, anorexics assert righteous self-control amid unruly surroundings. Here, clinical inference suggests that anorexia adapts constitutionally good children to an adolescence they can neither embrace nor escape.

Putting these parts into a whole—an "intelligible frame"—suggests anorexia is an ascetic pathology incited by contemporary adolescence. While culture inspires the syndrome, the pathology itself is neither culture-like (it is a practice, not a symbol), nor culturally constructed (outsiders' cultural view of it is not the reality anorexics know experientially), nor even culturally construct-able (it eludes anorexics' cultural tools for explaining). As a practice it is accessible to outsiders like us because recovered adepts remember how they did it. Building on what they tell us, anorexia need have no deeper or darker cause than the relentless asceticism that every interviewee reports.

Conclusion

Anorexia flourishes where modern thought goes blind. From Descartes comes the mind/body divide, which conceals anorexia's constituting wholes (person and practice). From Plato comes faith in a single underlying truth, which hides anorexia's diversity. And biomedicine's specializing and professionalizing moves the disease out of life and into lab and clinic, places whose logics reject what the recovered could teach.

Our research makes the recovered our teachers, putting the person in anorexia at dead center and contextualizing the disease. In this chapter we have done that through framing, a holistic strategy that turns raw information into useable knowledge. By finding the boundaries rigor requires, framing realizes four interlocking benefits. First, by preserving the person's viewpoint, framing gives the interviews greater value. Although twenty-two sufferers are a paltry source of *information*, each interview as a source of *perspective* has inherent value that the set multiplies. Getting the anorexic's viewpoint fills in a missing piece of the puzzle and suggests anorexia is a perspective-driven disease. Second, framing keeps the person whole. Valuing each story in itself lets our interviewees define themselves. Kept in frame, where no story is more typical than any other, the individuality of each case shines. Third, in recognizing that individuality, framing establishes anorexia's diversity and thereby pictures the syndrome more realistically. Fourth, framing facilitates curing, healing, and prevention by binding the disease to ordinary people's knowledge of it in real life.

Notes

1. As Colton and Pistrang (2004: 315) said, "Research into anorexia has tended to neglect an invaluable source of information—the views of patients themselves." That is changing (Jenkins and Ogden 2012; Nordbø et al. 2012; Offord et al. 2006), although thus far it is to improve treatment, not recognize the relevant wholes.
2. Interviews have pitfalls: no memory is ever complete or incorruptible (G. Becker 1997; Garro and Mattingly 2000; Linde 1993); what our informants were remembering—a practice—beggars description (Bourdieu 1990); and an interview's "facts" are less autonomous truths than interpretations constructed jointly by interviewer and interviewee (G. Frank 1979). One cannot, in short, treat our interviews like court testimony. That said, as fieldworkers, anthropologists not only readily correct for such "distortions" but use them to parse context.
3. We did five other lengthy interviews. One was with an anorexic's mother, another with a woman who could starve intensely yet stop freely, and others with bulimic women who were not previously anorexic. Their numbers are too small to report here, but these nonanorexic interviews inform our comparative perspective.
4. Our transcripts alter identifying details and add clarifying words in brackets. While we use only our interviewees' words, we edit for coherence and brevity, dropping confusing clauses, repetitions, and needless details—all without ellipses to mark gaps. We also rearrange passages to bring scattered ideas together.
5. Take the idea that anorexics diet for beauty. It is true that the media hypes supermodels and beauty ideals oppress women—those are structural conditions. Do they cause anorexia? By itself a very general condition cannot explain a very rare disease afflicting less than 1 percent of the population. Why the other 99 percent do not become anorexic is never explained. Moreover, if beauty is the impetus, how does one explain male sufferers (up to a third of partial syndrome) or women who know skeletons look ghastly? Then

there is the historical incoherence: when Bruch identified a distorted body image, Marilyn Monroe's sensual fleshiness was hot; only later, when emaciated models like Twiggy became the 1960s vogue, did body fashion fit—and seem to explain—anorexia; yet still later, when the 1990s celebrated a well-toned body, anorexia should have disappeared as unfashionable—but of course it did not. How could body fashion explain anorexia at one moment and not the other two? Fashion changes erratically, but anorexia's incidence does not jump around (Lucas et al. 1991).

6. Are these stand-alone facts anorexia's true nature? Were the recurring alone to define the disease, we could now drop all other frames. We will not do that. Stand-alone truths do not make our other frames any less true. Moreover, in placing anorexia within someone's life, case-by-case diversities are as vital as cross-case similarities. To have both we pile frame upon frame.
7. The two clear exceptions, Sarah and Francesca, involved depression.
8. "Religious themes and symbolism seem to arise more frequently in patients with eating disorders," and anorexics in particular describe "restriction . . . as holy, pure, and good, whereas bingeing and purging is weak and evil" (Baxter 2001: 137). See also Banks (1996), Lawrence (1979), Lupton (1996), Miles (1995), Mogul (1980), Rampling (1985), Winkler (1994).
9. Davis and Claridge (1998) call this auto-addictive behavior. Ethiopian hermits, Bushell (1995: 554, 560) argues, reprogram themselves so that not eating gives the rewarding experience that eating once gave.
10. Why does asceticism not ravage religious orders? Take Buddhism. As a solitary ascetic the Buddha went too far, almost dying from self-starvation. In consequence his monastic line now vows moderation (The Middle Way). Similarly, early Christianity saw a "heroic fanaticism" of desert ascetics competing in "feats of self-denial" (Harpham 1987: 20). Then fourth-century religious leaders, seeing "where spirituality went awry" and the need for "greater love of the self," held monastic communities to moderating rules (Dugan 1995: 547). Of course anorexics know no such rules. Alone when their austerities turn life-denying, they lack spiritual guardians to counsel "greater love of the self."

CHAPTER 2

Medicine
Reworking Cartesian Knowledge

> Modernity prides itself on the fragmentation of the world as its foremost achievement.
>
> —Zygmunt Bauman, *Modernity and Ambivalence*

Biomedicine fragments brilliantly. At its best it pulls a disease apart to find underlying causes. Yet that strength is a weakness, with anorexia. Pulled apart every which way, the syndrome has long defied reductive explanation. And no wonder—anorexia is a complex system, not a collection of fragments. Such diseases must be understood holistically, not just reductively.

To study anorexia holistically we must rework what biomedicine has learned reductively. To that end, this chapter relates biomedical knowledge to our biocultural approach. We first discuss our sample—does it represent anorexia? Next we contextualize anorexia as an affliction and an activity. We then go on to characterize the person—who gets anorexia? And lastly we consider causes—how do context, actor, and activity interact to create anorexia?

Our Sample

Our research comes from in-depth interviews with twenty-two recovered anorexics (chapter 1). Is this group, our sample, typical? To answer precisely we would need to know the precise nature of anorexia—which no one knows. We do know that the standard answer, the DSM-IV, is *not* representative for three reasons. First, the more serious a case is, the more likely it is to enter the health-care system and get correctly diagnosed. Many mild cases are missed: it is "not unusual" for people to recover from anorexia "with little or no formal treatment" (Lucas et al. 1991: 921). Second, the cases in health care (the DSM's sample) are more likely to have two or more afflictions. A person who is depressed and has anorexia may enter treatment for either problem and then have the other recognized. Such compounding misrepresents straightforward anorexia. Third, the longer a case goes uncured in health care, the more resistance and treatment distort its original character. The DSM, in short, overrepresents the atypical.

How does our sample compare to the DSM's? On the one hand, mild and subclinical cases make our sample closer to real-world anorexia than the DSM's. On the other hand, our set of cases has three limitations the DSM lacks: first, recruiting through universities excludes less educated anorexics; second, interviewing only recovered anorexics excludes the incurable and thereby under-represents the most severe cases; and, third, our cases are remembered by anorexics, not observed by clinicians.

Our sample fits the broad picture of anorexia rather well. Several interviewees report the perfectionism that typifies the disorder (Fairburn et al. 1999) as well as the common comorbid conditions (depression, OCD, anxiety disorder). Most informants have supportive homes, and only one had a seriously troubled prior life. That sounds atypical, but childhood adversity is not higher among anorexics (Webster and Palmer 2000). Two suspect they were molested on a single occasion, but none reported serious sexual abuse. We may underrepresent the abused—who presumably are less likely to recover as well as to volunteer for interviews—but this is not a major bias: sexual abuse among anorexics is no greater than among the general population (Gillberg and Råstam 1998: 130–131). We under-represent male anorexics: perhaps seven would be proportionate, but only two volunteered for our study (Woodside et al. 2001).

What finally recommends our sample is that each case is well contextualized. We reconstruct each anorexic's lifeworld and life course, whereas the DSM *assumes* it can extirpate cases from their surroundings. We dispute that assumption categorically. If we are right, then the DSM does *not* represent anorexia anywhere near as well as our approach does. Indeed, a National Institutes of Health workshop concluded that strict adherence to the DSM has "hampered research," as it does not represent the actual character of anorexia (Agras et al. 2004: 518).

Context: Placing the Activity

Today's anorexia is a modern ascetic response to modern life. That puts anorexia in the two larger explanatory frames of asceticism and modernity. We call these frames because each has a distinctive character and integrity quite apart from anorexia. Were anorexia to vanish, neither frame would change. Not so the other way around. Were asceticism's willed austerities to vanish, anorexia would disappear. And were the modern to vanish, today's anorexia would lose its initial motives and current symptoms.

Saying anorexia is modern and ascetic means the disease is not a discrete entity that we can explain by itself. Instead, we need to consider the ascetic and modern as outside inputs that require their own explanations. To that end, we will start with anorexia's symptoms and work toward the modern.

From Anorexia to Eating Disorders. Surely ancient, anorexia was not discovered until the 1870s, when medicine became able to differentiate self-starvation from other emaciating diseases like tuberculosis. Today's standard authority, the American Psychiatric Association's (1994) Diagnostic and Statistical Manual (DSM-IV), is quite precise:

A. Refusal to maintain body weight at or above a minimally normal weight for age and height (e.g., weight loss leading to maintenance of body weight less than 85 percent of that expected or failure to make expected weight gain during period of growth, leading to body weight less than 85 percent of that expected).
B. Intense fear of gaining weight or becoming fat, even though underweight.
C. Disturbance in the way in which one's body weight or shape is experienced, undue influence of body weight or shape on self-evaluation, or denial of the seriousness of the current low body weight.
D. In postmenarchal females, amenorrhea i.e., the absence of at least three consecutive cycles.

The DSM does its best to make anorexia discrete and unique, as the manual's purpose is to differentiate diseases. But *classifying* so narrowly impedes *explaining* this syndrome realistically. The DSM-IV defines anorexia too narrowly to cross cultures (A. Becker 2007; Khandelwal et al.1995; Lee et al. 1993); excludes many sufferers who do not fear fat (A. Becker et al. 2009; Palmer 1993), lack a distorted body image (Hsu and Sobkiewicz 1991), or have a low drive for thinness (A. Becker et al. 2009); and generally "fails to cover the range of experience covered by self-starving behaviour" (Garrett 1998: 48). One reason for these failures is that the DSM over-represents the most serious and distorted cases. Cases that clear up naturally or quickly—perhaps the majority—do not enter the health statistics that drive the DSM. When researchers studied physicians' records to recover anorexia as it entered health care, they found the "clinical diversity . . . was striking" (Lucas et al. 1991: 921). No wonder a gathering of experts found "[s]trict adherence to the DSM-IV diagnostic criteria . . . has . . . hampered research." Their report calls for broader diagnostic criteria to "permit more productive exploration of the nature and variations of anorexia" (Agras et al. 2004: 518). We do too.

Broadening criteria blurs the lines between anorexia and other eating disorders. That is a necessary inconvenience. Arguably anorexia is evolving.[1] Certainly old symptoms remain even as new ones arise: ninety years after anorexia's discovery, body image appeared (Bruch 1962); idealized thinness followed ten years later (Hof and Nicolson 1996: 589); still later bulimia became common (Russell 1985); and currently around two-thirds of adolescents presenting for treatment have such a "wide heterogeneity of symptoms" that they fall in the catch-all EDNOS, Eating Disorder Not Otherwise Specified (Darcy et al. 2012: 110). A study of nearly two hundred eating-disordered women found only one-third kept their original diagnosis over thirty months; for the rest, either symptoms or clinical assessments moved between anorexia, bulimia, and EDNOS (Milos et al. 2005). Indeed, in over 50 percent of cases, anorexia's simple restricted eating breaks down, and purging or bingeing complicates the syndrome (Agras et al. 2004: 510). That fits our interviewees: some started and stayed anorexic (just restricting); others tried purging but failed, or binged but reverted to just restricting; and still others subsequently became bulimic, either spontaneously or in resisting demands that they eat. Although anorexia retains its distinctive restricting, the larger syndrome has become a loosely bounded entity within eating disorders as a wider, changing field. Were this not loose enough, a high incidence of comorbidities (depression, OCD, perfectionism) suggests that these may be the primary problem and the eating disorder a secondary complication (Rosling et al. 2011: 309).

From Eating Disorders to Ascetic Activity Disorder. Our sample throws yet another monkey wrench into the DSM's tidy categories: nearly everyone exercised excessively, a few obsessively. In fact, some cases develop as exercise disorders that then distort eating. That is common: intense exercise and restrictive eating can occur separately or together, one can develop into the other, or anorexics can move between the two (Davis 1997; Meyer et al. 2011).

Is anorexia's disorder exercise or eating? While biomedicine might sort cases into these two categories, anthropology would stress their commonality: out-of-control asceticism. In our sample, ascetic activity always initiated anorexia. Whether it begins with eating or exercise, self-denial focuses and finally consumes the person's life. Here the history of religious asceticism tells us devout austerities tempt death. Today's anorexia secularizes that scenario.

From Asceticism to Modern Life. Asceticism haunts modern life. Even as our era celebrates abundance, personal life requires self-restraint and work expects self-denial. Indeed, "the asceticism of the really serious worker" breeds bodily discipline and "an intense concentration of outlook and purpose," and whether the task is "violin-playing or empire-building . . . it is accepted as the one thing that counts, and all else is strictly subordinated to it" (Hardman 1924: 2). Here "all else" includes bodily comforts, mental ease, and social pleasures.

Our informants all led achievement-oriented lives that collapsed into ascetic foci. While their "one thing that counts" varied—sports, dance, studying, art—everyone had mastered focusing (and thereby restricting) their interests and, in always demanding more of themselves, denied easy gratification. Here, like the aforementioned violinist lost in playing music others wrote, our interviewees incarnated ascetic scripts they did not write. The scripts we found—virtuous eating, bodily control, proper appearance—all date back roughly a century to the modern ascetic style with which the progressive middle class met urban industrial society.

Are we saying that modern culture creates anorexia? No, we are saying that the biology of asceticism, interacting with certain cultural currents, fosters anorexia—a self-sustaining biocultural hybrid. Our day's hybrid wears modern clothes, but Christian and Buddhist garb once was modern too, and within the modern, Japanese (Pike and Borovoy 2004), Mexican (Lester 2007), Israeli (Gooldin 2008), and our Canadian and U.S. hybrids, each has its own style.

Gender Dimensions. Popular thought sees anorexia as a female quest for beauty. That is wrong on both counts. On beauty, anorexics put discipline above looks—witness their grotesque appearance—and in any case, the disease centers in actions, not intentions.[2] On gender, it afflicts not just women in their prime but children, the elderly, and men. Male anorexia is seriously underreported: often disguised by athletics, perhaps a fifth (full syndrome) to a third (full or partial syndrome) of anorexics are male (Woodside et al. 2001).

Anorexia's gender dimensions are complex. At its core—that is, as a discrete activity and as an ascetic practice—gender apparently matters little if at all. That would explain why it is the same disease for men and women (Braun et al. 1999; Woodside et al. 1990). It is getting into the core—becoming anorexic—where gender matters. Arguably, women are more likely to become anorexic because the cult of thinness and traditional gender norms fit anorexic patterns. Indeed, carefully controlling one's body, watching diet, and eating sparingly are stereotypically feminine and express how women are held to higher standards of bodily virtue and sympathy than men. Yet the picture is not straightforward. Starving heroically and exercising intensely display a toughness, athleticism, and recklessness that are traditionally male and now accepted—perhaps even expected—from ambitious women (cf. Gooldin 2008). In this latter, specifically modern discourse, a woman strongly committed to progressive values (achieving, self-denial, control) is at risk for anorexia.

Person: Characterizing the Actor

Anorexics live within modern and ascetic frames. Although they are not consciously ascetic or modern, living their values and expressing their feelings invokes three complexes.

Ascetic Values. Anorexics live value-driven lives. These life-shaping values are taken for granted, not consciously chosen. Picking up what is "good" or "right" from their surroundings, they value ascetic restraint, tireless achieving, and sympathetic involvement.

Ascetic restraint, by deferring gratification, built the middle class. A child who studies instead of playing wins praise. That typically teaches that hard work—and thus self-denial—is virtuous. Certainly that is often how progressive-minded adults live their lives and how children grasp the way life works.

Valuing ascetic self-denial makes anorexia expressive, "a way of demonstrating self-control, autonomy, and individuality" (Rich et al. 2004: 183). That is the insider view reflected in what anorexics say (Banks 1992: 1997; Gooldin 2008; Lester 1995, 1997; Warin 2010). Outsiders may disagree, seeing anorexia as instrumental (e.g., a means to beauty or attention), but our informants were living out modern ascetic scripts where a slim, attractive, or disciplined body expresses virtue. Here anorexia is a distinctively modern expressive act.

A Sympathetic Capacity. The anorexic person readily embodies surrounding values and worries. Although all humans do that to varying degrees, anorexics appear to either use or have more sympathy than most people. Certainly clinicians describe them as especially attuned to the feelings of others (e.g., "acutely sensitive to the needs of everyone and even everything else in their environment" [Claude-Pierre 1997: 45] and "particularly concerned about social problems and the lot of others . . . less fortunate than themselves" [Lawrence 1979: 96, 100]). Just as saints once incarnated popular religious hopes and worries, anorexics feel and master today's concern for bodily control and personal self-discipline.

Growing up sympathetically sets a collision course with adolescence. How does someone who is good at being good handle a misbehaving life stage? Worse, how does a sympathetic person keep control amidst peers experimenting with drink, drugs, and sex? Here anorexia does triple duty: it asserts a disciplined identity, isolates you from difficult surroundings, and rebels with virtue.

A Metaphoric Sensibility. The more sympathetic anorexics are, the more metaphor shapes their feelings. Again, this is a human capacity that anorexics either have or just use more than most people, which is why they score high on "magical thinking" (Aharoni and Hertz 2012). Anorexia's inner logic is analogical: eating and body become metaphors for person and world (Lester 1997: 486). Once metaphor links the little (eating, body) to the large (person, world), controlling the little controls the large. Anorexics say as much: virtually all our informants said controlling food made them feel in control of their lives.

Is this madness? Well, it breaks a precept of modern knowing (dividing self from other) and spurs clinicians' curing (Aharoni and Hertz 2012), but it is not crazy. To the contrary, seeing body/cosmos harmony—what we call person/world oneness—is as old as astrology and as new as ecology. It flourished in early Christian, Greek, and pagan thought (Lincoln 1986a, 1986b), and now it challenges how modernity alienates us from nature. Here anorexia, in controlling oneself to control the world, makes perfect emotional sense.[3] Only if we stay outside person/world oneness, just looking in as skeptics, are anorexics simply mad.

An Anorexic Lifeworld. An anorexic lifeworld arises out of a person's ascetic values, sympathetic capacity, and metaphoric sensibility. Here we distinguish these parts, but in anorexia the three function as a single morally intense whole. Anything but abstract, virtue is as visceral as hunger, as concrete as what you eat. Ordinary actions thereby carry great consequence. So anorexics become strict with themselves, always striving to do better.

Anorexia functions as a lifestyle alternative to modern indulgence. A disciplined path, it holds the moral high ground. Given their values, it is easy to see why anorexics can feel superior to their surroundings. It is also easy to see why they resist therapy: it asks adolescents to yield on values that express who they are—their identity.

Causes: Sorting Out Factors

The foregoing considerations—context, activity, actor—give us all the influences and ingredients that make up anorexia. But how do these pieces cause disease? Simplifying radically, we distinguish agency, structure, activity, and function.

Agency: Good Intentions and Deadly Techniques. In social theory, agency captures how the actor pursues what he or she wants. Only two or three of our informants intended to become anorexic, and so at first glance agency explains little. Yet intentions drove attitude and actions. On attitude, most began what became anorexia as a project of self-improvement, what Lester (1997) calls "self-tailoring." Starting with good intentions, all came to take pleasure in how virtuous their activity felt. A sense of superior virtue thus energized their activity, dismissed objections, and resisted therapy.

In actions our informants were effective agents of their own illness. All but one quite consciously developed manipulative procedures that made them into anorexics. What they manipulated was not—or not just—objects and other people, but also themselves. Using what Foucault (1990) calls techniques or technologies of the self, they tricked, praised, and browbeat themselves into their self-improvement schemes (cf. Lester 1997). One willful part of the person thus ruthlessly enslaved the rest. Working alone, each person more or less reinvented the secular asceticism of Greek antiquity, a tradition where one trained to control one's appetites for both moral formation and health (Foucault 1990: 28). Yet where Greek mastery meant moderation, our sample sought to deny desire altogether. That, Foucault (1990: 63–70) argues, is how Christianity changed antiquity's asceticism.

Structure: Embodying Values. In anthropology agency contrasts to how structure has people doing what culture and society prescribe. Is the anorexic's restricting done freely (agency) or to follow some outside script (structure)? And is that script beauty—or achieving or discipline or even asceticism? All are valued in one social niche or another and any might lead to self-starvation. Here structural explanations are easy to propose but hard to prove. They are, in psychology's parlance, overdetermined (Lester 1999: 140). So we focus on not society generally but the anorexic person in particular. Here, in lifeworld and life course, what matters is unambiguous: disciplined achieving, not beauty or weight.

Critical though structure is to explaining anorexia, it leaves the anorexic's passion unexplained. Whether striving for beauty or achieving, how many would court death to do what society says? When that urging seizes only one in a hundred, a structural explanation needs to account for the other ninety-nine. Then, too, why does the one who hears society suddenly turn deaf when it says "stop—you've gone too far!"?

Activity: Losing Self and Defying Values. Activity can explain the passion that neither structure nor agency can. Consider how anorexia develops. At the start our informants demonstrated agency (choosing virtue) as well as structure (following societal values). Yet becoming anorexic ends agency (they could not stop) and defies structure (social pressure to stop, to be normal). Anorexia becomes an autonomous activity. What gives it that freedom? Any well established practice, Bourdieu (1990: 11–15) says, escapes the actor's consciousness and goes beyond what culture imagines and society urges.

Once established, an activity exercises amoral power over the actor. Suddenly the activity alone is good, its cost irrelevant. Family, friends, and prior life all shrink. Although our informants began diverse, anorexia got everyone acting and thinking alike. How? As mind is embodied in our acting bodies (Lakoff and Johnson 1999), all-consuming activities like starving or training can swallow a person's life and mind. Then control rests neither with the actor (agency) nor society (structure) but with an activity pursuing its own inner logic and unfolding possibilities.

Function: Meeting and Making Needs. Anorexia serves multiple purposes. Its ascetic closure very effectively counters modern openness and adolescent chaos. The syndrome can also establish identity, express values, escape peers, explore self, develop confidence, satisfy achieving, and—as the cliché has it—give a feeling of control amid tumult. Although no case did all that, every person experienced multiple payoffs.

Saying anorexia "works"—that it is functional—is obvious yet confusing. It is obvious that the pathology works well enough to seize someone's life, frustrate therapy, and impede recovery. Yet this is confusing in that "disease" implies dysfunction, a falling apart rather than a new creation. Here anorexia is less a disease than bioculturally constituted development like learning to speak. To be sure, anorexia is misdirected development—mis-development—but it is not *just* a pathology. It is a new steady-state that, like ordinary developmental change, restructures everyday life.

Conclusion

No one can deny that modern fragmenting has borne fruit. Once the Enlightenment severed mind from body, it began the fractioning that advanced science so remarkably on so many fronts. Yet fragmenting loses perspective, which is how the researcher's mindset and medicine's specializing miss the anorexic person's viewpoint. Fragmenting also hides wholes, which is how anorexia's actualities vanish amid the pieces that research makes to measure.

Against these losses, this chapter stresses how context, person, and causes show that anorexia is neither biologically determined nor culturally constructed. Were biology determining, neither agency nor structure nor activity would matter—but they all do. And were anorexia culturally constructed, the disease would be beauty-mad dieting as popularly imagined—but that would mock our informants' lives and stories.

Notes

1. When Bruch (1985: 11) began treating anorexia, the disease was so obscure that patients did not know they had it. Once anorexia became widely known, Bruch's patients lacked the earlier ones' passion.
2. No rigorous study has shown that pre-morbid anorexics value beauty more than their healthy peers. Although widely accepted, a beauty explanation flaunts logic and evidence: it forgets male anorexics, ignores anorexics' physically repulsive bodies, dismisses a century of clinical observation (the beauty motive gained acceptance only in the 1970s), disregards chronology (the disease appeared a century before ultra-thinness became fashionable and persists decades after well-toned bodies came into vogue), and overlooks counterevidence of other cultures (e.g., anorexia occurs where fat is attractive).
3. One of Jules Feiffer's cartoons first shows a man's horror at what is on the news ("Rivers of blood!") then his own bystander attitude, witnessing suffering he is not working to relieve. Beating himself up ("Don't I care?") he looks inward and ponders long to discover that what he really does care about is losing weight. The cartoon works because we can sympathize with the character's sympathies and response.

CHAPTER 3

The Stories
Respecting Diversity

Everyone, the saying goes, has a story to tell. Not so anorexics. When ill they speak for the disease, not themselves. Or, to be exact, they act rather than speak. Living out a relentless inner logic of doing, they neither explain nor justify their regimen as a proper illness story does. Instead they pursue starving unapologetically. That silence stymies caregivers.

Anorexia is not an idea or mental state. It is a practice, a bodily state with its own inexplicable momentum that, like practice generally, "excludes . . . mastery of the logic that is expressed within it" (Bourdieu 1990: 11, 81–82). Like a player "caught up in the game," intense involvement excludes "distance, perspective, detachment, and reflexion"—exactly what storytelling requires. So British schoolgirl anorexics refuse to "package their illness narratives" in an appropriate story but make "'chaotic', 'regressive' and 'rebellious'" statements instead (Rich et al. 2004: 185–186). That is not new: nineteenth-century anorexics left no adequate stories (Brumberg 2000: 164). Or take recent Australian cases: practicing anorexics offered no "fully coherent account"; the recovering jumbled their still-under-construction stories; and only the recovered told an adequate illness story (Garrett 1998: 58–62). It is as if no-story is the disease that a narrative could cure. This chapter seeks the story that practicing anorexics cannot tell.

One Disease

Our interviewees tell roughly similar stories. While anorexia's start varies, accounts are alike in their relatively simple middle and abrupt ending.

A Similar Story. In the stories anorexia is (1) an episode with (2) its own logic, and (3) a complex cause that involves (4) one's character and (5) actions that, in most cases, (6) adapt to a difficult situation.

- **An Episode:** Every interviewee treats anorexia as an episode—a distinct, protracted, largely bounded life-course event. Most treat it like a relationship that ended naturally. A few own the episode without regrets—it has made them who they are—but others declare it a total loss.
- **Its Own Logic:** Anorexia has its own compelling inner logic, a bit like a foreign culture. Everyone thus struggles openly to make the episode sensible and reconcile past thinking with how they now reason.

[You are] *thinking "I'm not going to gain a pound today" and that's the best thing that could have happened. Oh who knows! When you verbalize it, you think "God that was so dumb."*—Megan

Only a few attribute their anorexic thought to a cognitive or perceptual deficiency, as medicine does.

- *A Complex Cause:* Every story piles up influences, rejecting any single simple cause. Although a few mention beauty ideals and media influence, no one accepts these as primary and most reject their significance altogether. Instead, almost every story takes a narrower psychological-cum-practical tact that locates the problem either in the person's character or between the person and his or her surroundings.
- *The Anorexic's Character:* Every story recognizes outside influences, but the outcome still hinges on the narrator's choices. The story thereby pivots on character, although this is not richly developed. Nine spontaneously label themselves perfectionists (or words to that effect), and nearly everyone highlights a successful, achievement-oriented past. No one directly attributes the illness to ingrained striving, but nearly every story invites that conclusion.
- *The Anorexic's Own Actions:* In every story the narrator is an agent of his or her own fate. To be sure, in two cases anorexia is entirely unseen and accidental, and it is unintended in perhaps all but two instances, but everyone traces their affliction to their own actions. Here our interviewees typically find self-interest. So, for example, anorexia pays off in getting attention, manipulating others, or controlling oneself. Out of these self-serving motives, control was stressed by 20 of 22 as a personal need or desire.
- *Adapts to a Difficult Situation:* Although a few stories depict ideal circumstances, most describe trying conditions where stress provokes anorexia. Most present control-seeking as anorexia's psychological cause: an out-of-control life or body—or simply feeling that way—makes restricted eating a way to get control.

A Marginal Middle. Our stories have realistic beginnings and then move into a simplistic and typically short middle. In the middle, exactly where a fully developed story reveals an underlying conflict or unfolding complications, most stories strike just one or two notes. One note, deception, describes fooling everyone to foil intervention. The other note, extremism, chronicles how far weight loss and exercise go. One note or two, we hear little or nothing about how healthy practices turn deadly. We cannot, for example, trace how Megan's exercise or Jim's eating morph into pathologies. How anorexia actually develops eludes our informants.

Was there no developmental middle to remember? As we shall see, the middle's distinct components disappear into what is remembered as whole. Not seeing what was happening at the time, our informants' stories stay true to that blindness. Lacking an elaborated middle, most stories thus collapse into a clear start that mysteriously morphs into a horrible disease. Like breaking a leg, an incidental act has dramatic results—or so the stories make it seem.

An Abrupt Ending. Our stories come to various yet typically abrupt endings. In some stories the disease simply runs its course. Others end when anorexics inexplicably decide to get well. In still other cases parents or medical professionals suddenly intervene—as if they had had this power all along.

In a well-developed story we might expect the ending to spring from the plot or characters. Yet these endings close without closure. They neither return to the beginning, nor decipher anorexia's alien logic, nor resolve the dilemma's tensions. Of course, without a substantive middle, the end has little to wrap up. Still, one might expect talk of "lessons learned" or recovery's ups and downs. Not so. Instead, like a bad play that rescues the hero improbably, *deus ex machina*, anorexia is just vanquished—dropped like a bad idea. So anorexia leaves but no story masters it. Not surprisingly, some fear its return. Four relapsed.

Various Motives

Although our twenty-two stories describe the experience in similar ways, they differ in what initiates the disease. Here stories divide more or less naturally into *incited* as distinct from *incidental* anorexia. With the former, the story ties the disease to some prior event or motive where the narrator aims to stand out (distinguish oneself, outdo others), fit in (gain acceptance), or drop out (escape social life, wither away). With incidental anorexia the person unknowingly slips into the syndrome while pursuing other aims. Our typing is not to pigeonhole—cases mix motives and only liken as the disease progresses—but to capture how our interviewees depict four differing paths into anorexia.

Standing-Out Anorexia. Over the last forty years, experts have repeatedly characterized anorexics as top students and high achievers. Bruch (1979: 22), in particular, saw an "urgent desire to be special and outstanding." Sometimes that excelling goes into exercise, athletics, dietary restraint, or weight loss. Consider Megan.

> *My battle with anorexia began in the tenth grade. I had an older sister who was a senior. We were cheerleaders together and I hated being in her shadow, living this rehearsed life stuck as Janie's little sister. I went, "I don't want to do any of these things" and kind of threw them out and started again. I was going to graduate higher than she did, to take everything and do it better and make a better AP score. I was going to be the best person, going to do everything right, and well, and better. I mean, I adore my sister—I still think she hung the moon—but high school is just a hard time finding out who you are and want to be.*
>
> *May my sophomore year I broke up with my boyfriend and quit cheerleading. I wanted to be something completely different. So I signed up for track and got a job. All summer I'd run twelve miles every day. Started losing weight, which was cool. I'd never been thin before and it was kind of new. I was happy. No one could tell me not to run. No one could tell me what to eat. I just said, "This is what I'm doing."*
>
> *I got back to school and weighed twenty pounds less. Everyone said, "Omigod, Megan." "You're crazy." I'd stopped menstruating. My mother's going, "Oh my god." I had this great pediatrician. And she goes, "Well, we have to put more fats in your diet," and I'd go, "Sure! Yeah." But it became progressively worse. I joined cross-country. After practice I'd go home and run and then I'd go to the gym and then come home and do all my work. My grades were phenomenal. I was our best runner, the only one who went to State. So I got glorified, which was weird because there's this terrible, terrible thing going on but I'm winning awards. I looked so put together. My grades were stellar. People were envious. By Christmas I'd dropped below a hundred. My pediatrician would say "You need to do this," and I'd say "Sure!" I resisted the whole time. I've always been hardheaded, especially with this. I isolated myself. I pushed my friends away, pushed my family away. My friends would just humor me—bless their hearts! I just kept getting skinnier and skinnier and skinnier, and then—once it got ridiculous—I looked like a twelve-year-old. It was bad.*

Already a successful student, Megan adds athletic laurels. Then, what began with identity angst—getting out of her sister's shadow—unleashes an intense drive to be a good person.

For Lynn, standing-out anorexia meant winning in even your weakest area.

> *Late fall we started softball workouts. I was a freshman and there were all these much older sorority girls. They were gorgeous athletes. I could pretty much hold my own as far as intellect. And I was really good at soccer—started all the time. But softball I was not good at. I'd just started playing. And all these girls were phenomenal players. Our coach is like, "We're going to have weigh-ins." It was, "Oh god, you're*

kidding." I'd never really dieted. No, no, pretty much ate what I wanted and didn't think about it. The first day we got on the scale I was like, "Oh god!" I didn't know I weighed that much. I've never been small-framed.

I saw this movie in health class. Two girls: one had bulimia and one had anorexia. This movie was "This is what can happen." But it told you how to do it. I was like, "That's not a bad idea." I started paying attention to what I ate. I was losing weight and people were like, "You look great!" That was just more reinforcement. Then I stopped losing weight though I was exercising the same. I was like "I need to get in gear." So I got up at 6 A.M. and ran on the treadmill, three or four miles. I stopped eating pretty much anything—definitely no fat! I ate for lunch celery, diet Dr. Pepper and fat-free saltines. I was tired, really, really tired all the time. So I drank more caffeine.

Now we were having indoor [soccer] practice and then softball practice. We'd run two miles outside and then run stairs inside. I'd finish first. Everybody was like, "You're such an overachiever," but my coach was like, "That's great, you're going to be a base runner." So I had my place—I was the fastest runner. Running stairs I remember closing my eyes because I'd get dizzy. Before weigh-ins we had to jog up for cool down. That was the worst. By that time I could barely speak—my eyes were black and I was dizzy. Everything was spinning.

I don't know when I got bulimic too. It all linked together. Somebody would have a birthday party and leave cake on the counter. I'd be soooo hungry. I'd eat four pieces. Didn't even breathe between bites, almost choking I ate so fast. Afterwards I was like, "Oh god!" I felt immediately fatter. So I started running past my house where they were doing construction. I'd throw up there. I never threw up at school, though. Ever. That was too risky.

I never really felt sick. Everything was great. I was class president, I was getting good grades and I was always first on the softball team, and my indoor team—I'm a goalkeeper—I was quicker because I wasn't as heavy. Couldn't see anything wrong.

My mom started asking questions because I didn't eat at dinner—ever. But [it is] not a sit-down-everybody-have-dinner kind of thing. It's kind of "Come and get it, there's dinner on the stove." So I'm like, "I already ate." My mom's like, "I didn't see. There's not a plate in the sink." "No," I was like, "I put it in the dishwasher." It taught me to lie on the spot.

I didn't want Christmas break because there was going to be all the best food that I loved! I knew I was going to have to eat some. My mom had started dropping questions. I bought Ipecac and took it. It was awful stuff. But it worked. It was quiet and it was quick. And it didn't hurt. I was, "Oh my gosh. This is awesome." I had my own bathroom. I'd always do it while mom was bathing my sisters in the other end of the house.

I went back to school. Friends on the team were like, "You look so thin." It wasn't, "You look great" anymore. We got back for softball and weighed in. The littlest girl *was Jadi, probably 5 feet even. I'm 5 feet 5. I weighed 117 and I'd lost six pounds from before break. And Jadi weighed 118. It was the biggest victory for me. I was the only person on the whole team that'd lost weight over break.*

When it finally came to a halt my hair had started to fall out. My mom went into my room and found Ipecac. So they watched me eat. I was constantly supervised. I just didn't do it for a while. I ate normally for about two months. By that time it was like, "OK, now you're fine." So they didn't pay too much attention. But I never could get back like I was. I don't have the same willpower. The worst of it was definitely over.

Competition fuels Lynn's anorexia. Once she triumphs, her eating disorder no longer engages her. Even Lynn cannot figure out why winning matters so much ("*every time I finished first it was like, 'I did it!' Like some personal victory. For what I don't know*"). Contrast this to Megan, who likes running but "*hated the competition.*" Whereas Lynn delights in her victories, Megan gets "*glorified*" for succeeding but "*was unhappy,*" "*falling apart inside.*"

Fitting-In Anorexia. While standing out drove Megan and Lynn, Molly just wanted to fit in.

I was raised in Huntsville, Alabama and I have two wonderful parents. I've always been very athletic. My dad coached me all through elementary school and even junior high. It was something I really loved. Always straight-A student, competitive, Type A, perfectionist. Church activities too were big. I went to a small private Christian school, kindergarten through twelfth grade. So I knew everyone I went to school with for thirteen years. It was a pretty tight group.

In junior high I was really thin, one of those kids that ate and ate and could never gain weight. I guess I got my period in ninth grade. That's when I started gaining weight. But it didn't really bother me. Then junior year, I was playing basketball and having difficulty with the coach. Practices were really slow. I wasn't getting as much exercise as I was used to. I was about 130 pounds. I went up to 140 because I was mad all the time, eating a lot and not doing anything in practice. That caught me off guard. So I was like, "I've got to start watching what I eat. No more twelve pieces of pizza. Maybe just six." It wasn't extreme but I did start to lose weight. And I was like, "Wow, this is cool. I like this."

I did have close friends, but I floated between the really cool group and my other friends. Also in my class all the girls were gorgeous, like a modeling agency. I was always the athlete, friends with all the boys. It started to bug me that I wasn't considered hot. That made me want to lose weight. Started counting calories. I was still playing basketball and I'd run when I got home. I lost weight really fast. My parents didn't really notice, but once I got down to 120, people were saying stuff to me, like, "You look great!" The girls. The boys didn't notice. I was getting comments and liked the way it felt. Some people call me slightly OCD and I got obsessed about losing weight. I started skipping meals. I'd go to study session during lunch and pretend, "Oh I already ate." Then I'd pick at my dinner. I was really scared of anything that had fat. Then my mom finally noticed. I was in my bathing suit. She freaked out. "What's going on?" I was like, "Oh it's fine. It's just soccer and my stomach has been bothering me. I'll gain it back after soccer." So she was like, "All right, but you'd better start eating."

We made it to the State Tournament that year. I still don't know how I was able to play as well as I did when I wasn't eating. It was like my mind could just like "click" and not be hungry and go into this trance. After soccer season, it got really bad. I was constantly skipping meals. Looking back on pictures now, I was disgusting. I was going to the doctor constantly. I kept lying. My parents were like, "This is up to you." I just fought with them and fought with them, saying it was my stomach.

Senior year my parents were watching me. I had to eat three meals but wasn't eating enough to gain weight. Then I got accepted to Sewanee and they're like, "You're not going unless you gain weight." My soccer coach wasn't going to let me play unless I gained weight. I still didn't want to. It was like gaining weight was the worst thing in the world. The rest of the family gained weight because mom was cooking high fatty meals. Steak. We never eat steak and she was cooking steak and omelets for breakfast. Anything to get some fat into me. My friends started saying stuff to me. I was still like, "OK, whatever." I still liked being thin.

I don't know what triggered me getting better. I saw how upset mom and dad were. I was like, "I don't want to but I'll gain the weight." So I got back up to 120–122. I'm probably 125 right now. That's where I like to stay. I like to eat now.

Where Molly turns to fitting in with the cool girls, Susanna molds her body to dance.

I grew up in a white upper middle class family, an only child. I guess my family is well-educated, very involved in literature and books. Money was never an issue. I was very close to my parents and spent a lot of time around adults.

I fell in love with dancing when I was about two and started lessons when I was four. That's been a really big part of my life. I became more and more involved in the dance world. I had struggles in school when I was younger. I was very shy. I was dyslexic. It took me a long time to read. So I had to work really hard and I became an "A" student. I was a real perfectionist.

I wanted so much to be like Evelyn Hart. I read how she developed her eating disorder. It was like studying a manual. When I was eleven I started training every day. And before it [anorexia] got really out of control, it was working. I was an "A" student, doing really well in dance. I was in the band playing trumpet; I was in the musical; I was training every day in dance; I was taking violin. But at a certain point I just focused on dancing and acrobatics. I guess the year before I left home—*when I was fifteen I left to train at the Royal Montreal Ballet School—was probably the most consistently intense year of my eating disorder.*

Deception started to play in. I had a whole routine. School until 3, dance class to 7 or 8, and then I'd go home and do some work. Then sleep, get up and do it all again. I convinced my mother that I'd eat all my protein in the morning so all I'd need at night was vegetables. I'd wake up really early before my parents. I'd take a bit of bacon to create fat in the pan, cook it up, and then throw it out. Then I'd take a cereal bowl, swish it around with milk and half wash it to make it look like I'd used it. I'd generally throw my lunch out. I'd go sometimes for a couple days without eating anything. I remember getting to physically shaking. By high school it was easy to hide things. No one to really know what was going on.

My parents didn't really know. I remember picnicking. I wasn't eating anything and my mother said "We're not getting into this car until you eat something." So I grudgingly chewed up a cracker, stuffed it in the back of my cheeks and threw it out later. The way my parents dealt with it was kind of wished that it wasn't happening. They were scared and they didn't know how to deal with it and often reacted with anger.

Things came to a head near the end of that school year. I got really sick, strep throat, and lost even more weight. I was obsessed with the scale. It seems like another lifetime ago, but I was eighty to eighty-five pounds. I had all sorts of obsessions. I didn't want to get my period. I got it when I was fourteen or fifteen and then didn't get it for a whole other year. I was determined to never have it ever come back.

So I went to Montreal. There wasn't anyone there who didn't have some issue with food. If someone was really fucking crazy skinny, they wouldn't let them come to class unless they gained weight. But people fell through the cracks. We felt like we were being watched, but people were also being watched for being too fat. After I left a student sued the school for eating disorder stuff.

I knew I had a problem. What started to scare me was that I didn't control it anymore. I was really conflicted. On the one hand, I wanted to be a really good anorexic—I always felt like a failure that I was never a bulimic and couldn't make myself throw up. On the other hand, I had something in me that wanted to survive and be healthy. I thought that giving in to my body, or giving in to being human even, was a failure. [In dancing] I thought the ultimate goal was to be a conduit for music. So as little of myself ought to be there. I thought that was purity. But things started to break that down and the more they got broken down the more fucked up I felt.

Then I got a boyfriend. I got out of residence and stayed with his family. They got me in to see this psychiatrist. They fed me every day. I wasn't happy, but I was moving towards being healthier.

Susanna shows great plasticity, fitting herself to a series of molds. Watching her mother dance, she mimics her parent; later she models herself on a famous dancer, adapts to ballet school, and comes to idealize becoming just a "*conduit for music."* Does all this self-denial finally deny her personhood? No, not to Susanna—dance fulfills hers.

Dropping-Out Anorexia. The more anorexia disrupts eating with others, the more isolated the person becomes. Some want to escape social life; others, living itself. In the latter case, depression can lead rather than follow anorexia. Take Sarah.

> *I've had pretty severe depression since middle school. I think the eating disorder started around the same time. I've always written journals and I've read some of my seventh-grade entries about not eating because I felt like I didn't need to eat to live. I guess it sprung out of depression—another way of getting back at myself.*
>
> *I don't think it got really bad until ninth grade when I was very, very shy, very awkward, really depressed. I didn't know how to talk to my parents about it. I had this boyfriend who was two years older than me. He also had depression. We were both all over the place, drove each other crazy. Looking back, the eating disorder really kicked off because of sexual activity that freaked me out. It was so scary. I think I just wanted to not be a girl, not be a boy. If I didn't eat, I'd get very, very small, not look like either or. I cut all my hair off. I was trying to remove myself from gender. I was emotionally all over the place. I hated my boyfriend but was too scared to do anything about it. The weight and the food was all I could control by myself. I wanted nothing to do with sexual pleasure. Getting pleasure from not eating was all I needed, all I wanted.*
>
> *That was when my eating disorder became conscious. Before it had been something I didn't really think about. Then it became all of my thought. I never really exercised. I hate exercise. So it'd just be food restriction. I just wouldn't eat. At first it would hurt—I'd get stomach pains—but then it'd just go away to where I couldn't feel it at all. Calories never mattered to me. I don't understand why people do that. Losing weight was the visual payoff. So you could tell something was working. It's not that I thought my emaciated body was attractive. That's not what I was going for. I was going for shrinking away, not being a person.*
>
> *I was going to a psychiatrist and a nutritionist. I hated putting my parents through that. I didn't want to do it to them, but I couldn't help it. I was put on severe weight watch. If I lost any more weight, I was going to be hospitalized. Anorexia often turns into bulimia. So that happened to me. I became pretty severely bulimic, throwing up after I ate every time. Secrecy was important. I didn't want to talk to anyone about it. I didn't want anyone to feel obliged to talk some sense into me. I didn't talk to anyone about it until it came to a head and my parents were watching over me. I think also the bulimia started out of secrecy. I could still keep myself in control, but secretly.*
>
> *I'm a petite person. So when I do lose weight, it's drastic. I think I was weighing 105. If I got down to one hundred I was going to be hospitalized. When the*

nutritionist told my mom that she started crying. It was so painful. That's when I tried to pull myself together. That was the starting point of recovery, wanting to not hurt other people. It kind of resolved in not wanting to hurt myself. It was a long road. I got different friends and that helped a lot. They were so much more balanced and that helped me be more balanced.

In saying "*I just wanted to not be a girl, not be a boy*" and "*I was trying to remove myself from gender*," Sarah rejects any identity at all, dropping out of personhood altogether. In fact she voices this directly: "*I was going for shrinking away, not being a person.*"[1]

Depressed like Sarah, Francesca was eager to drop out of life. Yet where Sarah stayed close to her parents, Francesca felt abandoned.

My parents are still married though growing up the marriage didn't seem very healthy. In my family the most stressful time occurred around dinner. There just wasn't a very supportive atmosphere. One way of trying to control that was just not eating.

The time I got my worst my parents were going through a lawsuit. He [father] *lost his business. My mother has always been neurotic about money but the thought of losing the house, she just couldn't deal with it. And she became abusive towards her kids. Mainly verbally abusive. Not physical or sexual or anything like that. My dad, trying to preserve normalcy, would support her. But it was as if he was supporting our abuse. It was just such a mind-fuck.*

School was terrible too. Parts were good. I was getting into this weirder subculture hanging out with Goth-Punk kids and Skaboys, and I had a few teachers I looked up to. But there were problems. One of the biggest was my first boyfriend, Mike, who I'd say—this is so hard—molested me when I was fourteen. He reshaped the way I looked at the world. I came to high school having some faith in my parents, trying desperately to justify the way they acted. Mike challenged that. Kind of in a good way, kind of in a bad way. I became very hateful, very angry. I withdrew into this private hell, [asking] *whether how my parents interacted with me was acceptable, thinking, "Maybe this isn't quite right."*

One thing that started the depression was that my grandmother died. My parents left to go to the funeral and I was left [for days] *to take care of my sister. I felt very, very abandoned. My parents didn't even ask if I wanted to go. They just kind of left. I just broke. I totally broke. I just—I couldn't stand up I was so grieved. And it wasn't because she had died. It was because they'd left. I remember sitting in my room weeping for hours. Nobody listened. Nobody knocked. Nobody came in. My parents came back to find me pale and thin and extremely disturbed. I wouldn't eat at dinner. It totally gave me a feeling of control. It made me feel much better. And it was also "Red Flag! Look at this! There's something wrong." I knew that. I realized*

> that if I sat at the dinner table and didn't eat anything, somebody was going to ask about it. And I wanted that.
> When I got really depressed, appetite just went. There was no hunger. The thinking just took over any kind of hunger pangs for a good six months. They just weren't there, and the medication made it even worse. My father, being a psychologist, decided that maybe I should go into a hospital program. So I went into outpatient day-treatment and did a lot of intensive counseling and art therapy. It just got worse and worse and worse. I was obsessed with death. I couldn't think of anything else. I just couldn't function. I remember one of the nurses saying, "In the twenty-five years I've worked here, I've never seen a more depressed patient." I didn't even react. I hit rock bottom. They found me on the bathroom floor crying and saying I wanted to die. That was when they put me in the in-patient program.
> So I went to Methodist Hospital. I lived on the psych ward for I think three days. They said if I don't eat I can't leave. So that encouraged me to eat. They put me on Welbutrin, the worst idea ever. It made me lose my appetite even more. I could go days without eating. It didn't even occur to me. I managed to convince people I was OK enough to leave the hospital. So I continued in day-treatment and then went back to school.

Like Sarah, our earlier dropping-out anorexic, Francesca loses her appetite. For both, starving expresses their feelings directly. Both see themselves as artists and, unlike almost all of our other interviewees, have no interest in athletics.

Slipping-In Anorexia. Where Susanna consciously copies an anorexic dancer and Lynn uses a health film as an eating disorder guide. others, like Jim, slip into anorexia unknowingly. Growing up in suburban Charlotte, he had a *"pretty close-knit"* family.

> A lot of this is hereditary. My mother was a semi-professional ballerina and had an eating disorder. The onset of puberty, maybe twelve, thirteen, I was diagnosed with OCD and a couple other problems that everyone in my family has. When I was younger I had asthma really bad. So I was kind of an indoor kid. Read a lot of science fiction and stuff. So mainly I did karate and indoor stuff. When because of medicine I was able to do outdoor stuff, it was always by myself. With running if I had an asthma attack, I could stop. So it's a very individual thing and goes with my personality anyway.
> Running didn't get competitive until seventh grade. With track there's this dual world—your own time and points for your team. Our sprinters placed well in State every year. So there was pressure for distance runners like me to score points so the sprinters could go on to State. One guy told me he thought he wasn't going to get a scholarship because I screwed up the point standings. He later apologized, but there was a lot of pressure.

> *Because of my mother I was always really health-conscious. I stopped drinking whole milk and eating red meat in third grade because I thought it'd give me heart problems later on. That was back when the big health trend was fat. We didn't eat anything fat. No fat at all. Never. None. I remember I wanted more vegetables. I stopped drinking soft drinks and gradually eliminated sugar. When I started getting involved in athletic competition, I started cutting out even more. Fat became an obsession. I couldn't eat any fat and if I did, I had to run to make up for it. Then it got to the point where I was scared of eating calories. I'd eat soup and cereal with a fork because I didn't want to get extra calories with the milk or broth. I eventually got to the point where I wasn't eating because I thought it was going to help me become a better athlete.*
>
> *When it was really bad, like eighth grade or maybe freshman year, I started passing out when I was running. My parents wanted to take me to the hospital. I convinced them not to. I was like, "You guys aren't disciplined. You don't understand!" I completely blew them off. I know I yelled, "Get the hell away from me! You don't know what's going on. I'm doing this to be a better athlete."*
>
> *When that started I was, like, "OK, I don't really know why this is happening. If I pass out during a race, I'll disqualify my entire team." That's when I started listening to my mom. Mom started talking medical help.*
>
> *I don't know if this figured into it but I started doing karate because my dad wanted me to. He was an absolute all-star athlete in high school. He got real excited when I got into track. I was never able to connect with my father, ever. He was out of town so much for his work. I was able to connect with my mom a lot. We're a lot alike—same humor in books, films, and stuff like that. But my father I can never really find anything to connect. One reason I was pushing myself so hard was that it was a way I could communicate with him, I think. If I did well he'd call me from out of town.* [I] *was internalizing someone else's drive.*

Jim's case recalls Megan's, as both channel an intense drive to succeed into running. Yet Jim slips into anorexia, blind to his pathological eating and exercise, whereas Megan knows something is wrong and hides it from others. Her obsessive running follows from a conscious *"breaking point"*, after which *"small, gradual, very invisible steps"* make her anorexic. For Jim there is no break, just invisible steps. Having begun pushing bodily limits with karate, he now senses no change with anorexia. In the end, sports get Jim out of anorexia (starving was not working) but Megan's secrecy holds her in.

Running was also Elizabeth's gateway:

> *I grew up in New York City and went to an all-girls school. I had three older sisters. From a young age I wanted to define myself. All of my sisters, especially my two older ones, were very smart and very pretty and seemed perfect in every way. But I was a*

much better athlete than they were. So from a young age that was my obsession. I swam, did gymnastics, started running pretty early. It was something I put before anything else.

I went to a really big boarding school. Every kid there had come from being a big fish in a little pool to a small fish in a big pool. It was cutthroat. I went from the same school for ten years, forty girls in my grade, and then got tossed into this class of 300 from all over the world. For the first time in my life I was unhappy. That was just foreign to me. I was a very happy kid, never depressed or made fun of at school.

I was running cross-country. The girls on this team were so much better than at my old school. I was very intimidated. My first day we were doing a hill workout. My coach looks over at me and he was like, "I guess no one told you," and I was like, "What?" and he was like, "Why this is called Sick Sally Hill," and I was like, "No," and he was like, "Because Sally ate lunch!" And I got sick in practice. That's how everyone learns you don't eat lunch before cross-country.

By the time I was a senior I wasn't eating breakfast or lunch and I'd probably run twice or three times that day before any meal. I was running times I'd never run, shaving huge chunks off times. Before boarding school, I'd been an outstanding athlete. Then I wasn't getting any better. [Now] I'd gotten out of this plateau. I was one of the best again and that was a really good feeling.

I definitely didn't recognize it [anorexia], *which is crazy for me to think about now. When anyone mentioned anything about it, it was like, "What are you talking about?" I felt as if I was functioning better. I was doing better in school and my times were faster.*

Something that played a role—at least that's what my mom says—was that the first major bad things in my life kind of set it off. Chronologically it makes sense but I don't know if that's true. Anyway, I had a really serious boyfriend. My senior fall all these girls were saying they'd had their underwear stolen. And I walk into my friend's room and this girl was sitting with a bottle of vodka just crying and I was like, "What's the matter? Are you OK?" She's like, "They found out who the underwear thief was." It turned out her boyfriend had been stealing my and four other girls' underwear for three years, going into my room. He played lacrosse with my boyfriend. That shook me up [and], *more than anyone, my boyfriend. He started ignoring me and not treating me well for the first time. I think that had a lot to do with that* [anorexia], *tying into how it affected the closest person in my life and our relationship.*

Like Jim, Elizabeth slips into anorexia. Years of training give them the constitutional fortitude to push through pain. Unlike Megan, neither Jim nor Elizabeth resorts to secrecy, seeing nothing to hide. Elizabeth says "*I definitely didn't recognize it*" and still finds it shocking that everyone knew but her.

Does the underwear incident explain Elizabeth's anorexia? Her mother suspects trauma. Elizabeth is skeptical—she remembers surprise, not trauma. Her boyfriend suffers, not her. So she attributes her anorexia to trying to get his attention. Follow-up questions suggest a simpler explanation: her boarding school life had two narrow circles—running and a few close friends. When that clique—including her boyfriend and the underwear thief—breaks up, all her energies go into what is left, running. She reverts to an earlier passion: in growing up she put athletics *"before anything else."*

Elizabeth's slipping-in contrasts with our earlier standing-out, fitting-in, and dropping-out cases. Although these types are heuristic, and a different sample might change their number or kind, anorexia clearly begins for quite various reasons.[2] That is no news to clinicians who regularly deal with such variety (A. Becker et al. 2009) and may already distinguish paths into anorexia to help tailor ways out (Vanderlinden 2010).

The Elusive Will

Though motives vary widely, there is one great unity: willpower. Some interviewees mention it directly (e.g., *"I had a will of steel"*—Susanna), and everyone exults in feeling its strength. That experience—exerting one's will over oneself—anchors every ascetic tradition. Yet what we hear is traditionless. It is not, say, to train the person (as in ancient Greece) or transcend self (as in Buddhism). Quite the contrary, this freelance asceticism celebrates the self: *"'Look what I can do!'"* (Natalie); *"I can't believe I made myself do that"* (Melissa); *"Yeah, I put that [feeling] there. I can make it go away. I can put it there"* (Lynn). Such first-person phrasing, what Throop (2010: 34–35) dubs the own-ness in willing, expresses modern identity. What exhilarates our interviewees, then, is not just the will's triumph over body, a pleasure all ascetics savor, but also the double discovery that they have extraordinary powers and their peers do not (e.g., *"I loved it at lunch when I looked over and my friends were eating all this food and I'd be eating five carrots"*—Melissa). However the self-denial began, here anorexia serves adolescent self-discovery.

The will's role in anorexia is elusive. For medicine it is paradoxical: the will is central to what happens yet peripheral to professional explanations. On the one hand, nothing could matter more: starving demands *unrelenting will*; interventions meet *willful resistance*; recovery requires a *will to get well*; and the disease entails *moral willing*. On the other hand, in explaining what happens, will could hardly matter less: "explicit reference to 'the will' has disappeared from psychiatric classification and theorizing" (Good 2010: 167), and even methodical analyses of anorexia and its sufferers (e.g., Casper 1990; Jordan et al. 2008) omit will or anything that global. How can experts ignore something so obvious? Well, as professionals, experts rely on research, and today's research relies on fragmenting. So the will's oneness disappears into pieces to study one by one. How do these pieces work together in the person? No one knows—that emergent whole is too unwieldy to study. Here, by perfecting only itself, research fails the clinic (Clinton 2010).

Are our interviewees any better at grasping the will? In their accounts willing first explains everything (they choose to starve) and then nothing (starving is compulsive, not chosen). In this black-and-white mindset the will is either omnipotent or impotent, present or absent. Yet were an outsider telling the tale, the drama might depict a trickster will where one half rules consciousness grandly while the other runs the cognitive unconscious quietly, sweating details relentlessly until one day, the mind awakens imprisoned by those practices. Yet we hear nothing that ironic or thoughtful. Even those in recovery do not wonder at the vagaries of a will that led them into hell, then left.

In the end, neither experts nor sufferers can parse the anorexic will. Experts dissolve the will that sufferers reify, but neither strategy reveals much. The reason, we argue, is that both are Cartesian. In this epistemology, where subject (mind, self, spirit, culture) differs naturally from object (body, other, matter, biology), either the will breaks the body or reality breaks them both. To be sure, a triumphal but then broken will sums up anorexia nicely, but that scenario blinds everyone—sufferers, caregivers, clinicians—to how the will works bioculturally and what self-help or therapy requires.

Conclusion

To get at anorexia, we listened closely to the recovered. Treating anorexia as an event (Mol 2002: 15–20), they placed it within the life course and identified prior motives. Their stories justify three conclusions.

First, beauty has little or nothing to do with anorexia—a point anthropologists have repeatedly established across multiple cultures (Banks 1992, 1997; Gooldin 2008; Lester 1997; Pike and Borovoy 2004; Warin 2010). Some, like Megan, enjoy looking better, but that is a secondary benefit. Beauty is never primary.

Second, anorexia develops from diverse orientations. Our informants differ widely in social attitude and niche. Lynn is a school leader, Molly feels left out, and Susanna is hardly in school at all. Then again, Megan is into everything, Jim cares only about running, and Francesca cares about nothing at all. Although we have heard only a few stories, all twenty-two say the same: there is no anorexic social type.

Third, anorexia develops from diverse motives. Our informants enter anorexia with various and even opposite intentions. Molly wants to fit in and Lynn to stand out—completely opposite aims. And while their aims are social, Elizabeth loses herself asocially in running. There is no common anorexic motive.

Notes

1. Is starving a strategy to hold on to childhood or hold off womanhood? That Freudian interpretation, "the core of medical theorizing of anorexia" (Lester 2001: 202), misconstrues Sarah. Follow-up questions found she had no nostalgia for childhood, always felt far more mature than peers, and felt pride that friends came to her for advice.
2. Are these more than heuristic? In analyzing Japanese anorexia, Pike and Borovoy (2004: 518–522) characterize one person's motives as to "fit in" and another as "opting out"—two of our four types. As Japan and North America differ markedly, this cross-cultural similarity suggests our types have gotten "out of perspectivalism and into the disease 'itself'" (Mol 2002: 12).

CHAPTER 4

Bioculturalism
Seeing Holistically and Historically

> Divorcing the body from subjectivity and from human relations was a brilliant move, central to the success of modernity—a violent move, cloaked with reverence for progress, and one that must always remain incomplete, provisional, and unsatisfactory.
> —Margaret Lock, "Decentering the Natural Body"

Modernity's "violent move" rips objectivity from our subjective lives, a stable universe from humanity's shaky hands. That Cartesian move, "brilliant" indeed, bids science divorce biology from culture. Add the equally brilliant Platonic move that violently rips one "true" form from deceptive diversity, and presto, a universal biology commands center stage, sweeping aside life's petty local particulars.

In their violence these moves shrink science too far. Anorexia gets swept away—it is a disease built of petty particulars, a syndrome centered exactly where biology and culture do not divide. To be sure, the universal biology that replaces it has advanced science enormously. Yet now we need no longer choose universal or particular. Instead, further advances call for a science that embraces the biocultural character of not just rare pathologies but all humans' evolution, development, and life. In this chapter we show why that is so and develop a biocultural alternative to the biology-or-culture logic that has long left anorexia unexplained and uncured.

Working with Cartesian Dualism

Although Cartesian dualism cannot explain anorexia, we must begin with this dualistic logic. It organizes the anorexic's mindset as well as today's medical knowledge. On both counts, to get at anorexia's biocultural character, we need to go through these Cartesian constructions.

Popular Dualism. All humans live whole lives, but modern folk learn to talk and think dualistically. So we split mind from body or spirit from 'matter' the way we divide religion from science and individual from society. Although these imagined halves are deeply interdependent, contemporary thought expects conflict. That is the specious logic wherein beauty ideals (society) oppress women (the individual) as if the two arose separately and then suddenly collided. In this popular dualism humans have warring halves.

An eating disorder functions as a whole. It arises where reason and emotion fuse, where bodily sentiments and societal logic resonate. That blindsides sufferers. True to our tradition's intellectual tools, anorexics reckon their ailment dualistically. So mind wars against body, and will (spirit) fights flesh (matter). Using dualism lets anorexics pursue their illogical starving logically (counting calories, hiding evidence) and explain it to others as well as themselves (*"I'm just losing weight." "I'm eating healthy"*). What they cannot explain, of course, is how their controlling spins out of control—how this reasoning becomes unreasonable. To do that they would need to see the mind-with-body oneness that our dualist tradition hides. So they *live* the eating disorder as a whole but *think* about it in conflicting halves.

Medical Dualism. Modern medicine struggles to do better. Indeed, many doctors grasp that health is spiritual as well as physical, yet medical training, instruments, accountability, and standard practices all distinguish subjective from objective knowledge, imposing a mind/body distinction that makes anorexia incomprehensible. So anorexia's challenge is not just practical (how do we cure it?) but epistemological (how do we know what current knowing excludes?).

Social Science Dualism. Social science stumbles too. An eating disorder arises from how society's values and the person's body live through each other. Yet Cartesian social science separates the individual from society, only to reconnect the two artificially by belief *or* behavior, a mind/body distinction. So two great schools debate which half matters most. On one side, materialists (stressing body/nature/objective conditions) render anorexics victims of their own manipulations (dieting for appearance) or societal interests (the media, patriarchy). On the other side, mentalists (stressing mind/culture/subjective meaning) attribute anorexia to a cognitive disorder (distorted body image) or malignant meanings (embedded misogyny). Mentalist or materialist, each has a perfectly logical Cartesian explanation. Yet this language of battling halves can only hide how eating disorders function smoothly as wholes.

Demoting Dualism. Today dualism rules the roost. In popular, anorexic, and scientific thought, it is the way the world "really is." We disagree. Yet our research must give dualism its due. It is a viable practice, even if it is not an adequate explanation. So we treat dualism as not an epistemology but as a subject to study holistically and a heuristic tool to apply bioculturally.

Bioculturalism

Our epistemology follows Bateson (2000). In his all-embracing ecology, humans are always in the world, caught up in emergent wholes (like culture) and subject to feedback loops where our actions react back on us. In that oneness of the intricately interdependent mind and body, humans function as historically contingent wholes that arise from and then interact with their surroundings. That truth holds for one person's development or the evolution of our entire species; it encompasses social and cultural realities from small groups to complex civilizations; and it captures how a pathology like anorexia comes and goes.

Bateson's epistemology encompasses today's bioculturalism. In medical anthropology this scientific yet nondeterministic holism dissolves the old Cartesian divides to study how disease, person, and culture all co-create each other (Csordas 1994; Morris 1998; Worthman 1993). To trace co-creation's dynamic, one must see not just the pathology but the individual and our species as thoroughly biocultural creations. We liken all three to hybrids in that each weaves biology and culture into a new whole that then sustains itself adaptively. Of course Bateson, in his logical purity, would not call these hybrids (as that would privilege biology and culture as natural entities). We, however, are intellectual pragmatists. So we work with disciplinary truths by highlighting realities where the division between biology culture hides the integrity of what is happening and thereby cannot answer the questions we are asking.

Answering our overriding questions about how anorexia arises, functions, and persists takes us beyond this one pathology to highlight the biocultural character of our entire species and each individual. As historically contingent, one-off hybrids, all three are structurally alike—homologous. Three traits—history, hybridity, and homology—unlock anorexia's secrets. Yet the prior point is that bioculturalism captures how humans function in health as well as sickness. So the following sections apply bioculturalism to ordinary human phylogeny, ontogeny, and ontology before we apply these same principles to anorexia, an extraordinary disease with ordinary beginnings and development.

Biocultural Phylogeny

Humans evolved to live in groups. Like chimps, bonobos, and gorillas, we are highly social primates (King and Shanker 2003). Our sociality dates back five million years or more (Ward 2003) and is "as much as product of evolution as is [our] . . . bipedal posture and a larger brain" (Zihlman and Bolter 2004: 23). As an adaptive strategy, living in groups makes humans moral creatures (de Waal 2001: 350–363; Howell 1997: 10). That is not to say we are naturally good or cannot easily do bad, but only that humans are physiologically adapted to live in value-based groups that function sympathetically. Like it or not, we feel sympathy as a direct bodily sensation (e.g., wincing at a stranger's pain), mimetically (wincing at a stranger's wince), through respiratory co-rhythm (Lyon 1999) or olfactory cues that entrain individuals' emotions and allow group contagion (Brennan 2004: 10), and even imaginatively by oneself (e.g., worrying about global hunger with not a hungry person in sight). Without some such moral sensibility, no human individual or society could prosper.

Human groups, shared values, and our moral sensibility all co-create each other. Picking up values begins at birth, when we enter a custom-carrying group where we become "active agents bent on mastery of a particular form of life" (Geertz 1997: 192). To master the specifics of knowing when and how a custom applies, the young must also learn the larger lesson that context counts. That sensibility lets us keep up with changing values, move between groups, and live through the largely inherited traditions that anthropologists call culture.

Culture and human biology coevolved. How far back their highly evolved interdependence goes depends on how we define culture, but the depth is great enough to say that humans are cultural beings by our biological nature (Geertz 1973). That biocultural hybridity, in erasing the Enlightenment's nature/nurture split, is how both individuals and groups build themselves out of values that are as various as the world's cultures.

Human evolution put this species-specific package together. Calling this a package disputes the Cartesian separation of biology from culture, of the individual from society. Our species did not first evolve biologically and subsequently add culture. Instead, proto-culture altered human adaptive conditions and thus our biology. Nor can a human be seen as a biologically complete individual who then joins a group, for infants are born biologically incomplete and become complete through the caring of others. So calling this interconnectedness a package says human phylogeny, ontogeny, and ontology co-evolved to make the character of each highly dependent on the others.

Biocultural Ontogeny

Ontogeny roughly recapitulates phylogeny. That is, working within our primate heritage, human infants develop bioculturally much as our species apparently evolved bioculturally. Helpless at birth, every infant must, to survive, enter society by interacting with caregivers, all enculturated social beings. That early interaction, deeply socializing a highly plastic neonate (Worthman 1999: 63–64), has a profound impact "from the molecular level upwards," as early patterns of use establish neural circuitry and fine-tune how anatomy, physiology, cognition, and emotion all develop (Armstrong 1999: 269; Blonder 1999: 275; Worthman 1993, 1999). So instead of nature or nurture, environmental inputs at critical and often epigenetic moments of the infant's built-in developmental sequence shape lifelong organizational patterns.[1] Taken together, these bioculturally decided patterns give each individual a unique constitution and yet typically attune that person to familial and group ways.

How does deep socialization unfold interactively? Within hours of birth, an infant can imitate facial expressions and show interest in others' feelings (Bronson 2000: 111; Field 2001: 48; Worthman 1993: 347–348). All it takes for a newborn's social life to begin is the sympathy an infant evokes in others and then returns, either naturally or via learning. As mother and child mirror each other's feelings, the infant's body appears to become a template for experiencing others' emotions empathetically (Modell 2003: 119). An emotional skill—experiencing others' feelings—thus directs early development, initiating a social sensibility that guides us ever after.

Equally critical to infant development is that this sympathy—or even recursive mirroring—is a two-sided exchange. Sympathy binds two bodies together (feeling other-in-self oneness), while exchange holds them apart. In that separateness, self-interest arises. Does it eventually replace sympathy? Modern thought supposes so. Yet if sympathy truly and totally were lost, life as we know it would end abruptly, for without sympathetic adults to evoke that sentiment in infants, how could the young develop normally? Moreover, a healthy society requires not just self-interest but an emotional sensibility that joins its members. It is this human capacity, perhaps epigenetically tuned, that the anorexia-inclined first exaggerate and then, once afflicted, cripple in isolating themselves.

Biocultural Ontology

In today's academic division of labor, where biology virtually owns phylogeny, human ontology is up for grabs. Biology, psychology, philosophy, and anthropology all stake claims. Anthropology's entrant is culture. Although the discipline debates the character of culture (is it values, beliefs, discourse, story, web?), all agree it pervades everyday life and is thus key to human ontology. Here anthropology used to color neatly within Cartesian lines. Given the mind-or-body choice, most favored mind, centering culture in each group's unique commonalities while leaving the body to biology's universals. Lately, however, some have used culture to claim the body too. Arguing that humans *embody* their culture, these scholars make the top-down claim that the individual is how the group constructs the person. Here ontology sometimes reduces to culture.

We do and do not agree. We agree that humans enculturate the body deeply, but we would argue that human ontology has an individualizing biocultural core that does not reduce to its cultural interpretation. So we would place a person's existential experience less *in* culture than *between* culture's centripetal pull and three sorts of centrifugal individualizing: each person's unique constitution (chapter 5), the practical autonomy of activities (chapter 6), and the societal differentiation that flourishes within cultural wholes. Here, negotiating a middle ground, human ontology unfolds bioculturally.

Brain science favors a biocultural ontology. To be sure, culture has a key place in the brain, but this group-constituted logic does not work alone. Contrary to Descartes, human reason uses emotions to weigh logical outcomes (Damasio 1994). The brain separates the two, localizing reason's symbolizing in the cortex and emotions in the limbic system. Yet the two are interdependent, apparently having coevolved to create "a brain in which symbols interest, motivate and satisfy many of our desires" (Armstrong 1999: 257). In these two brain regions, emotions "emerge from the synergistic interaction between biology and culture" (Hinton 1999: 13). Culture's commonalities thereby get grounded in each individual's biocultural unique body. Moreover, because human "affective systems" became "specialized for the mediation of social relationships" (Reynolds 1981: 82), these culturally inflected emotions link not just mind with body or thought with action, but individual with group (Lyon 1999: 183; Scheper-Hughes and Lock 1987: 28–29).

These emotion/reason and individual/group linkups inevitably individualize culture's collective character. Calling culture collective means it is a shared set of symbols whose language-like discourse pulls a people together. Yet within this commonality, each person individualizes culture idiosyncratically—once because social life particularizes, and again because humans live interpretively within biographies, ontogenies, and biologies that vary from person to person. Here human ontology is incarnate, not disembodied; emotional, not dispassionate; and metaphoric, not literal (cf. Lakoff and Johnson 1999). An individual's everyday existence thus goes outside the skull into a unique body and life that irresistibly engage their local surroundings. Ontology teeters between these inner and outer worlds.

Metaphors bridge this inner/outer divide. Mapping the new onto the old, the human brain relates the strange to the familiar, the distant to the close. Reasoning, then, is largely analogical and imaginative, not strictly logical and literal (Lakoff and Johnson 1999; Tilley 1999). Moving outward from the person, we find culture also revolves around metaphor. Of course, while the brain analogizes promiscuously, culture does so chastely, pushing some connections but not others. Here contemporary culture, by imagining person, body, society, and the nation as homologous, gives anorexics all the metaphors they need.

Within this wider cultural web, the closer we come to individual ontology, the more local regimens organize everyday life around disparate or even defiant meanings. Indeed, to live in complex society, a person gets involved in highly particular institutions, lifestyles, cliques, rituals, procedures, and customs. As these regimens get lived concretely, not just thought abstractly, they interweave mind with body bioculturally as they enmesh the person in social life. Here, amid these highly historical hybrids, anorexia arises for quite particular local and personal reasons.

Anorexia's Ontological Beginnings

Anorexia begins in everyday life. Most interviewees describe an achieving but otherwise ordinary prior life. To take up yet another self-improvement project is nothing new. Then life gets upended—anorexia seizes them unexpectedly, out of nowhere. Later, in recovery, everyone searches for a deeper cause, but to no avail—no one finds much out of the ordinary. That stumps Cartesians and Platonists who, expecting a serious cause for a serious disease, look through rather than at life's accidents and surface. Thus they miss how ordinary practices, metaphors, and logic create this extraordinary disease.

Gateway Practices. To discern *how* anorexia begins, you pinpoint *where* it begins. Here we need not—indeed should not—dig deep: our interviewees' lives revolve around achieving. They all see themselves as achievers, and family and society treat them as such (praise, awards, etc.). This, then, is the personal place where an anorexic practice gets its life-changing leverage.

As achievers, they commit wholeheartedly to a project of self-improvement. Some are taking up a new project on a roll, expecting yet more laurels; others are reacting to troubles or worries, mustering an old strength for new angst. Still others are pursuing prior projects, blind to their new significance. Although projects vary—dieting, healthy eating, exercising, athletic training, studying—they share three commonalities: they are *activities*, not just ideas or daydreams, and doing well requires an *inward focus* and sustained *self-denial*.

Gateway Metaphors. Anorexia's gateway practices all lead a double life. Publicly, each is a practical means to a practical end: dieting is the means to weight loss, healthy eating serves health, and so on. Yet these gateways also lead a metaphoric life: dieting, training, and healthy eating are modern metonyms—parts that represent the whole, the person. That is how an instrumental activity (the means to an end) becomes expressive too (an end in itself). Once that happens, the need to succeed balloons. Now, one's identity is at stake—who you are, not just what you are doing.

What magnifies these practical actions into person-defining activities? How, that is, do dieting, exercising, and healthy eating become vastly more than they are? Metaphor makes a second leap. Where the first jump connects actor with activity, the second one adds the modern homology where person, body, society, and nation all echo each other. All at once your actions can sway the world. Your discipline and virtue build—even create—a disciplined and virtuous world. In modern thought that is delusional, but it is how modern lives get lived nonetheless. Indeed, given how modern ontology lives within human ontogeny (Damasio 1994), it may well ground everyone's life.

Gateway Logic. What weaves these practices and metaphors into a pathology is relentless rationalization. That is the unbending logic that cross-examines every thought, act, or feeling, asking just one question: Is this the most efficient means to my chosen end? That is the tireless logic that changes achievers into anorexics, that sweats every personal detail until the person disappears.

Where do achievers get this deadly idea? We need not look far. It pervades modern life. Modern organizations—governments, businesses, professions, schools—impose means/ends rationality on themselves and those they serve. That is how you get results. So it is no surprise when exercising sucks in more and more of an achiever's life, or calorie cutting expands to fill every waking moment. That is the modern way.

Biocultural Mis-development

How does anorexia develop within this biocultural matrix? Our answer begins here and continues over the next two chapters. Eventually we analyze the anorexic's agency empirically. First, however, we need a structural overview of how the pathology develops.

Constitution. Anorexia develops out of a prior constitutional makeup. Our informants' intense childhood involvement in athletics, dance, art, or even study arguably developed a biocultural ability to lose themselves in activities. This ability would later serve the total commitment that anorexia requires. Certainly their ascetic inclinations were a nature/nurture hybrid long before their situations evoked obsessive exercising, dieting, or disordered eating.

A fateful change taps this constitutional background. Out of these old capacities, self-starvation creates a new biocultural hybrid. Although some cases develop more abruptly than others, eventually the whole person (mind, body, spirit) gets reprogrammed (perhaps epigenetically) from, say, dance to anorexia through what we will call structuring, analogizing, aligning, and energizing. These are not separate steps, but as analytical distinctions they help us think sequentially about what is entangled and concurrent.

Structuring. Anorexics invent their own ascetic disciplines. Each regimen interweaves mental rules and bodily schema to create a uniquely local hybrid. Becca, for example, let herself eat freely at two particular restaurants, whereas Isabel standardized on cereal. Different as these regimens are, all structure life around restricted eating, vigorous exercise, or both. Once begun, the structuring follows its own inner logic, typically growing in scope and rigidity until a single principle rules the anorexic's life.

Analogizing. Anorexia restructures anorexics via metaphor. Instead of being apart from mind, body becomes a structure for thinking expressively about the world (M. Douglas 1973: 72; Kirmayer 1992; Lester 1997)—a little arena for larger issues. That is how human brains work (Damasio 1994), so such "magical thinking" (Aharoni and Hertz 2012) is not pathological in itself; rather, the abnormality is how anorexics live metaphors that others merely imagine. The abstract becomes concrete. As a lived metaphor, food evokes purity, not nourishment (Warin 2003a); eating invokes control, not sustenance; and hunger incarnates virtue, not death (Gooldin 2008). None of these transformations are logical. To the contrary, they are all *ana*logical—reasoning from parallel cases. Analogy is not naturally bounded: once food is not food, what it can be by resemblance multiplies wildly (Foucault 1970: 17–54).

Nor is analogy measured: once eating is a metaphor for purity, any pollution is abhorrent. You *are* what you eat. Shades of gray are lost, as metaphoric thinking is in all-or-none extremes. After all, once the body is a metonym for the person—a part that represents the whole metaphorically—you *are* your body. You do not ask, "Is my body half of me?" or "Is it 63 percent?" Once the body *is* the person, mirrors and scales tell anorexics who they are. All or none, metaphors enmesh anorexics in black-and-white choices, stark tests of will where they are strong or weak, good or evil. Suddenly one's discipline is like virginity—either kept pure or totally lost.

Anorexia literalizes a part-to-whole metaphor we call person/world oneness. In themselves these little-to-large analogies are quite conventional and pervade Western thought from the Bible to contemporary individualism (Dumont 1986; Lincoln 1986a, 1986b). In these analogies, big and small telescope into each other: a person is society or cosmos writ small, whereas society or cosmos is the person writ large. Taken literally, little/large schema organize anorexia. Then, just as the person (whole, large) is the body (part, little), the body (now itself a whole) is what it eats (part). Once their experience moves metaphorically, anorexics feel that if they eat any fat (a part), they will become a fat person (the whole)—a person who eats fat *is* fat. Although in actuality a fat person may show great self-discipline in everything but eating, in metaphor this one weakness (a part) makes the person (the whole) weak. Nor is obesity just personal: weak people (a part) make society (the whole) weak. Not surprisingly, anorexics show an acute concern for like-with-like grouping and a magical fear of contagion (Warin 2003b: 88).

Aligning. Anorexia's metaphors align like with like across multiple domains (food, eating, person, body, society) to create an all-encompassing single-principle world. In itself that is not abnormal—monotheism does exactly that—but actually living that way is. Daily life pulls principle and practice apart, for most people. That gap is just realistic, not hypocritical, or so they would say. Anorexics, however, align their entire lives around disciplined eating and living as an all-or-none moral commitment, social stance, and cultural value. To get that concordance actors must rearrange their outer expressions (what they do) and inner realm (how they think and feel).

How does the self rearrange the self? In other words, how do you accomplish the psychological equivalent of pulling yourself up by your own bootstraps? You externalize. The more expressive you are—that is, the more you manifest your thoughts and feelings outwardly—the more tangible and thus potentially tractable your inner life becomes. Just as writing out a to-do list allows us to manipulate ourselves, the outwardness of eating allows an anorexic to work on body and self as everyday projects, objects for endless improvement. Our informants, for example, wrote out eating plans, charted their performance on paper, marked success with gold stars, admired their willpower in mirrors, numbered their discipline on scales. Unlike daydreaming's passive inner discourse, the anorexic's active externalizing creates a lever to act on oneself.

Where would someone learn this bootstrapping? Sports, school, dance, art—the more performance-oriented these activities become, the more the outward sign leverages or even replaces the inner state. Of course, were humans truly dualistic creatures—mind apart from body, spirit distinct from matter—none of this self-manipulation could ever work. Fat or thin, you would still be the same person inside. Yet precisely because inner and outer do in fact bleed into each other, because they are richly connected bioculturally, a strong-willed person who demands top performance can become anorexic, just as another such person becomes an Olympian.[2]

What is the new interior arrangement? As every self has many sides, an anorexic in the making has a lot to work with. Judging by how they come to live by a single principle, their executive self (Baumeister 1997)—the conscious leader of the person's parts that our inner voice expresses—denies their more sympathetic, sociable, sincere sides. The latter qualities, in giving other people and unfolding events a say in one's life, lessen one's autonomy and control. The executive self, in contrast, readily asserts control and manipulates others to get what it wants. Only the executive can deliver a single-principle life. Or, as it is a loop, we could also say only living a single-principle life can give the executive such dictatorial power. That is how Molly's virtuous eating and Elizabeth's devoted running (single-principle lifestyles) can gear their minds to restructure their inner facets into what accidentally becomes anorexia.

Energizing. What empowers anorexia to displace healthier ways? As the executive self becomes dictatorial and anorexia's elements align, they begin to function as a single self-energizing system. What does this new psychic economy offer that the older arrangement lacked? Case by case, we see incidental payoffs, consequences of anorexia's life-focusing intensity. For example, anorexia improved Elizabeth's running just as its expressiveness pleased Francesca. Intended or not, these consequences energize anorexia—they work to solve prior problems or meet practical needs, and that success inspires further effort. Other than these particular payoffs, consider five other potential gains:

- As an ascetic discipline, anorexia orders and simplifies living. A single principle settles life's endless complications and contradictions—the tangles that stymie and confuse us.
- Shrinking life into a ritualized regimen establishes control and relieves stress.
- Anorexia embodies virtue. Initially slimming, exercise or healthy eating feasts on praise from others. Later it feeds on "doing what is right" and "staying strong."
- Anorexia isolates. Withdrawing into their rituals, anorexics escape difficult involvements as well as social stress.
- Anorexia establishes an identity. In adolescence, anorexia is a recognized social niche.

One or all, these payoffs energize the structuring, analogizing, and aligning that together give this deadly disease an emergent life of its own.

Opposing. As payoffs energize the pathology, it becomes a hybrid, a self-sustaining biocultural whole. It thereby functions as a system, including some phenomena and excluding others. Here, as sympathy aligns what is within, antipathy to what is outside creates a system-making boundary. Our informants spoke about disgust at fat in food or on people, and began to define themselves in opposition to easier lifestyles as well as caregiver efforts to get them to ease off their regimen.

Bioculturalism and Epigenetics. What then pulls anorexia together? Dualism cannot say. It makes the anorexic a puppet of gender or genetics, never mind how. So anorexia just happens, its inner workings a mystery. Instead of this black box, bioculturalism organizes evidence to give productive answers that root the disease in the very void that dualism creates by divorcing culture from biology.

Is anorexia's biocultural integrity built or buttressed by epigenetics? So far there is "scant direct evidence" of an epigenetic role in psychiatric disorders, but the process of modulating or even silencing genes could explain "how features of the social environment translate into psychopathological outcomes" (Toyokawa et al. 2012). At least for anorexia, the regulation of weight and appetite has multiple genetic dimensions that epigenetics could modulate. In one scenario the "maintenance of an eating disorder could be due to epigenetic changes that allow individuals to escape physiological processes underpinning appetite and weight regulation" (Campbella et al. 2011). In fact anorexics do show epigenetically induced changes, but whether this is a cause or consequence of their disorder is unclear (Clarke et al. 2012: 185; Toyokawa et al. 2012: 72). For now, given that anorexia's epigenetics is still "largely in its infancy" (Clarke et al. 2012: 185), those changes have three implications for our work: epigenetics provides a mechanism for emergence; it suggests how brief historical moments have lasting consequences (sometimes called "molecular memory"); and, by stabilizing anorexia biochemically, it makes substance-denial similar to substance-abuse and, arguably, harder to break.

Conclusion

Medicine can neither cure nor prevent nor control anorexia. That is not for want of time, trying, or talent. It is for want of an apt epistemology. To that end this chapter goes back to basics to show how understanding life bioculturally can solve anorexia's mystery.

All humans live biocultural lives. Our species-specific adaptation, culture, taps social, moral, and cultural *capacities* that are built into our biology. That is human phylogeny. To exercise these capacities effectively, normal humans develop *sensibilities* bioculturally, beginning in the womb and building rapidly postpartum. That is human ontogeny. It equips us to weave ourselves into and out of local social and cultural worlds. That is human ontology, an ongoing *meaning-making* that our phylogeny allows and ontogenies crave. Phylogeny, ontogeny, ontology—these three biocultural realities all meet in anorexia.

Anorexia mis-develops its sufferer bioculturally. Although mis-develop is not a word in today's biology-or-culture episteme, it is how biocultural maladaptations like eating disorders arise. In these syndromes a once normal human grows into a self-destructive way of functioning. Then the human body, well designed to fight off invaders, does not know how to defend its health. Its destroyer is itself, not an alien. A mis-developed body thus defends its self-made malady. That befuddles Cartesian biology and defies reason. But it is exactly what bioculturalism explains historically. Here anorexia's accident does not differ from the way our species evolved and every individual still develops. All follow from how contingent events spawn synergies that take on lives of their own.

Notes

1. Once genes epitomized how nature stood apart from nurture. Now epigenetics shatters that split to reveal a biocultural middle ground where humans have always lived. Your genes are not a set-in-stone plan for your biology. Instead, some genes allow a set of possibilities that epigenetics can decide in response to environmental influences. True, some areas are under tight genetic control. But others are looser, and some depend heavily on epigenetics to decide a wide range of possibilities through environmental inputs. Many key epigenetic moments come in the womb or infancy. Others come later as life's biological possibilities narrow progressively in growing up. And a few can occur throughout the life span.
2. Olympic swimmers, Chambliss (1988: 13–14) finds, win not because of extraordinary gifts but "by doing what needs to be done, by doing everything right, by concentrating on all the silly details that others overlook. What makes them champions is the knowledge—and the action following from that knowledge—that champions are only real people."

CHAPTER 5

Bodily Bent
The Individual's Constitution

What kind of person gets anorexia? Epidemiologists know most are female adolescents, but beyond that the field's other markers—class, income, education, lifestyle, residence—give no clear picture. Testing does no better: psychological measures turn up various incremental differences such as a higher incidence of OCD, but nothing as coherent as an anorexic personality.[1] History hardly helps: the experts (Brumberg 2000: 47; Bynum 1987) say each era has its own anorexia. Bruch (1962: 192) does better, for characterizing the anorexic as a perfect child hints at the prior person, although this makes the defiant anorexic all the odder. Over a century into the question, what kind of person gets anorexia still stumps researchers. Our chapter tackles this old mystery with a new idea—constitution.

Anorexic Constitutions

In growing up everyone develops a distinctive constitution. Anorexia manifests late in this game, but as the following cases show, it can arise rather naturally out of the person's long-established practices and attitudes.

Becca's Healthy Eating. Becca was introduced in the Preface. Someone with no weight concerns (*"people would always tell me how skinny I was"*), she grew up in Austin, Texas, where she had a happy and stable school life—the *"same school district with the same kids,"* kindergarten through high school. She describes herself as *"very energetic and very bubbly"* and close to her family (*"I have really loving and supportive parents"*). Asked to tell her story as if speaking to a friend, she began with her perfectionism:

> Well, I'm a real big perfectionist. They'd already know—"Yeah, Becca, you're a perfectionist." I'll start there and kind of go backwards. In sixth grade, when my sister went to Sewanee, she came back and had the freshman fifteen.[2] My mom wasn't hard

> on her, but my grandparents were. I'd overhear my mom talking about it with my godmothers. Of course my big sister wasn't around.
> Eighth grade—it was weird—I just started limiting my food portions. I went on a cruise with my family. They'd be like, "Don't you want more?" Buffets and everything. It's like, "No, no." And when I came back I started exercising a lot more. The thing is, I was [already] a big healthy eater. I didn't like junk food.
> That's how it all began until I finally realized that I had an eating disorder—that was ninth grade. A whole year went by and I dropped at least twenty-five pounds. Like in bathing suits you can see my ribs! My mom'd say, "You need to eat more." "Oh, I'm just not hungry." "Well, why are you going for another run?" "Oh, I just feel like being outside." I'd just find ways. I didn't see it wrong in my eyes. Up front I didn't, but in the back of my mind I knew there was something not right. But it was like, "You know, I'm fine. This is good for me."
> I remember the day I finally realized. I was at a Mexican restaurant. Mexican food: fat, fat, fat! Calories! Oh my goodness, galore! My family ordered nachos. My mom was like, "Becca, have a nacho." And I'm like, "No, mom, I can't." "Yeah, yeah. There's plenty." I'm like, "NO, MOM, I can't." And she goes, "Rebecca, Rebecca, c'mon have a nacho." And I'm like, "NO!" and just broke down crying. After we got back I sat down with my mom and we realized that we needed to get help.

Did fearing her older sister's freshman fifteen provoke Becca's anorexia? The criticism is gossipy, not confrontational. Her telling is matter-of-fact, not troubled. If it set her to brooding, she does not say so. Two years elapse. Suddenly, to her own surprise ("*it was weird*"), she starts restricting and exercises more. It makes no sense ("*To this day, I really don't know why*"). She blames her perfectionism but recognizes that "*a skeleton as a body really isn't perfect.*"

Can overheard criticism of someone else activate one's own deadly disease years later? Follow-up questions show her mom shares the perfectionism that is Becca's lifelong trait: "*My mom says I always—even since a little kid—tried to make or build things just the best way I could.*" That trait moreover becomes a family role and perfectionist identity.

> *My big sister is laid back, my little sister has learning disabilities, and my little brother—we're working on him. He's smart but he needs to apply himself. With me I had this image of myself. My parents looked to me as the kid that liked to do everything to the best possible. And so I had this image of Becca. I wanted every little thing about me to just—I guess—be an example. That people would look at me and, like "Wow, There goes Becca! Oh that's the perfect child!"*

All of this suggests her perfectionism is constitutional. If the "freshman fifteen" shows imperfection, we might expect her to react viscerally, to fear that flaw in ways her consciousness can neither follow nor calm.

Why did she "perfect" eating and exercise rather than, say, health and appearance? Later we discover restricted eating models her mother: "*I look up to my mom a lot and my mom eats really small portions because she gets full easily. So I often ate the same portions my mom ate. Half portions. I'd model my eating after my mom's.*" Still later, in describing eating at college, Becca turns out to practice virtuous eating (chapter 10), a moral discourse where the good person has a healthy lifestyle and eats austerely.

> At our dining hall people say, "Oh, you eat so healthy!" I'm like, "Yeah, I like healthy food." And they say, "That's strange." And I'm like, "Yeah, but you eat what you like." In third grade I almost had an eating disorder. I just got scared of fat. I'd look at nutrition panels and really got scared of fat. I'd only eat Kellogg's. Mom was like, "I just cooked dinner and you're eating Kellogg's cereal!" "I like Kellogg's!" "Rebecca, if you don't stop eating just Kellogg's corn flakes I'm going to take you to a doctor." And that scared me. I didn't want anyone to think there was something the matter with me. So my mom and I started going to this health food grocery, Whole Foods. We'd go every Sunday, quite a distance. I'd get really upset when we didn't.

Although she eventually drops her whole food craze, healthy eating still distinguishes her. Where others indulge, she restricts—and people notice:

> My best friend's family—whenever I'd come to their lake house or something—they'd always, "Goodness Gracious, we gotta have fruit for this child! We have to have carrots. All the other little girls are having cookies and this kid's eating healthy snacks."

Five years into a bodily practice that is her social identity as well, eighth-grade pressures intensify restricting and she starts "*exercising a lot more*" after sports practices. It turns out this too is built into her identity: "*I was a big athlete too—basketball, softball, volleyball and I liked running too.*" Nor is it just her:

> My family is very big on exercise. My parents love to do it, not only for health but it's a stress-reliever. In fact our Austin newspaper did an article on how parents influence their children's outlook on exercise. And there's a picture of our whole family playing basketball.

Anorexia blindsided Becca and still mystifies her. Yet she looks in the wrong place for the wrong cause. She clutches at the odd while ignoring the ordinary, suspects trauma rather than her constitution, and stresses strife instead of values. A single troubling incident (her sister's freshman fifteen) thus supposedly incites a syndrome that was actually years in the making. Had she grown up thinking constitutionally rather than psychologically, she would see how anorexia intensifies the life-organizing values and practices that she began long ago.

Beth's Work Ethic. Like Becca's, Beth's anorexia taps deep roots. Both women embody their family's lifestyle virtues. Where Becca's family has a healthy living ethic, Beth and her parents value work. So while they lead an active and healthy life (*"I'd consider us a very healthy family"*), when asked about fitness, Beth replies, "We've never really been huge on 'gotta go the gym,' 'gotta do this,' 'gotta do that.'" Indeed, their "gotta do" is work.

I come from a small town in Alabama. I grew up in a wonderful family. My father is a family physician. My mom manages my dad's office and I worked from an early age. I'm pretty much a perfectionist, having grown up with two extremely hard-working parents.

My grandparents are very active in my life. My mom's mother is really gorgeous and very concerned about appearance. My mother and aunt were in a lot of beauty contests. My aunt's sort of bigger. My grandmother always comments on how she's killing herself. She's fat, is what she'll tell her—just horrible. Mom and I are more ideal types so she praises us. I have a brother, a year younger than me. Very quiet and reserved. We're polar opposites. I've always been involved in everything and he's done what he wants. I'm the daughter who does everything the parents expect. I grew up a very good child.

I was an overachiever in school. Did piano and art. I stood out in every aspect of small town life. I enjoyed school. Overworked everything, made great grades. My friends on the other hand couldn't have cared less what their grades were. I played sports, but I'd have to go home to study because I had to be the best in both. Sports I've done all my life—basketball, volleyball, softball. I waterskied before I could walk. I had to have hip surgery. I forgot to mention that. I was born with bilateral hip dysjunction but that's all been resolved.

I've always been one if I set my mind to it, I go all out. I started out junior year just wanting to lose a little weight for the prom. I got into this habit of eating very little, shaving more and more off. After sports, I'd run an additional mile. After prom, instead of stopping right there—I was an ideal weight—I just kept going. It became a way of life. By senior year my dad referred me out to someone in Birmingham, a specialist. But I wasn't ready. So I played little games with him.

I came here to college. First semester was really hard. I overcompensated for being from a small town. All I did was study, just killing myself with work. I hid behind that. Never ever have I had a problem making friends. But I closed myself off.

I remember them telling me I couldn't go to Italy for Summer Abroad [unless I gained weight]. *As always I'd set goals and achieve them. I HAD to go to Italy. So I did what I had to do to. Then I went to Italy, not paying attention anymore to it. By the time I got back I weighed under one hundred pounds, lost about twenty pounds. I wasn't aware of it. I wasn't doing it on purpose.*

Beth struggles to stop the weight-shedding she has built into her body. She changes her mind only to find her body will not. How did she lose control? Beth overworks everything—hard work is how she knows herself, identifies with parents, plays her family role, succeeds at sports, engages school and college—and once she adds weight loss to that package, she cannot get it out. Her constitutional bent—go all out in all areas—denies doubting her commitments, just as her achieving sense of self will not let a challenge go unmet.

Compensating intensifies Beth's work ethic, as when she overworks college to offset small-town deficits. But perhaps it began with her hip dysfunction. Saying *"I've never been confident about my body,"* she stars in sports nonetheless. Earlier Susanna recalled a similar triumph. The only child of two well-educated parents, she says, *"I had a lot of struggles in school. So I had to work really hard and I became an 'A' student."* In love with dance, she shines at ballet even without a ballerina's body: *"It's just the way I'm built. I kind of felt that there was something fundamentally wrong with me, something I had to fix about myself that was quite essential. And I had to take great measures to do so."*

Becca, Beth, and Susanna all embody life-organizing values. The values differ—healthy eating for one, dedicated work for the other two—but the consequence is the same: each develops a constitution that carries her into anorexia.

Outer Expressions

Like Becca and Beth, all other interviewees evidenced anorexia-inclined constitutions. If we stress outward expressions—what is empirically evident—everyone mixed performative, ascetic, and virtuous dispositions.

A Performative Disposition. Most kids perform for others to admire. Were our informants especially performance-oriented? That would explain their childhood success. As Bruch (1979: 55) says, "most anorexics are outstanding students who are praised for their devotion to work, enthusiasm in athletics, and helpfulness with less advantaged schoolmates." That is our sample: all have records of high achievement, most see themselves as high achievers, and roughly a third call themselves perfectionists.[3]

Again and again our stories show constitutional achievers who have built who they are and how they think, feel, and act around sustained superior performance. Take Beth's overachieving. It is not due to parental pressure—they accept her laid-back brother—but she will not let up. Or recall Megan. Already excelling academically and socially, she commits to doing even better—*"I'm going to be the best person, going to do everything right, and well, and better."* Lynn sees how this achieving turns anorexic: *"It's like athletics in a way. You've got your 'how long does it take me to run this distance?' Then next time you're going to cut a couple seconds off it. It just attaches itself to thinness.*" For a top student, three-sport athlete and class president, weight loss is just the next mountain to climb. Ever an achiever, at college she studies "*as extremely*" as she once starved, double majors, graduates with honors, and begins a masters before medical school.

All but four or perhaps five of our twenty-two grew up not just with but through dance, athletics, or both, performing regularly before the critical eyes of coaches, competitors, and judges.[4] To succeed, performers hone three anorexia-favoring capacities. First, performers play to an audience. Satisfying others to satisfy oneself enmeshes you in what others see. Second, performers master committing decisively and carrying on courageously, blocking out all doubt. Third, performers manifest ideas directly. A slim body is one such idea.

Are these performance-honed capacities integral to anorexia? Just over half of our sample (12 of 22) were elite athletes or dancers. At the top in sports and the performing arts, a height where "criticism is frequent and severe," Goode (1978: 306) finds the performer usually "internalizes this recurrent disapprobation and scolds himself or herself for the least falling away from an ideal performance." However they learned it, several informants live that self-critical attitude, what Francesca dubs a default tape player in the back of her mind.

Our interviewees depict themselves as high achievers. Fifteenth in a graduating class of 325, Becca observes that "*there's definitely a correlation in the perfection I was seeking for my body* [and] *my grades.*" Our informants' achieving intertwines with how they understand themselves. Take Megan:

> *In high school, my sister graduated in the top of her class and was in this all-around homecoming court. Our parents were involved in the school. We were the Jones sisters and all that good stuff and my parents instilled in me the need, you know, if you're going to do something, do it well.*

So too Jane: "*I'd always been very determined in anything that I did. In elementary school I was always very determined to achieve. So the determination—the will—that* [anorexia required] *was nothing new.*" Once self-denial and control measure achievement, anorexia has its engine.

An Ascetic Disposition. Whatever else they may be, anorexics are ascetics, devotees of self-denial who shun creature comforts. Yet which came first, anorexia or asceticism? Evidence that an ascetic attitude is not only prior but constitutional comes in statements about seeking challenge. Rather than accept the self "as is," our informants demand more from themselves. Take Susanna, a professional dancer:

> *I was having this conversation with other performers like me. You know we laugh, you find yourself in the studio killing yourself, like you've asked yourself to do really*

really hard things and it's because it doesn't feel like you're working unless you are doing that.

Or Jesse:

I want to do a half marathon. I hate running—I find it boring and terrible—but I want to be able to do it. Any sort of physical activity, to get better, it's not enjoyable in itself. But it's about getting there. You never improve fitness and strength unless you push beyond what you can do with ease.

Or Lindsay:

The things I choose to do are always very rigorous and very challenging. I remember at camp there was a bunch of canoe trips. There was only one super hard one, almost impossible. Of course I did that one every year. I was like "I have to!" I've always done that.

A producer, Lindsay relishes high-stress jobs where *"you work your ass off."* When she says, *"I have a really hard time letting myself take a break or relax,"* she describes an ascetic constitution where denying oneself feels right.

What is this asceticism's origin? Other than work-before-play in school, most informants spent years under the even more demanding self-denial of dance and athletics. Molly credits her capacity for anorexia to sports:

I've always been self-disciplined but athletics actually taught me self-discipline. So I knew how to push myself and be mentally tough. I learned you can always push yourself further. What you think you can do, you can do more.

Jim does too:

Even if you're almost blacking out you keep going. You're taught to discipline your body and overcome it. It definitely figures into the eating disorder things. As long as you can keep going, do it. I literally get a black outline around anything I'm looking at and that's when I know to back off—unless I'm at the end of the race.

Of course performance activities are not the only path to self-denial. Although Francesca did neither dance nor sports, she knew that attitude:

My parents were all about self-denial. To this day my mother doesn't buy herself new clothes, ever. She doesn't think we have enough money—although we do. She's all about these bogus perceptions. My father's all about "Don't disturb your mother, even if it means you don't get what you need. Deny yourself." He does it too so he can take care of Mom. Since I was a baby I can remember these things for the longest longest time.

A Virtuous Disposition. Earlier, in characterizing anorexics as virtuous, we quoted Bruch (1962: 192) on how they had been "outstandingly good and quiet children, obedient, clean, eager to please, helpful at home, precociously dependable, and excelling in school work." In follow-up questions we sometimes read that statement to get our interviewees' reactions. Out of the twelve we asked directly, eight thought it fit them exactly: *"sums me up"* (Molly); *"textbook!"* (Francesca); *"That's me as a kid. That's very much me."* (Fred). The remaining four had some qualifications—*"I was really really eager to please but not always helpful"* (Natalie)—but otherwise agreed. Sheena elaborates:

Even as young as three or four, people would baby-sit me and I was very, very good on my own. I'd keep to my activities. And that continued on. I never got sent to the principal's office, stuff like that. I always strived to please family, make them proud.

Although no independent evidence backs up their professed virtue, our informants' self-image highlights being good and doing right as children. Indeed, some link anorexia to pursuing virtue. Lindsay, for example, says, *"I think most people that have had an eating disorder think they always could do more; they could be a better person. It's like this constant feeling you can always do better."*

Inner Coherence

Are these three dispositions—performative, ascetic, virtuous—separate attributes or a single trait variously expressed? Staying close to life's surface, we arrived at these three inductively, but they are entangled. In school, for example, being good would lead into the self-denial of hard work and result in the achieving that accents a person's performative side. Indeed, in an achievement-oriented society, where does the performative end and the virtuous begin?

While these three connect closely in *society*, are they intertwined in *the person* as well? We can approach this empirically or theoretically. Empirically, it varies case to case. Recall Lynn and Megan. While both aim to stand out, Lynn celebrates beating rivals. Megan, in contrast, disavows any real rivalry with her sister, says she *"hated competition"*, never mentions competitors, and quite unlike Lynn never gloats in victory. For her the performative is about feeling worthy, not triumphant, and ascetic self-denial—always asking more of herself—is being worthy. All three fit closely together for Megan, but for Lynn winning rules the others.

The theoretical approach to this three-or-one question asks whether we can deduce some core complex behind these three dispositions. Our informants, we propose, have long combined a sympathetic attitude with somatic expressiveness.[5] *Somatic Expressiveness.* Our primate past makes our brains and bodies highly refined communicative organs. We all somatize: our bodies broadcast thoughts, feelings, and intentions while receiving and reacting to what others give off. Long before mastering language, infants thereby develop group as well as personal communicative styles that become core constitutional patterns.

Anorexics are skilled somatizers. In dance and athletics they translate ideas, feelings, and intentions directly into actions. Susanna says the dancer's *"ultimate goal"* is to be *"a conduit for the music,"* which evokes how A. Frank's (1995: 41–44) disciplined body "defines itself primarily in actions of self-regimentation" and "stresses performance." That describes even Melissa and Francesca—gym avoiders who take pride in how intensely they can study. As Frank says, the "disciplined body-self is not likely to tell stories about itself; rather, its stories are told through the pursuit of the regimen." Indeed, anorexics act rather than speak. The saying 'actions speak louder than words' becomes 'somatizing speaks louder than explaining.'

Do anorexics somatize where other psychologize? In psychologizing, a person voices worries and feelings, expressing distress verbally rather than somatically (Kleinman 1986: 55–56). Although this contrast is neither absolute (all humans somatize) nor culture-free (it is a Western mind/body dualism), it helps describe the anorexic state. The afflicted act rather than narrate, so they tell no story—they somatize rather than psychologize. Is this anorexia's effect or the person's prior style? Our evidence cannot say. At least in recovery we find articulate individuals like Francesca who excel at psychologizing *and* somatizing. She is, in short, highly expressive. When Francesca gives up on life, she somatizes it directly by loss of appetite. We saw the same in Sarah, another highly verbal yet highly somatic person. In Natalie's story appetite and digestion somatize stress.

Ahh, the story of my eating disorder [takes a deep breath]. *If I were telling someone who knew nothing I'd start with what it is now, which is it's more stress than body image. Like, I have the same concerns most women have—"Oh I look fat in this dress"—but it never factors in with food these days. When I stop eating, it's more stress. I get nervous. Maybe something triggers it, has me buzzing, upset, shocked, whatever. And suddenly food takes on this feeling of vulnerability. Like I can't look at food and eat, have a desire to eat. Even the act of buying food is difficult. These days it's manageable, but I think it was overall a self-image thing. Like I don't want to be seen as the sort of person who needs to eat, you know, strangely* [laughs]. *Sometimes eating is attached to ideas—greed and gluttony and badness. Then other times I think it's wonderful. Like this week, I was away with some friends and I actually really enjoyed cooking and eating. So sometimes food is comforting.*

My eating disorder started around twelve or thirteen. Before that I had some kind of weird illness. I just couldn't eat. I felt sick sick all the time on the point of throwing up. So I gradually lost my appetite. It was completely a physical thing. I was still going to school and I was still dancing. So I dropped weight like crazy and I got skinny skinny skinny. Everyone started to notice like, oh, suddenly, "She's a beautiful dancer now," "She's got a body of a dancer, you know—perfect." And my dancing got better because I was getting all this recognition.

Things were busy. I was starting to dance a lot more, and all the extra-curriculars were picking up. I was only getting four to five hours sleep at night. My mom had chronic fatigue. Oh that was a hard year for her, so hard. No one knew what chronic fatigue was. Well they sort of knew but most doctors didn't take it seriously and she was still going to work, still doing twelve-hour shifts, still coming home and cooking and cleaning and making my costumes. Then her dad died. I remember that being the point of gravity—me being sick, my mom being sick, my grandfather dying.

Then I sort of outgrew this stomach thing. I started gaining weight back. I don't know what I got up to before I said, "Wow, I don't want to get too high." I just remember this summer where me and my friend Steph were fanatically weighing ourselves. We didn't want to get over eighty-three pounds. First year of high school I pretty much didn't have breakfast and lunch. I could only really eat if I had a close friend around. That was around the time it was straight from school to dance where you would dance until 9 or 10 at night.

Being light had a lot of connotation with goodness and doing everything right and purity. It also meant that I was doing everything I could as a dancer. It felt like a responsibility, and also like a goal. To be seen too often with food in your mouth was shameful. Everyone [in dance] felt like to be the best they could be also meant abstaining. There was a really overt culture of not eating.

Home life kind of blew up for me. I left when I was sixteen. I did the bratty teenage street life thing where I met really great people, really crappy people. But the great people helped me. They introduced me to the joy of food. Anytime I was in a relationship, a happy one anyways, I ate more. Food became more tasty. When things were topsy-turvy, the eating disorder would start to come out. I only know that it's almost like you have to take off armor to be able to eat, and it leaves you sort of belly exposed.

I have some really clear memories from when I was very young. My mom, when she was working days, she needed a babysitter for me and my brother. She used to bring us to this woman who was kind of a Nazi. She was babysitting a handful of other kids, and she wouldn't let my brother in the house. As soon as my mother left, she'd lock him outside for the day and say "Go play." Me and the younger kids she'd just leave on the floor. We couldn't touch anything—"Don't touch the TV! Just sit on the floor." Feeding time was particularly weird. [At that age] I could eat solid food, but if you put a ham sandwich in front of me, I didn't know what to do with it. Then she'd hit me, yell and throw things because I couldn't eat it.

In calling her mystery illness "*completely a physical thing*," Natalie makes a mind/body distinction to say it was not a mental illness. Yet instead of choosing mind *or* body, calling her family's mounting troubles a "*point of gravity*" better suggests how events pull the whole person in. Although stress impacts everyone's digestion, Natalie's social, emotional, and dietary sides are too well integrated somatically for her own good. Where life's bumps and bruises send others to comfort foods, they estrange Natalie from eating altogether.

Sympathetic Attitude. Anorexia's distinctive somatic style is sympathy. Take the way Natalie's eating sympathizes with her relationships: when they are good, so is eating; when they are difficult, so is eating. We also see that harmonizing in ballet: she not only feels what the others feel about eating—picking up their "*culture of not eating*"—but to excel at dance, her body has to sympathize with other dancers, the instructor, the music, and the dance itself. And her eating disorder echoes her social surroundings: it waxes around restricting dancers and wanes around people who enjoy food. Here sympathy is at once a contagious state of agreement (accord, harmony, a fellow feeling) and a telos, a life-organizing purpose.

Natalie's sympathies appear redemptive. As her mother and brother suffer, so does she. When the sitter locks out her brother, she locks out food; and when her mother suffers fatigue, her starving fatigues her. Initially, just as her stomach ailment is mysterious, so is her mother's fatigue ("*that was back when no one knew what chronic fatigue was*"). Then she corrects herself: ("*Well they sort of knew*") to say her mother's suffering was unredeemed ("*most doctors didn't take it seriously and she was still going to work*"). Does Natalie suffer sympathetically, even sacrificially? Certainly a family's bodily states get entangled. Take Becca's family: her sister's weight gain becomes a mutual bodily involvement where Becca's reducing redeems her sister's failing. Or Jim, whose vegetarianism and exercising bring back his mother's earlier mindset: "*she brought* Diet for a Small Planet *back down* [from the attic] *so we pushed each other into having these athletic, healthy lifestyles.*" Although somatic entanglement may characterize all close relationships, Bruch (1979: 122) found "a tendency in anorexic families for each member to speak not for him- or herself but in the name of another member. . . . They function as if they could read each other's minds." Actually, as the mind lives in and through an expressive body, we are all mindreading loved ones all the time. Even so, if Bruch is right, anorexics' families are more somatically entangled than most.

Sympathy goes in all directions. Take fitting-in anorexia: Molly and Susanna somatize their sympathy for the group they want to join. In contrast, Jim's and Elizabeth's slipping-in anorexia harmonizes their bodies with running, an activity. For Megan and Lynn, standing-out anorexia orients their bodies toward an ideal, and for Francesca and Sarah dropping-out embodies their peers' nihilism. Whatever the direction, none feel sympathy passively and vicariously. Instead all incarnate sympathy quite actively and directly.

Take Sheena. Raised in a small town north of Toronto, she was popular and athletic, and had no real weight problem. Yet her active sympathies twice draw her into and then out of anorexia.

> *In grade nine a friend of mine went into vegetarianism. So I became vegetarian. Then I just started to worry about weight more. There was a new focus on food, being really conscious of what I was eating, reading labels. Grade ten my best friend was trying to stay thin. We fed off each other. If she was really at it then I was really going at it as well. I became more and more religious about exercise. I never ate breakfast. I tried to skip lunch if I could. I always had to eat dinner—I was with my family— but I wasn't eating meat. So I'd pick at the vegetables. I weighed myself every day.*
>
> *My friend—she went more bulimic and it was quite easy for her to do. That never really appealed to me. I did get to a point where I was just so desperate. So, a few times—I wouldn't binge—but I ate and then purged. But it was very tough for me and I didn't see a change. So I stopped that.*
>
> *Near the end of grade ten I kind of thought "You know some of the girls are more curvier." And I got way more into fashion, makeup, hair. Until that point I was very into sports, but all of a sudden my hair was done everyday. I was wearing makeup to school and tighter clothing. My priorities kind of changed.*
>
> *So that [restricting] continued to grade eleven and then I started going out with an older guy. During that time, I kind of laid off a bit. I wouldn't say that having a guy around is what changed it, but having new priorities and being in a relationship, and all that. It was just so much effort to keep the anorexia up.*
>
> *We broke up and I pretty much stayed the same. Then grade twelve, being thin was still on my mind and I kind of went back into restricting. Then first year university I was on the dance team. We had to wear these really small outfits and it was like "Oh I'm going to be seen in front of all of these people" and it was important for me to look fit and toned and thin.*
>
> *Then second year I moved into residence and met a new group of people. And again priorities changed. Since then, it slowly kind of dissipated. Being on the dance team, there was more focus on being fit versus just being thin. That kind of helped me.*

Exercising vigorously rather than restricting is less a change than it looks:

> *I'd always been very into sports. My mom was always active. My dad as well, into hockey, squash, everything. I did dance when I was younger for four years. I got big into figure skating and soccer, did a bit of piano lessons. Dabbled in everything. Was in a choir for a few years.*

It is all part of a *"super busy"* family lifestyle.

Our family was go go go go. I don't really know anything different. Sometimes it would have been nice to have a night here and there, just relax, but if it was too much the opposite I'd go crazy.

Activities orient Sheena just as healthy living guides Becca and work directs Beth. Like Natalie, Sheena moves in and out of anorexia via social involvements. Her restricting adjusts to these moves, but unlike Natalie, she does not vary her attitude to her body: "*I felt kind of a need to keep this kind of body type.*" She wants it to express her lifestyle directly ("*I wanted my body to reflect the activities that I was doing*") and publicly (she wanted "*other people to recognize that*"). Where Natalie somatizes her changing relationships, Sheena somatizes her fixed identity and works to keep it stable. Although acutely conscious of how she looks to others, she has no particular interest in pleasing them. She wants to look *too* thin and does not care if it is less attractive than curves. Asked how to help anorexics, she says, "*Don't comment,*" because "*whether it was a good comment or bad comment, I wanted to keep that up.*" Once personhood is your body, then you must stay the same physically to be true to yourself. So Sheena seeks not approval but direct acknowledgement that she is as she is.

Crises of Autonomy

Sympathizing threatens autonomy. The more deeply and directly one sympathetically incorporates other people, the less bodily control one has. Anorexics' control-seeking response—restricted eating—meets their social desires somatically and literal needs metaphorically. Once you are your body, to manage your life properly you need only manage your eating strictly (cf. Lester 1997).

Consider Lindsay's dilemma. She loves people who do what they please, ignoring her wants. She does not take this passively. Talkative and outgoing, she is a "*very take-charge kind of a person*" who is so confident ("*can handle anything*") and imperturbable ("*never upset, always smiling*") that she can give freely and not get in return ("*you cheer everyone up, but you're always fine and always ok*"). Well liked ("*I always had tons of friends, and I was kind of always the center*"), she is socially established (her clique is "*a little 90210*" of beautiful people[6]) when anorexia develops.

I'd say a high school breakup triggered my anorexia. I was sixteen, in grade eleven. Prior to that a couple things contributed to my susceptibility. The first was my father. When I was about twelve, thirteen, I gained some weight. I was kind of chunky—by no means obese—but I was going through puberty. When I went to my dad's place, I was totally made fun of, called fat by my dad and his wife's children. Another reason I was susceptible was I'm a bit of a control freak and a perfectionist.

> *Basically what brought it on was I broke up with the love of my life* [Jason]. *I guess I felt totally out of control and I, I don't know, maybe I thought I wasn't good enough; or like, you know, I guess I always have been very insecure about—ahh, not anymore—about looking a certain way and having to be perfect. I guess it was a combination of all that stuff. I remember I was really upset over the breakup.*

Knowing what happened but not why, Lindsay psychologizes as she guesses at her own somatizing motives. A later explanation, speculating she was depressed, is no more certain:

> *It took me off and on five years to get over the guy. We talk now, we're friends, but we're completely opposites. He lives in Barrie and didn't finish high school. I just felt a real loss I guess. I guess I was depressed, but no one would know it right? Because I was still doing all these things and still being myself and happy and what have you. But I just, I don't know. Maybe I got it into my mind that if I was thinner, or something, or if I could control this somehow I could control my life. I don't know. I just started cutting back on food.*

Apparently no one—not even Lindsay!—knew she was depressed. A third explanatory effort reveals what she could not control was Jason, not her life.

> *Jason was my first love and maybe I thought in my juvenile mind that if I lost weight, or something—I wasn't thin enough, perfect enough, pretty enough—do you know what I mean? I felt really out of control. I couldn't control the situation. I was actually the one who broke up with him.*

If she rejected him, why strive to be thinner, prettier, or more perfect? Knowing her reaction makes no sense, she blames her "*juvenile mind.*" Of course, were anorexia's payoff not beauty but autonomy, then restricted eating would achieve separateness and control metaphorically. That autonomy would also shrink her world to what she could control while redirecting her emotions from an uncontrollable boyfriend to eating, where her willpower rules. Is she also avoiding social contamination metaphorically? Consider why Lindsay broke up:

> *He was getting into drugs and dropped out of school. I was like, I can't be with someone like that. I wanted him to change. He was a kid. I think it was a control thing too, because I'm like, no matter what's happening, I can control my weight.*

If breaking up asserts her control, why does she then feel out of control—exactly the opposite? Her inability to "*control the situation*"—that is, to control Jason—makes *her* feel "*totally out of control.*" Jason has her heart and he is out of control. A less sympathetic person might dump him to free herself. Lindsay, however, not only keeps caring about Jason but (as a later example shows) lives as if perfecting herself could redeem her loved ones' failings. That is her reaction's intuitive sense. If she is her body and bodily sympathies bind her to Jason and him to her, then were she more perfect, Jason would not ruin his life. Where Natalie echoes her mother's suffering, Lindsay reverses what Jason does, controlling while he goes wild. Can Natalie substitute for her suffering mother while Lindsay offsets Jason's faults? Medieval Catholicism worked that way!

Did love throw Lindsay into this thicket of metaphors? No, she grew up there. Long before and after Jason, her sympathies bound her to the wellbeing of others.

> *I was always more concerned about everyone else than myself. If I was cold and someone else was cold, I'd give them whatever to keep them warm. I was always very I-take-stuff-last, always very good at reading people's emotions,* [at knowing] *what it'd take to make someone happy or to keep peace. When I was a kid I was always trying to keep everyone happy. Even now, I never say "No"—I say "No problem I can handle it." With family, with friends, if they have a problem—"Don't worry, we'll take care of it," like everyone's cheerleader—very reliable, very responsible.*

Embracing friends and family sympathetically, she then feels she can and must make that world right. Of course asking so much of herself jeopardizes her own control and self-worth.

> *My sister and my mother used to fight a lot and I was always the mediator. I made sure the garbage got out, that the laundry was done, that there were meals made and the house was clean. My mom was working all the time and my sister wasn't helping out. I had a lot of responsibility at a young age, but I always felt a lot of responsibility.*

Where others get angry and break bonds, Lindsay keeps people together. Extending her sympathies so widely and into struggles, she labors so it all comes out right.

> *As much as my mom loved me, she was very unreliable. It used to upset me when I was a kid. I used to make all the meals. She was like "Oh, I'll make dinner tonight." And I'd be like "Ok what time?" And she said seven. So at seven, she hadn't started; eight, she hadn't started; nine we're ordering pizza. It's not because she meant to hurt me. It's just who she is. She's got ADD. Severe.*

Note her deep but controlled feelings: she gets "*upset*," not mad; feels "*hurt*," not angry. Anger would pit Self (Lindsay) against Other (her mother). Yet Lindsay feels her mother's failures directly, sympathizing with her "problem parent."

Extending her sympathies so widely and deeply, Lindsay puts everyone in a boat that she steers and keeps afloat.

If you're looking after everyone, you're controlling everything. A lot of times someone that I trusted, who I loved very much, was constantly letting me down in saying they're going to do stuff and then not. I developed a sense of "if I don't do it then no one will" and "no one's going to do it right." So then you have a hard time letting people do anything for you because you think they're going to let you down anyway. So just do it yourself.

Although this last sounds like go-it-alone individualism, the need arises only because she opens herself—extends her sympathies—so that everyone gets bundled together. Is it the failure that hurts, or what it represents? Elsewhere she says you fail others only if they are not a priority.

Disappointing me is one of the most hurtful things. So when I had a medical procedure and Lillian was going to pick me up, I was like "No I'll walk home." She got lost and couldn't find me. So things like that—just do it right or don't do it at all.

With such high emotional stakes and failure personalized, she micromanages:

I'm a bit of a control freak. I think it's because I did grow up a bit in chaos. My mom—she was the best in every other area—but she was totally disorganized, totally clutter. I was constantly trying to control my environment as a kid.

She presents this as controlling objects, but it is loved ones she wants to manage. Here her strategy is metaphoric (she controls eating) as well as literal (*"very direct and very proactive"*). Outperforming all, she claims the authority that effort and high standards earn:

Everyone else can be a slob and do all these maybe awful things and things you think are maybe morally wrong. And they can do all that stuff and they're still great, but it's never ok for you to make a mistake or screw up.

Sound like self-pity? In fact Lindsay's attitude is heroic—I do more because I can do more. Others can walk away from the awful or wrong, but Lindsay will not break the bond. Instead she finds a new and more reliable partner—her eating disorder.

It becomes your whole life. It's like you have a relationship with it. You've got your eating disorder over here beside you. It just comes around with you everywhere and it's dependable, it's always there.

She depicts her eating disorder as outside herself. So too are her loved ones. Does an eating disorder's constancy compensate for unreliable loved ones? Lindsay's psychologizing captures an eating disorder's emotional payoff *after* rituals rule. What first establishes them? In this instance anorexia somatizes her struggle. Eating and the body become proxies that she can manage perfectly. Of course, to take this path, one must first be a sympathetic somatizer.

Crises of Control

Lindsay makes anorexia all about control. Were the syndrome's cause up for a vote, control would win in a landslide. Many feminists like Bordo (1997) say it is control. Our informants agree: eighteen out of twenty-two saw control as *a* or *the* key factor in their anorexia, and another two factored it in. Most depicted their need for control as causing anorexia. A few treated that need as constitutional (e.g., "*I'm a control freak*"). More blamed a difficult situation (e.g., middle school chaos). None saw a third possibility: anorexia created the need for control, not the other way around.

Anorexia-Created Control. Is control anorexia's cause or consequence? Take Amorn. Initially control is not an issue: "*I just started restricting my food, and then it just eventually was no longer about the food at all. It was more about the control I was exerting over myself.*" Or consider Susanna. Confident in her gifts, she feels so in control that she chooses anorexia to mimic a great dancer. That then brings controlling to the fore: "*at the beginning there was an air of both I was controlling it and that there was excitement about it, with an underlying feeling that I really had no choice and I really had to do this.*" Is this no-choice feeling external pressure? Or is it internal, in that once she challenges herself, she must meet every test? Either way the dynamic becomes internal: "*But as I went on it felt more like I was trapped. It started to dawn on me that I'd created something that I couldn't control anymore. The idea that I might be trapped in this cycle for the rest of my life got really scary.*" Starting as the master of her realm, anorexia turns the table on Susanna, giving her good reason to feel out of control.

Asked about control, Natalie says it did not necessarily cause anorexia—"*it wasn't especially the goal of being in control, but you needed to assert a lot of control to be able to do it.*" Indeed, by testing one's willpower, self-starvation foregrounds self-control. Of course, if each daily victory proves one's mettle, past successes still ride on the current match. The victory is not like an award that, once won, can sit on the shelf. To the contrary, like gamblers who keep their winnings on the table, anorexics' stakes keep rising: each match puts all the proof of character at risk.

Further intensifying the thirst for control is the progressive tightening of their eating/exercise disciplines. Bit by bit, eating and living slide from pleasures to enjoy into temptations to deny and situations to avoid. Anorexia thereby creates a craving for control that its own exercise/food rituals come to satisfy addictively. As all anorexics starve themselves, keep unbending regimens, and stake their character on getting results, all exaggerate control physiologically, psychologically, and morally. Here obsessive controlling is more anorexia's consequence than its cause.

Control-Created Anorexia. Although controlling's addictive loop factors into every case, some show situational control as an adaptive response to disordered surroundings. In contrast, keeping control as a temperamental imperative regardless of surroundings is constitutional control. Of course these overlap, and though we can hardly quantify Natalie's controlling (e.g., 50 percent situational, 30 percent addictive, 20 percent constitutional), proportions clearly vary. Take this chapter's first four cases. As all somatize local values quite directly; all are equally constitutional. They differ in whether the local is fixed early in life or changes fluidly as situations do. Here Becca's and Beth's syndromes have strong constitutional roots: anorexia simply extends, intensifies, and ritualizes childhood patterns. Natalie and Sheena, on the other hand, live so freely in the present that their syndromes come and go as their situations change. Social chameleons, they move between groups, taking on new values as they go. Had they not met a restricting situation to embody (Sheena's vegetarian friend; Natalie's ballet) they might never have become anorexic. Countering that "When in Rome" ethic, Becca and Beth hold, "When in Rome, do as I did at home." Not ones for adolescent breaking away, they remain moral homebodies, sticking to their family values. They are not prigs, but were we to imagine a continuum, Natalie and Sheena would be towards the go-with-the-flow situational end, and Becca and Beth towards its set-in-stone constitutional opposite.

Jesse's case distinguishes the situational and constitutional in yet another way.

> *I was born in Cape Charles and lived there until I was fourteen. A small town, the kind of place where everybody knows everybody. A friendly, very friendly place. My parents were sort of hippies. So they built a cabin in the woods. My mom worked and my dad stayed at home, painted. It was pretty happy. I spent a lot of time by myself because we were so isolated. I had friends up the road but you had to drive to get there. So I spent a lot of time running through the woods, dancing with trees, that sort of stuff* [laughing].
>
> *As a kid, my mother would say I was dramatic, drama queen. I was very sensitive, for the most part happy. Always been the type of person who gravitates towards being just happy, content. I've always loved animals, always wanted to be around them, look after them. You know, find wounded squirrels and bring them home and care for them. But I was easily upset by people saying mean things. My mother would always say "Oh you need to toughen up" because I'd come home* [makes crying sound].

I remember in junior high—that age when boys and girls are taking notice of each other—liking that I was getting attention. But it also made me super conscious of what I looked like and should look. I started getting seriously into dieting when I was fourteen. But it went over the edge when we moved to Kingston. It started in high school, in a brand new city. Didn't know anybody. Plucked away from friends, my small town, and put in a totally different environment. I went haywire. It was so lonely. I was so sad. I went into grade eleven where people had already been in school together for two years. It was really hard to make friends.

Well, I just started getting super obsessed with what I was eating and dieting, doing research on food and calories, slowly reducing what I was eating. It just seemed to snowball. I became completely obsessed, terrified I wouldn't lose weight. I was obsessed with food. Like I read recipe books all the time. I watched cooking shows. It was torture. I had a book were I kept track of everything I ate—how many calories, fat, all the stuff. I'd plan out meals for a week. I also did research on anorexia and I was like, "This is what anorexics do? Well, ok." I was trying to eat less than 500 calories a day and no fat. When I was in a social situation where I was forced to eat, I'd throw up. But that wasn't something I did very often.

So just became really unhappy, desperately unhappy. And I just got sick of being unhappy. I had friends who had similar issues and one had been talking to her high school counselor. She got me to see her. I talked to her, and she convinced me to talk to my parents—'cause I had this delusion that nobody noticed. So [I] talked to my parents, went to my family doctor, and got referred to an eating disorders clinic. The big turning point was really just my own desire to not continue.

Moving to a new town, being in a new school and in a new grade threw Jesse into settings where she had little control. Add in adolescence—how she was getting boys' attention and had begun restricting—and external events would seem to explain her concern for control. Yet elsewhere her interview suggests a prior constitutional anxiety about keeping control. Asked if control matters more to her than other people, she says, "*My husband would say so,*" and then elaborates:

I don't like being out of control. I don't like being lost. I panic very easily. I'm a little bit better because I have things now that make me feel safe. I've got my credit card. I can take a cab home. But I don't like doing things where I don't know what will happen. Like a new bus route is very stressful. I've gotten a lot better, but when I first started university it was really difficult to stay overnight anywhere. In Cape Charles people would have parties at their house and just crash there. I couldn't do it.

My mother loves to be adventurous and get lost on the country roads. So she was always always randomly turning down dirt roads—"Oh lets see what's down here." I hated that! Control, I really wanted to be in control. So [in Kingston] my life was completely out of my control. My own interpretation is that anorexia was having some semblance of control. I mean being a teenager you don't have any control over anything. But then the move. Like you don't have any way of deciding what your life is going to be like. It's a terrible thing, terrible thing.

Jesse craves control. That is constitutional for her, just as it is for Lindsay. Yet they are social opposites: Jesse is solitary and retiring, extending her sympathies to animals perhaps more than people; Lindsay is sociable and assertive, extending her sympathies to friends and family who upend her controlling. Occupationally, Jesse's thesis research will observe animals in their natural habitat; meanwhile, Lindsay is a producer, managing various people in ever-changing tasks. The two take constitutional controlling in opposite directions, and yet both contrast with take-what-comes Natalie, someone who shapes herself to ballet as readily as to street life.

Conclusion

Anorexics are made, not born. Their affliction is years in the making. From conception to adolescence, everyone's wide possibilities narrow as the organism grows. Day by day biology, culture, and chance interact. Over and over they fix points that shape later interactions, and bit by bit this biocultural hybrid—a constitution—gains guiding force. Here, saying anorexics are made means that these early developments give them capacities and inclinations that only later invite anorexia.

What are these constitutional characteristics? Our interviews reveal clear patterns. Some characteristics, like skill in sequencing or manifesting ideas directly, we infer from prior success at dance and athletics. Other characteristics—their performative, ascetic, and virtuous dispositions—are empirical generalizations. Still others—a sympathetic attitude and somatic expressiveness—follow deductively from life-course patterns.

Lifeworld and life course: each embeds the actor in value-laden thoughts, feelings, and practices. Here everyone makes choices. What distinguishes those who become anorexic is not their chosen values—many people esteem discipline, achieving, a thin body—but rather their constitutional capacity to order life strictly around their choices, orchestrating every detail around a single principle as an absolute value. Lost in their own self-imposed ethic of restricted eating, they become as rigid as fundamentalists.

Notes

1. While there is not *a* personality, Casper (1990) sees distinctive *features* for those recovered from one subtype, restricting anorexia, that has a "prototypic personality profile . . . well

known to any clinician in the field" in its *presentation* as "constrained, conforming, obsessional, rigid and perfectionistic" (Wonderlich et al. 2005). We stress presentation because even though these features may describe active sufferers, only perfectionism fits what our interviewees saw in themselves and we encountered. While our interviewees did share somatic expressiveness and a sympathetic attitude, these traits fit quite various personalities.

2. In their first year in college, coeds often gain weight. The "fifteen" is pounds.
3. Beresin, Gordon, and Herzog's (1989) tests of recovered anorexics found perfectionism was the one subscale where subjects differed from controls (see also Fairburn et al. 1999).
4. Four avoided sports and dance, lacking interest and ability. Of these, two saw themselves as artists and could commit to that activity as others did sports. For the two artists, depression seriously complicated and perhaps preceded their anorexia.
5. While everyone is somewhat sympathetic and somatically expressive, those who become anorexic appear to have a constitutional bent toward sympathetic somatizing.
6. A TV show about privileged and glamorous teens in Beverly Hills.

CHAPTER 6

The Activity
How Ascetic Doing Takes Over

Anorexia makes the actor into the activity. How does that happen? Our informants could not tell us directly. Yet piecing together what each said separately reveals regularities in how the actor's "techniques of the self" establish "a perfect supremacy of oneself over oneself" (Foucault 1990: 10, 31; cf. Lester 1997). Isabel, for example, describes how she invents and intensifies a discipline that becomes her life.

Isabel's Story: The Activity Takes Hold

I grew up in a very small town in Western North Carolina. I went to public school through ninth grade. Everyone's comfortable with everyone. Lunch hour you'd just eat whatever they had. No one seemed to have a problem. Then I went to boarding school in Virginia, Rosemont Academy. That's where my problem began—in boarding school. It's a common problem.

My mom is a big family person. She always likes everyone to eat together. Even though she'll have everything ready, she'll be the last to sit down and still wait on you—which is annoying! But we'd always have dinner together. We're a really close family. When I went to boarding school I was shocked at how people didn't get along with their parents, cussing at them and verbal abuse. I was just shocked!

Before I went off to boarding school—because I was a little unsure and maybe a little afraid—I got into the mindset where I wasn't going to let myself eat chips or candy or French fries or anything of that nature. I was still in that mindset when I went to Rosemont. One of the first things all the girls told me was that no one really eats the food. They just eat cereal and bagels instead. If you see other girls eating not as much as you, you feel guilty. I've never had a weight problem ever—I've always been fairly petite—but in boarding school everyone's watching everyone else. When girls get obsessed with who's skinniest, it gets in your head that you need to fit into that mold. You don't even know what you're doing. I got into the routine where I wouldn't eat normal food, like a meal. My body got used to eating only cereal, maybe a bagel, a jelly sandwich. It wasn't that I didn't eat at all. It's like when I did I hardly ate anything. It was more of a loss of appetite. The look of something fatty makes you disgusted. And you get into the mindset that if you eat the smallest amount of anything, you're just going to gain so much weight. You're very narrow minded because you're so strict with yourself. Things become black or white. If I saw a friend eating something I wouldn't eat, I'd think, "I have a lot more willpower than she does. I have a lot more control than you do. Why is she eating that?"

Sophomore year I got into the routine of eating cereal for basically every meal and obviously you're going to lose weight. I didn't break out of that. Then when I came back junior year, I thought—I don't know why but I thought—if I eat anything but cereal, I'll probably gain weight. [So] I really was strict on myself and I wouldn't snack. I just decided like I'd get so mad at myself if I'd cheat on eating anything with any fat. You get into the mindset where you just can't consider it, or you don't want yourself to at least.

That's when teachers and friends really started to notice. You look so pale. I had dark circles under my eyes. I was really thin. People would say, "Are you feeling well?" And that's the last thing you want to hear. You don't want anyone to suspect anything and you're so embarrassed. I'd try much harder to look good. You use make-up and cute outfits to disguise that so they don't get suspicious.

It was just a bad period in my life. Before that I never had any problem. I've always been a very happy person. I think it's an issue of being depressed. It's something where you don't ever think you have a problem.

Isabel's case lacks the usual suspects: with no weight problem, she's a naturally petite, happy person who is close to her family and popular with peers. She pinpoints boarding school as an environmental cause, which it was, but her restricting begins *before* she leaves home. Facing a worrisome change, she denies herself a few pleasures in preparation, cutting out unhealthy fattening foods—an austerity any health-conscious parent would love. She is, or intends to be, the classic good girl. About to be on her own, she initiates self-management proactively. Any diffuse desire to do right or be good is now concrete rules for living.

Boarding school intensifies her discipline. Now the virtuous course is restricting in itself, and she feels guilty if she eats more than other girls. As she remembers it, her restricting progresses in steps: first, at home, she prohibits some foods; second, school sparks a narrower habit (eating only cereal); third, the habit tightens ("*I didn't break out of that*"); fourth, the habit fends off dire consequences (if she breaks it she will gain weight). At some point it is no longer about weight or eating. It is about holding herself together—"*you think everything's going to fall apart*" if you break your habits. Now it is anorexia or chaos.

Isabel captures how ascetic regimens intensify. Others had other habits, but all pursue anorexia's ascetic logic in a similar manner. Our next section dissects that pursuit, identifying regularities as well as diversities.

The Activity's Features: Experiencing Anorexia

In narrating their illnesses, informants told stories with simplistic middles. We heard about resisting intervention or the extremes of starving, but no one covered how anorexia grew. Were there turning points? Was it step-like or seamless? No one could say.

After they told their stories, we asked follow-up questions to jog memory and recover what the narrative dropped. It took time to find the right phrasing, but once we did, follow-ups brought back experiences in ways our interviewees found satisfying and even surprising. When we asked Fred if starving felt exhilarating, he replied, "*Absolutely. You feel like you can manipulate your body. It's really hard to describe, actually. I'm surprised you said that. I've never really thought about it that way but that's absolutely right.*" That phrase "*I've never really thought about it that way*" might suggest we were planting ideas, but in fact the ease, conviction, regularity, and detail of the replies got "into the disease 'itself'" (Mol 2002: 12). Our questions opened new doors to old experiences.

Through those doors came regularities we will dub features. A feature of, say, a landscape might be a mountain or stream—too obvious to miss, too conventional to debate. By that rough and ready standard, what is conspicuous about anorexia is a mixed bag: some features characterize a feeling (exhilaration, surrender), others a practice (goading, feedback), still others a consequence (isolation, consolidation). Are such features anorexia's symptoms? They could be. Certainly they cluster around what is known as anorexia. Yet a symptom implies an underlying reality, a deeper cause. Our radical empiricism (Jackson 1989) favors the surface instead. We are flat-footed ethnographers here, looking *at* features, not *through* them. A feature, then, is a low-level empirical generalization denoting whatever is felt, done, or occurring clearly and regularly enough to be notable.

Eight features recur in our interviews. All first develop mid-course, arising after serious restricting but well before death's endgame. Each interview shows most features clearly, some contain all eight, and none counter these findings. Late in the research, when a few follow-up interviews double-checked findings, everyone recognized all the following features.

Exhilaration. Intense restricting or exercise exhilarates: "*a thrill at, well, I can do this*" (Susanna); "*a feeling of 'good on yah,'*" along with "*'I can do this, I can—look what I can do!"* (Natalie). Melissa's high was feeling the discipline: *"I was like, I can make myself do that. After I'd get done with my five hours of exercise, I'd be completely exhausted. I could hardly move and I'd be so happy: I can't believe I made myself do that."* Calling it *"the ultimate,"* Lynn shows no irony in describing extreme self-denial as intensely gratifying:

> *It's instantaneous gratification every day because every day you get on the scale. Every time somebody says something to you, it's instantaneous gratification. Every kind of hunger pain it almost feels good. It's like, "Yeah, I put that there. I can make it go away. I can put it there."*

What causes exhilaration? Reported by religious fasters, the feeling has physiological roots (Davis and Claridge 1998; Marrazzi and Luby 1989), like a runner's high. Some describe transcendence, a sense of being above their bodies. Others experience its opposite, immanence, savoring the sheer physicality of starving, of feeling *in* their bodies. So Lynn toys with hunger, letting the pain come. For Amorn it *"felt as good as an accomplishment,"* like the boost she got from gymnastics—a very this-worldly experience. Francesca said, *"You get addicted to not eating and you get addicted to cutting."* For her there is *"a similar kind of feeling in the fact that I had discipline. I'd cut and I'd feel the pain and I'd see the blood. I'd look at it and it fascinated me."* Here pain grounds the person in a unifying experience.

Our interviewees' exhilaration has four faces. One is achievement. All challenge themselves and succeed. The hurdle is artificial, but success delights them nonetheless. Achieving, it seems, is intrinsically valuable. Natalie connects it to self-improvement:

> *It was a feeling of making yourself a better person by doing this, by going through this and coming out and thinking, "yah it feels like crap and it hurts, but you can do this." And going days without anything but water go through you makes you go like "yah dammit, I can do it."*

A second face is power. Lynn recalls, *"I look back on that time not upset. It was dark, yes, kind of, but so powerful. It was a high."* Twelve informants remembered a sense of power, separating it from subsequent powerlessness. Some phrasings depersonalize (*"I had my body working almost like a machine"*—Fred) but in others it is power over oneself (*"I can't believe I made myself do that"*—Melissa), acting on either the person (*"teaching yourself a lesson"*—Natalie) or one's body.

A third face is *"this weird, indescribable thrill of controlling"* (Megan). Were anorexia gratifying a prior need for control, we might expect relief. But that is not reported. Indeed, even as Lynn feels hunger pains as exerting control (*"I put that there"*), she muses: *"I don't really know why. It wasn't that I wasn't in control of the *rest of my life.*" Amorn usefully distinguishes feelings from reality: "*up to a certain point fasting gave me—felt like it gave me—control over my life.*" Indeed, ascetic regimens make life *feel* controlled even if it is not. Here, the more someone experiences life metaphorically, the more controlling eating or exercise (a part) will feel like controlling life (the whole).

Lastly, some felt superiority: "*you actually get this feeling that you're above people, that you're more, not civilized, but you're able to control yourself better and that other people are a little weak*" (Lindsay); "*I thought everyone else had to eat but I didn't. That made me proud, I guess. I thought I was kind of special, that I didn't succumb to bodily functions*" (Sarah). Molly's superiority celebrates perfectionism: "*I definitely liked having that feeling, that I could control what I ate. That meant I was more perfect than Ginny sitting beside me, eating a Snickers bar.*" Melissa elaborates:

> *I loved it at lunch when I looked over and my friends were eating all this food and I'd be eating five carrots. I was so proud of myself and I wanted them to know. I got really judgmental. "They're such bad people. Look at all that they're eating."*

Here superiority comes from putting peers down, an attitude others shunned.

Beyond our sample, others recognize exhilaration. Warin (2006: 49) found Australian, Scottish, and Canadian anorexics expressed pride in starving; and Gooldin (2008) reports experiencing hunger gave Israelis a sense of power and achievement together with immanence ("*I can feel myself*") and transcendence ("*I can be outside of it*").

Discipline. Every interviewee creates a distinctive food or food/exercise discipline that becomes an absolute, life-ordering value. In Beth's words,

> *It start*[ed] *with food and then* [I] *added exercise. And then you realize to maintain those you also have to change your social habits, your relationships with family, your religious practices. You have to change a lot to fit into that scheduling, that plan you've created for yourself.*

Changing food and exercise changes one's life. Everything is now neatly ordered around a self-imposed discipline and, exactly as it feels, one controls this narrowed world.

Our informants invent quite various disciplines. Megan's has frenetic intensity:

> *Order was a big thing. I was like clockwork. I can remember my mom came into my room once. I was about to do my laundry and do all my history homework and I'd just gone for a run. My room was clean, my bed was made—I mean everything. I knew what I was going to eat. I'd religiously go at night to this yogurt place. She*

> came in and said "You understand, none of this is that big a deal," and I remember I just cried. I lost it because I was so anxious that everything had to be ordered and controlled by me.

Unlike most informants, Megan orders activities and exercise rather than food:

> The only technique I had was to come up with more ways to exercise. I remember telling Dr. Bates my goal was just to weigh 115 pounds. But once I was there, that wasn't good enough. I'd run every day and then running wasn't enough. I'd run and then go to the gym every day. Then that wasn't enough. So I'd run, go to the gym and swim three times a week. Then that didn't become enough. So I cut back on all sugar. Then that wasn't enough and then there wasn't enough of me.

She captures exactly how discipline tightens. Where monastic ascetics fulfill a tradition, anorexics chase a fugitive ideal. As restricting gets more restrictive, a once open life closes around a single principle.

Exercise-driven as Megan is, her food attitudes become like non-exercising restrictors:

> It's funny that as little as you eat and as focused as you are on food—paradoxical again—all food had a complete emotional attachment. Fried food was bad and sodas and sugars were bad. Guilt—when I ate pizza. [I knew] what was good to eat and what I should eat and what was going to happen when I did eat.

"Good," "bad," "guilt"—such notions capture how her discipline moralizes eating.

Some, like Jim, develop anorexia within an already established food system. Giving up whole milk and red meat in the third grade, he later cuts sugar and then fat. By seventh grade he wants only soup and cereal—all well before his anorexia. Others, like Lynn, develop a food system and anorexia together. Once she had "*the worst eating habits. Then I went polar opposite and started being really, really concerned about what I ate.*" Grocery shopping with her mom, she picks out low-fat items and says, "*'I'm going to eat healthy.' My mom was like, 'That's great.'*" Soon restricting intensifies:

> So from low-fat to fat-free to no-fat and then really low calorie. Stepping into it with the low-fat and healthier, healthier, healthier definitely let it go on longer. I was just trying to eat healthy. But it also trained me to be more disciplined about my eating. It wasn't everything at once.

And still others, like Francesca, fashion a food system after anorexia takes hold:

> It was kind of a slow buildup and eventually eating and food entered my journal writing. I think that's when I really started to realize how this was becoming a major thing. I remember feeling when I didn't eat I was clean and when I ate I was dirty. I clung to that for so long. Whenever I ate anything I felt disgusting inside.

Asked if the disgust centered on only some foods, she replies:

> When I was on the tail end of recovering, I did have a sort of a particular leaning towards vegetables and things that I called clean food. And, if I ate French fries or pizza, it was dirty food. But at the beginning I wouldn't say it was there as much.

Where Francesca moralizes, others depict growing restrictions more neutrally. Molly recalls a three- or four-step progression:

> It started out: "Don't eat as much at meals. Don't eat desserts as often as you do." Then it went to: "OK, good. Now let's start counting." I don't know exactly when the counting calories came in. But that was definitely next. It was like, "OK, I know the turkey has fifty and each slice of bread has fifty." Reading labels and stuff. That started and then it was, "OK, I can eat even less if I skip meals," and it progressed from there.

Lindsay also describes steps. Asked if she stressed fat or calories, she replies,

> It was counting calories for sure. I'd count every single thing I'd put in my mouth. I'd mentally calculate. I think I started off with a bigger zone, like maybe 1,500, and then I probably went down to 1,000. And then I went down to 500.

Unlike Lindsay counting calories, Beth focuses on fat: "*Fat was more important than calories. If there were muffins and they were fat-free, I could eat them. It didn't matter if they were 300 calories or one hundred calories.*"[1]

Our informants also differ in food variety. Beth cuts quantity but not variety: "*I did a lot of bagels and fruit, yogurt, things like that. Cereals and milk. When I got here* [Sewanee], *I branched out, eating from the food groups, controlled little tiny portions.*" In contrast, Isabel standardizes, "*eating cereal for basically every meal.*" Amorn stresses simplicity—no entrées with unknown ingredients. Although her food system begins with healthy eating, safe/dangerous or pure/dirty moralizing never develops.

Isolation. Turning inward, anorexics become mentally self-absorbed and often physically distant and socially isolated. Emotions are flattened (Davies et al. 2011) or avoided (Wildes et al. 2010), hollowing out relationships. Though a few interviewees wanted to withdraw, most did not expect or intend to isolate themselves.

Starving breeds inwardness. In World War II research, starving made once-gregarious volunteers "progressively more withdrawn and isolated" (Garner 1997: 158). As their "decline in [social] interest" fed "feelings of social inadequacy," they "became self-centered" (Keys et al. 1950: 837). In retrospect our interviewees see their anorexia as selfish ("*vain and self-centered*"—Lynn).

What turns their lives inward? The WWII volunteers found dealing with others "became 'too much trouble' or 'too tiring'" (Keys et al. 1950: 837). Fred says, "*You really don't want to have anything to do with other people.*" But other interviewees felt they had to attend to others to avoid interference or embarrassment. For Beth "*there was always this vague sense—mentality—that I didn't want to be bothered in my practices. I always put up barriers and defended myself.*" On the other hand, fatigue foregrounds their physical existence. In Francesca's words,

> *I literally had no strength to stand up. I became so physically centered that I could feel my heart beat and I could feel the fatigue in my arms, in a sense withdrawing physically into myself. As you start to become aware of every process that's going on, down to your breath and your heartbeat, you become preoccupied with the problem itself.*

Private rituals tighten the inward turn. Any ritual cuts off those outside the rite, but personal rituals can isolate you even in a crowd. Sarah, for example, would spend two or three class periods polishing the apple she would eat at lunch, absorbed in her own bodily actions rather than being present for others. Jane's food rituals developed unknowingly:

> *I didn't realize that I was cutting my food so tiny and then separating* [it]. *The way I'd arrange it on the plate was really strange. Once my brother was watching me and he was like "What are you doing? Are you anorexic?" It just clicked—what am I doing?*

Starvation does that: the WWII volunteers hoarded rations to eat later in "a long-drawn-out ritual" or "a private eating ceremony" (Keys et al. 1950: 833). Valuing their small portions fully, many ate very slowly, a practice that encourages playing with food and ritualistic restraints that extend the experience. Knowing this behavior looks odd adds to the isolation.

Obsessing over food narrows the starver's life. In Jesse's words, "*I was obsessed with food. Like I'd read recipe books all the time; I watched cooking shows. Constantly talking about food, looking into it.*" Fred remembers, "*When I couldn't sleep at night, I'd stay up watching the Food Network. For hours, hours. I wrote down recipes to try, easy stuff, for after the* [wrestling] *season.*" Food thoughts fill and organize one's life. Beth remembers:

I couldn't go to sleep at night before I decided what I was going to eat when I got up in the morning and planned out my meals for the next day and counted the calories I'd consumed that day. I used to plan out my outfit for the next day before I went to bed and that was quickly replaced by thoughts of food and planning meals.

Food thoughts replace more than wardrobe planning: "*my interest in most everything declined, beyond food. There were times when I'd grasp for things and try to pick up my Bible and read again or go to church. There was no room for it.*"

Inwardness does not always center on food. Amorn, who could forget her hunger, says food thoughts were "*mostly out of the way.*" Instead she obsesses over exercise and counting repetitions. Weight preoccupies Lindsay: "*all day that's all you're thinking about, is how can I burn calories and how can I get through the day not eating anything.*" Depression kills Francesca and Sarah's appetites and they forget about eating. Were they then free of food thoughts? Not exactly. At first Francesca forgets food. Then, "*the further I got into it* [anorexia], *the more it became about food and eating.*" Sarah follows the question's lead: "*food was always, always in my mind,*" but what she actually describes is hunger management—"*I'd think about ways to skip another meal without feeling too bad, without fainting.*" So although food thoughts do not preoccupy everyone, all our interviewees experience an obsessive, socially isolating inward turn.

Social inwardness and isolation feed on each other. In Amorn's words,

I just had no social interest at all. Very withdrawn. I didn't know who I was. My life became very secretive and very isolated. My friends would get upset with me because I wouldn't hang out with them, wondered why I'd rather be at home.

Food fears isolate Becca:

During lunchtime when most kids would be eating with friends and relaxing I was off working. I became like a little hermit crab. I didn't like being around people very much. I definitely didn't do much with friends. Like sometimes when I did I'd think about, "What if they don't offer healthy food?" My mom would say, "Why don't you go out and do stuff with your friends? They're calling." "I don't want to." I was that afraid that they wouldn't have food that I'd want to eat.

Jim shuns others to avoid interfering criticism:

I had to give up a lot of the stuff I was doing socially. I didn't want to eat with my friends and family. I felt their criticism of what I was doing was ridiculous and completely unfounded—that I was right. I didn't want to deal with them. I spent a lot more time alone.

Roughly half who could lose friends did so.[2]

Where Amorn, Becca, and Jim isolate themselves literally, others who cannot escape grow distant psychologically. Megan *"was around people all the time. I was pretty involved, doing a lot of things—student council, different things."* Avoiding what she can (*"I didn't want to go to church because I didn't want people to say things to me"*), she tries to hide what is happening (*"I wanted to keep inside and hidden that I was unhappy"*). Her friends are not fooled:

> *A lot of things fell by the wayside. I remember coming out of it and wondering, "God, all my friends hate me. Why?" And they went, "Well, you blew us off for eight months, of course. We don't even know who you are. We don't know what you're doing."*

Sarah, a reflective person, masters being socially present yet inwardly absent:

> *I don't think I really ever talked to them* [her friends] *about it. I was close to them but I was really distant. I didn't talk about myself. I mean, I listened to their problems and helped them out, but when it came to what was going on in my life, I kept it to myself. I didn't want to feel like I was bragging. At that point, all my friends were far too emotional for their own good. When they talked, it seemed like a pissing contest. I didn't want to partake in that so I just kept it to myself.*

Anorexia is a solitary pursuit for sixteen informants, whereas six find partners along the way.[3] When Janet discovers her older sister's eating disorder, shared austerities bring her anorexia to *"a whole new level."* In two instances co-starving is a passing involvement—a month for Susanna and a summer for Natalie.

Feedback. An Israeli anorexic captures how weighing oneself takes on ritual and drama:

> Every evening I would go into my room and lock the door. I would then take the scale out . . . and make sure it's properly adjusted. I would then take all my clothes off. I take a few deep breaths and go on the scale. I would stand there for a few seconds, without looking at the numbers. Then, I would look down to the numbers. If I lost weight, I'll be ecstatic. If not, I'm really down. I do this every evening. (Gooldin 2008: 286–287)

Like her, our informants all become intrigued—sometimes obsessed—with feedback that objectifies their body. Some fit the stereotype of mirror-gazing anorexics: Jesse says, *"I was weighing myself constantly, checking the mirror all the time,"* and Jim says, *"I had a scale in the bathroom and bedroom and I did look at myself in the mirror a lot."* Is this about looks? Sarah thinks not: *"Losing weight was the visual payoff. So you could tell something was working. It's not like I thought my emaciated body was attractive."*

Measuring varied. Take Megan's activity-centered regimen: *"I don't remember getting nit-picky about the pounds. There were so many other things I was concerned about I didn't have the energy to worry about the numbers."* In contrast Melissa stresses weight and avoids mirror-gazing: *"I never really looked good so I never looked at myself in the mirror."* Mary uses yet another measure: *"I knew that I wasn't fat if I fit into the jeans my parents bought for me in grade three."* Weighing is too crude a measure for Fred. He always knows his weight during wrestling season (*"At any point during the day I could've told you within two tenths of a pound exactly what I weighed"*). Getting the exercise/weight-loss calculus *"down to a science,"* he measures weight loss by *"watching the clock"* while exercising.

Several justify their objectifying as a tool. Francesca remembers, *"you get in front of the mirror and you stay there for a long time looking at every part you possibly can, to see how it's changed, where you've succeeded and not succeeded."* Natalie says:

> *It was really important for me to be able to gauge, like, progress I guess. Looking at the mirror, looking at the scale was a way of gauging, telling me where I'm at, assessing 'How well am I doing? 'What kind of person am I today? Oh, I'm an eighty-three pound person.'*

Taken literally, her explanation says the person *is* the objectified body. In contrast, for Jim the person is a runner whose body is merely its tool:

> *I had this really really big concern with my body. I did look at my body in the mirror, but whenever I did that, it was always tied into that "How do you look right now? This is awful, this is terrible, you look bad. You're not going to be able to run well." I never got away from that.*

Objectifying gives them a tool to act on themselves. In two instances where anorexia does not begin as weight loss, measuring develops as the activity takes hold. A person with no weight problem, Amorn initially aims only to restrict and thus has no particular interest in mirrors and scales. Yet eventually, *"what I allowed myself to eat or not eat depended on my weight."* Weight also becomes a way to set long-term goals. So at first, she says, *"the goal wasn't the pounds. But that became a part of it. When I'd see that I weighed ninety-nine pounds, I'd be like, 'Oh, I wonder if I can get down to ninety-five.' But I don't think it was necessarily the weight, the pounds."* Weight comes later for Francesca too: *"For me it never started out as, 'Oh, I'm fat, I need to lose weight.' It started out as, 'I'm stressed, I don't want to eat anything.' But then later it did become about the weight."* In time she uses weight to set goals:

I had weight numbers I wanted to get to and I wanted to stay at—right now I'm 135 and I'm very preoccupied with that number. I want to get to 125—that sort of thing. I associate the numbers with the control, the self-mastery, self-discipline.

Does quantifying feed the control concerns that feed anorexia? Surely numbers enable the objectifying that gives anorexia its distinctive mental hold. Yet when therapists withhold Amorn's weight, she invents a subjective standard: *"wanting to be weak."* Like Sarah, she goes for the feeling of shrinking, just as Francesca enjoys *"feeling small and thin and tight."*

Most objectifying stresses impersonal measures, but some anorexics need more subjective social confirmation. Jane could see her bodily changes, but *"I didn't really take it in until someone else said something."* Sheena required social recognition:

Comments from other people were the biggest motivation, you know. Whereas people from the outside might think that "'Oh you tell someone that they really look too thin, that they don't look good, that would make them stop and say, 'Oh I better eat something.'" For me it was quite the opposite. Someone would say "You're looking too thin." I'd think "Good, it's working!"

Outside our sample, an Israeli anorexic "used to walk in the roads of my Kibbutz and watch the reactions," staging what Gooldin (2008: 288) calls a heroic drama. Outsiders' subjective judgments provide objectifying feedback just as weight does.

Goading. Our informants use various techniques to motivate their restricting. Everyone breaks starving down into smaller, easier steps. Molly has *"mini-goals"*; Lynn incrementally *"trained"* herself to eat with more discipline, never pushing for *"everything at once"*; and Sheena recalls setting each weight-loss goal *"a little lower,"* raising *"the bar a little bit each time. I never set really unrealistic ones such as like, okay, I'm 115 and I'm going to go ninety."*

Some mention small rewards. Melissa recalls

a ritual when I got home, before I exercised. I'd let myself have a snack. So I got to where I loved air-popped popcorn. No calories. That was the highlight of my day. I'd look forward to that because I'd be so hungry. Every day I was like, "OK, I'm going to have my popcorn!" It's really sad looking back on it.

Jane remembers, *"even when I was dieting and starving myself, I'd reward myself with a piece of chocolate. I just love it!"* Then, given that love, she could withhold the reward: *"I'd go through periods of time where I was like 'Okay, I'm not eating chocolates."* Or she could create an arbitrary rule by telling herself "*I'm only going to eat like, ahh, vegetables and chicken.' Then I'd stick to it.*" By making up a rule that she can then keep to win, she can motivate and reward herself with nothing: "*it was like I achieved another goal; it was like I was successful! And I was good at what I was doing. It's so motivating when you know that you're good at what you do.*" Lynn weighs herself each morning. If the number goes down, good. "*If I didn't lose weight, it was like the rest of the day was bad. It was awful.*" That bad feeling pushed her to try harder: "*I'd run more or I'd eat less* [and] *the next day I'd lose weight.*" Jesse punished herself: "*If I didn't meet my goals, I was always picking at myself or scratching at my legs or kick the radiator.*"

Some describe a contest with oneself. Lynn's team weigh-ins pit her against peers, but the challenge is internal too: "*How much more can I lose?*" Amorn's restricting is not about weight but "*the control I was exerting over myself.*" Here the challenge becomes "*How far can I go?*" and, as an exercise in autonomy and self-denial, "*What can I get away with?*" Success raises the bar: "*As soon as I'd eliminate a couple foods or eliminate a meal, it was hard to go back. It was like I'd set a standard for myself and I had to beat that standard.*"

To compete against oneself divides the person. Initially, restricting gives Amorn "*a feeling of power over myself—my self that needed defeating, I guess.*" Her doubtful ending testifies to the mystery in how the self acts on the self. We have just heard this divided self in Melissa's "*I would let myself,*" and Isabel's "*I wasn't going to let myself eat chips or candy*" as well as "*I just decided I'd get so mad at myself if I'd cheat on eating.*" Is an executive rule-making self bullying a more relaxed self? Certainly our informants spoke dualistically. Jim, for example, splits person from body: "*I was disgusted with my body and trying to detach myself from it. I felt distance from my own body even though oddly enough my body was really driving me.*" Natalie talks about "*teaching yourself a lesson, teaching yourself restraint and discipline.*" Janet takes the split still further:

> I kept a little food journal and I wrote down every single thing. I'd circle the calories at the end of the day—usually negative. Sometimes I'd put stickers on the page or write notes saying, "This is great." Or if I gave in, I'd write things like, "You're a fat ass." It was like the physical me and the mental me were completely different. The mental me was talking to the physical me via this journal.

Once the person splits, self-criticism can become autonomous. Like Janet, Jesse journals "*as if I was talking to someone else—'you stupid, ugly'—that sort of stuff.*" Competition goads Fred: there is "*always that voice in the back of your mind saying you can do more. 'The guy across the street, the guy at the next high school—he's working harder. What are you going to do about it?*" Natalie did not need competitors:

I'd strive for that feeling of accomplishment and once I got there I'd talk it down and I'd be like, "Oh so what! So you made it here—that's the least you should expect from yourself. What you should do is go for the next level.

Where Natalie deflates any self-satisfied feelings, Susanna reverses compliments: "*I started feeding myself consciously bad messages. Like when people would compliment me on something, I'd very purposefully inside tell myself it wasn't true and that I wasn't good enough.*" She thereby creates an emotional unease that goads still further improvement, "*a feeling there was something I had to fix about myself.*"

Consolidation. Eventually the inward turn becomes inwardness, a stable trait. Not only do features stabilize as one acclimates to starving, but piecemeal responses coalesce into new wholes. As in learning to drive, halting moves start working together smoothly. Our interviewees undergo four consolidations. First, their taste changes, making restricting easier. For Molly, "*Anything with fat—like ice cream—I was like, 'Ugh, gross. I don't like the way it tastes.'*" In recovery Beth finds it "*hard to know what my tastes are.*" Jane's taste also changes permanently:

> *I got really used to drinking water and then, eventually, I didn't have a desire to drink juice or pop anymore. Now I can't drink it at all. Like I don't enjoy it. A lot of things that I kind of cut from my diet then, like pasta, I still don't eat. I trained myself not to enjoy it.*

As Isabel says, once you cut something from your diet, "*you don't see the need to go back. You don't care to*" as it does not "*even seem appetizing*" anymore.

Second, disgusts develop that strengthen one's discipline. Fat repulses Mary: "*Fat, is like, one thing that I still fear. When I did this course in grade eleven, I saw the stomach being cut open and I saw the fat there. I'm like, 'that's disgusting!'—the most disgusting thing ever.*" So too Natalie:

> *I had a repulsion to fat absolutely. It was scary to me. It had associations with bad things. So to have fat was also to be bad; it was to be a bad person. It was like a badge of your gluttony and your loss—your loss of something—I don't know what. It was horrifying.*

Indeed, morbidly fearing fat identifies anorexia diagnostically. Fred, who once felt sorry for fat people, "*got to the point where I absolutely disliked fat people. They truly bothered me. I'd think to myself, 'F-ing fatass. That's pathetic.'*" Others target foods. Isabel remembers, "*you look at one French fry, or one person eating that type thing and you think, 'How are they doing that? That's not good. You're going to gain*

10 pounds." Where others disgust Isabel, Lynn felt bodily horror upon gobbling cake: "*Afterwards I was like, 'Oh god!' I felt immediately fatter and I know that's ridiculous. But I could feel it.*" Apparently full now felt fat. Susanna had a similar perception: "*if I ate something that I thought I shouldn't have, it's like I could feel it growing on my body.*"

While restricting may incite disgust with food, that sentiment generalizes (Aharoni and Hertz 2012) and may turn to hating one's body. Asked how he felt about his body, Jim says, "*Hatred, definitely, is the one word I'd use to describe it. Disgust. I hated the way I looked. I suppose I saw my body as something I'd just use to do other things with.*" For Melissa, "*I'd think, you know, 'you deserve this,' talking to my body. 'If you were better and looked better, you wouldn't be hungry.' I liked to punish myself.*"

Where disgust targets not just one's body but oneself, the result is what Claude-Pierre (1997) calls the negative mind. Amorn remembers "*so much negativity inside that it completely took over me.*" Francesca speaks of a "*lurking derogatory presence in my head*" that is never satisfied. Beth hears "*a voice that's constantly in your mind, that's condemning of everything you do.*" She remembers such a voice "*from an early age,*" when "*it wasn't about my body*" but just critiquing her performance to improve it: "*you learn to be critical with yourself,* [and then] *with anorexia, that takes on an alternate persona inside your mind.*" This then is "*the mentality* [that] *tires you, the voice that's incessant, the thoughts that never end. Even when you stop consciously thinking about it, it's still there like an echo.*"

What causes this self-disgust? Were the motivational strategies we have heard to consolidate into a mindset, goading one's efforts could turn into loathing oneself. Earlier we heard how Susanna self-consciously reversed compliments into criticism. She does and does not buy her trick: on one hand, she starts "*really believing all the terrible things I told myself about myself,*" but on the other, she finds herself "*feeling this incredible amount of superiority and arrogance*" because "*as much as I'd berate myself for not being perfect, I knew that I was doing really well on a lot of fronts.*" This then is transitional: goading is not yet loathing. Perhaps what keeps greater negativity at bay is that she succeeds in all she does. Not so Amorn: having given up starring at gymnastics, she is an also-ran at other sports.

In the third consolidation, what we will call "process pleasure," starvation's effects become pleasures in themselves.[4] For Melissa, "*being hungry was pleasurable. I loved being hungry, so hungry that my stomach hurt. It was like a victory when I was hungry.*" In effect she felt victorious, not hungry. For Molly the substitute feeling is cleanliness, "*a sense that I'm clean because I don't have food inside.*" For Sarah it is clarity and alertness ("*When I wouldn't eat, my mind would feel very clear and I'd feel very alive*") that connects with feeling clean and being creative:

> Ever since I've been little I've always been a creative kid. I'd always feel when my body was clean, that was when my creative juices would flow the best and I could make the best things. And it was very clear. My mind would get clear!

Asked if starving felt like the painful yet pleasurable way sports and late-night studying push the body, she replies, "*It did. I guess it was again that my willpower was strong and that gave me pleasure.*" Not surprisingly then, when asked if she took pleasure from setting and meeting weight-loss goals—an important reward for others, like Lynn—she says no, "*it was more just the process that was the reward.*" An artist, Francesca finds tactile and expressive pleasure in starving:

> I remember loving to run my fingers over my bones and just feel them stick out and think, "this is the perfect manifestation of the way I feel inside." Feeling small and thin and tight—it feels so great! You just—I don't even know how to describe it. It's like you're a success suddenly.

Fourth, once anorexia develops, some take comfort or "pattern pleasure" in the condition and its routines—it is "*dependable, always there*" (Lindsay). Heading to college, Beth plans a sport to continue her eating disorder's exercising "*and know I would have that.*" Later, under academic pressure, relapse is "*a safe haven because it was familiar to me.*" For Francesca

> You become preoccupied with the problem itself. I remember exam week and I was just not eating enough. And I thought, "Oh my god, I'm going to fall apart again." And I became so focused on the problem and, "Should I go somewhere?" And then at the same time I loved the problem. I don't know. The whole process of being in that problematic state was somehow enjoyable.

In sum, these consolidations—taste, disgust, process pleasure, and pattern pleasure—normalize anorexia as a steady state.

Deception. Secrecy gives anorexia meaning and power (Warin 2006: 49). Knowing it is dangerous, Lynn hides evidence and lies about her eating—anorexia "*taught me to lie on the spot.*" In time, most end up lying methodically to family, friends, and therapists. As Lindsay stays close to a wider circle of friends, her challenge is to accompany peers yet keep restricting:

> Everything's very calculated. You have to plan. You know people are going to be, like, "Did you eat?" You stop going out for dinners. Stuff like "I'll meet you after." Or you go over, and they're like "Are you hungry?" "Oh I already ate"—that kind of thing.

Where Lindsay lies to avoid eating, Janet eats deceptively:

I had all these tricks. If I went out with my friends to Dairy Queen, I'd get something in a cup that wasn't clear. Then I'd sit there and chew on my straw for ten minutes and then throw the whole thing away. Or at home during dinner, I'd get a big tall glass, fill it up halfway with milk and I'd start eating my dinner. I'd chew it up, go for a sip of my milk and I'd spit out my bites into my cup.

For Isabel, guarding her secret creates a new mindset: *"you analyze people more. You're always sort of looking out to make sure people are not looking at you and being suspicious."* This in turn makes her suspicious: *"you think about things so much more. I remember thinking, when my roommate was in another room, she might be talking about my eating habits."* This made her more sensitive (*"you let things get to you more"*) and secretive (*"I'd just hold a lot of stuff in"*). As Melissa becomes more inward, she takes pride in her *"ability to make people think I was fine"* and fool clinicians.

Do anorexics become pathological liars? Molly remembers:

My mom would ask me point-blank: "Did you eat lunch today?" And I'd say, "Yeah. I had some of Sara's chicken fingers too." And I hadn't eaten a thing! But anything else—if it involved boys or coming in past curfew, I couldn't lie. But food, no problem.

Why no problem? One answer is that, once anorexia takes hold, they can either lie smoothly or rebel openly. Jim recalls how *"I yelled at my parents several times: 'Get the hell away from me!' 'You don't know what's going on—I'm doing this to be a better athlete."* Choosing lying saddens Beth:

I'm such a good liar. I hate it. I don't like being a good liar but you have to be ready for anything. To protect yourself. You get to where you're doing it without even realizing you're doing it. The lies come out as easily as the truth does for most people.

Surrender. Sooner or later anorexia takes over. How does one grasp out-of-control control? No one pinpointed the change, but most remembered feelings of control reversed to helplessness. While the syndrome orders everything, for Beth *"what stands out is the lack of order I felt when I started becoming aware of what was controlling me."* For Sarah, *"it started off as I was powerful and I was in control and I think it just collapsed into helplessness."* Within this, *"I think the first big shift was from it kind of being at the back of my mind, not really thinking about it, to controlling all my thoughts."* In that physical imagery, her anorexia moves and grows. Amorn takes that alien imagery a step further—*"I created a beast and now this beast is controlling me"*—and describes how *"once it took over I just felt completely out of control and helpless. It was controlling me and everything about my life, every thought, every action and then impulse and obsession."*

Although several thought about food incessantly, the stories connect lost control to compulsive feelings, not obsessive thoughts. For Amorn, eliminating a food or meal made it *"hard to go back."* In Susanna's words,

> *It really was much more that I didn't have any choice in the matter of whether I reached this goal or did better than the last time. It started to dawn on me that I well, that I created something that I couldn't control anymore. The idea that I might be trapped in this cycle for the rest of my life got really scary.*

Some likened anorexia's takeover to an addiction.

> *I knew that certain feelings felt good, like the bones, the emptiness. I knew I wanted to continue that. With any addictive behavior, you want to continue it as much as you can. So it would snowball. And I'd let it because I liked it. It's like drugs. You feel you're in control of those drugs. You're regulating how you feel. Then suddenly you realize: I don't have any control over this. I can't stop this.*—Francesca

> *When I lost the weight, it was never good enough when I got there. It's almost like an addiction, right? It's like smoking or alcoholism or drugs. I don't think drug addicts are, like, "Today I'm going to get stoned this many times." They just start doing it and they're like "Oh I like this," until it becomes your whole life.*—Lindsay

Sooner or later fatigue kills exhilaration. In Beth's words, *"You feel so trapped and so watched and so tired and unable to escape."* Amorn feels high from fasting until she gets down to a banana and toast a day. *"Then it really quickly spiraled because my health spiraled: I lost weight and my energy drained a whole lot. Then it was out of control. I was controlling it to start with, like counting calories and reducing meals, and then all of a sudden it was controlling me."*

Parsing Features

As empiricists we have used features to map anorexia's evident surface. Our rough sketch outlines eight features. Another sample might hold another number. And another ethnographer might regroup the evidence. For example, Warin (2003a) picks out hygiene and Gooldin (2008) heroism, highlighting single features where we see several. So our eight are not definitive. They do, however, root explanation in the everyday—in what is obvious and immediate—rather than posit deep or distant causes.

What Features Say and Do. Each of the eight recurring features is internally diverse. For example, Discipline can regiment daily activities or exercise or food, and food discipline can target fat or calories or health. Or take Feedback, which can come from mirrors, scales, charts, clothes, comments, or feelings. Such variety establishes three critical facts. First, anorexics do not follow a single, hegemonic cultural model. Quite the contrary, this diversity tells us each invents what suits him or her as the activity unfolds. Second, the overall activity is emergent. When parts vary widely case to case but the syndrome is the same, the cause cannot be in any one part. Rather, it lies in how the pieces interrelate. Third, when differing people restrict in differing ways for differing reasons and yet come to think and act alike, the only common denominator is the activity itself. In this sense anorexia is an activity disorder.

Connecting these features radically reimagines how the disease gets going. Apparently features feed on each other. For example, restricting develops a Discipline that typically Isolates you socially, making the restrictions all the more absorbing and life-defining. Further restricting responds to Feedback that achievers use to Goad improvement. Then the more your body resists, the more obsessively you must keep your Discipline inviolate. Sooner or later, when others intervene, Deception defends your autonomy and emerging anorexic self. The more deceitful and secretive you are, the more Isolated you become. And so the circle closes. That, anyway, is one likely scenario. Other synergies could integrate features in other ways. Or the critical change might come when Consolidation makes starving feel natural and right. However it happens, this is emergence: different parts (features) integrate to create a new whole (anorexia) that is greater than the sum of its parts.

Features Across Cultures. Are these eight features peculiar to our sample? Thanks to other researchers, we can situate our twenty-two North American informants among six other ethnographies covering over two hundred cases from Australia, Canada, Israel, Japan, Mexico, Scotland, and the U.S. (Banks 1996; Garrett 1998; Gooldin 2008; Lester 2007; Pike and Borovoy 2004; Warin 2010). Two points stand out: we agree implicitly on features and disagree explicitly on interpretation.

On the features: although these disparate studies work up their data in differing terms to make differing points, what is reported fits well with—and comfortably within—our sample's eight features. At this low level of generality (just mapping the obvious), anorexia looks remarkably similar across cultural, social, and gender lines. Thus Warin could discern a common anorexic discourse despite Australian, Canadian, and Scottish differences. And that unity amid diversity is also clear in our sample: a macho Georgia wrestler echoes a polished New York debutant, and a struggling Russian immigrant in Toronto relapses just as a prosperous doctor's daughter does in rural Alabama.

On interpretation: the other six studies propose six different meanings for anorexia. Lester (2007: 370) neatly captures this tension by comparing two eating disorder clinics, one in Mexico and the other in the U.S. In both places patients' "behaviors and clinical symptomatology . . . look practically identical" and "seemed to be coupled with the same sorts of personality characteristics." Yet the "two centers construct very different clinical realities" because cultures differ: each interprets the syndrome locally. Indeed, as the other ethnographies show, anorexia can be religious in the U.S. (Banks 1996); an adolescent female "strategy for delaying maturation" in Japan (Pike and Borovoy 2004); hygiene protecting bodily boundaries in Australian, Scottish, and Canadian treatment centers (Warin 2003a); and "heroic selfhood" in Israel (Gooldin 2008). Taken together these well-done studies demonstrate a crucial truth: each culture defines anorexia in its own distinctive way.

But culture in itself is not the underlying motive. Here we diverge from the other six ethnographies. In highlighting meaning, they suppose the anorexic enacts local culture or even reacts against it. We disagree: anorexia is a bodily practice, not an idea; and the anorexic surrenders to an activity with its own inherent character, a practice that no culture can adequately code or reduce (Bourdieu 1990). That character is why anorexia's features look alike across cultures. That is also why practicing anorexics have no story to tell: a culture cannot express a dynamic it did not create. Of course saying the syndrome is not explained culturally does not mean culture is irrelevant. As Sections II and III will show, culture decides who gets anorexia and why.

Parsing the Will

What we have just clustered into features are disparate forces, feelings, and ideas that nonetheless work together to reinforce or even create anorexia. A few informants see one feature feeding another (e.g., how Deception feeds Isolation), but anorexia's coup comes quietly, well below awareness. Only later does consciousness awake to its helplessness. How did starving get a will of its own? No one can say. That is the best Cartesians can do.

Phenomenology does better. Willing, Throop (2010: 34–35) proposes, has three "experiential correlates" that are variously foregrounded or backgrounded. One, feeling the "effortful-ness" that willing requires, is backgrounded by our interviewees. Is the effort just forgotten, lost to memory perhaps? Or do adept starvers downplay effort, making the hurdle feel lower? Apparently the latter, for when their words foreground effort (e.g., describing one's regimen as too exhausting), it justifies yielding to treatment.

A second correlate, the experience of "own-ness," is the "I" in willing that Exhilaration captures. What happens when the thrill wears off? Sooner or later, when starving becomes routine, not heroic, at least some disown the routine as alien and tyrannical (e.g., Amorn's "*beast*"). Indeed, once separate from themselves, some personify this alien will ("Ed" for eating disorder; "Ana" for anorexia) only to struggle over whether it is friend or enemy (Colton and Pistrang 2004: 313). Either way awareness comes too late. Starving now has a will of it is own.[5]

In Throop's third correlate, anticipation, one feels an intended future—what one wills—in present acts.[6] Arguably that is easy with tasks like housecleaning—what is intended gets felt as one does it. But anorexia's projects (weight loss, becoming a star ballerina) take lengthy unremitting effort. Yet present actions can apparently still feel a future so distant and daunting. As Feedback and Goading show, a humble deed (skipping a meal) savors a glorious future (a thin body) still far off.

Conclusion

Activities order our lives. One moment reading, another parenting, still another driving—our bodies know these moments well. Day by day, their sheer regularity comforts us in how one or another groove focuses, runs, and orders our life. That order is partly cultural, partly personal, partly the activity itself. Anorexia is just one such ordering activity. Like the others, it carries its own rewards and pursues its own inner logic. That is not anorexia's only engine, but it is the dynamo that overpowers many unwitting restrictors.

As an activity, anorexia exercises an ascetic inner pull that is fundamentally human and thoroughly biocultural. To be sure, starving is obviously heavily biological. But anorexia only develops out of an individual constitution where restricting desire and denying the self are well-honed biocultural skills. Various as they are, anorexics fit Weber's (1964: 173, 168) description of all ascetics: their "distinctive goal always remains the alert, methodical control of one's own pattern of life and behavior." Whether anorexic or monk, once absorbed in the discipline, one "neither inquires about nor finds it necessary to inquire about the meaning of [one's] actual practice."

Notes

1. Warin's (2003b) multi-site ethnography of practicing anorexics reports this calorie/fat distinction. Apparently, fat raises purity/pollution fears but counting calories does not. More generally our interviewees' food systems are similar to what Warin (2010) reports. While what we *heard* from the recovered was decidedly more variable and, perhaps, less obsessive, Warin was *observing* and talking to practicing anorexics. Moreover, as her sample likely had some who would never recover, these more serious cases may well explain any differences in our findings.

2. Seven interviewees were obligated to activities that impeded friend-loss, and another two made new friends through starving. Of the remaining thirteen, seven spontaneously mentioned losing friends, two felt they had no friends anyway, and the remaining cases were ambiguous.
3. Isolation often spurs developing anorexia, but once one is anorexic, camaraderie with other anorexics can provide "a whole new set of social relations" (Warin 2006: 43) through either a treatment center or pro-Ana [pro-anorexia] websites (Dias 2003).
4. Ascetics understand this principle. With the right training, Diogenes says, a person can "derive more pleasure from despising pleasure than from the pleasures themselves" (Foucault 1990: 73–74). Bushell (1995) describes this for Ethiopian desert ascetics.
5. If that erodes the "I" of own-ness, backgrounding it, why doesn't the starving stop? Own-ness, Throop (2010: 42) shows, can also be in the third person—how one sees oneself in the eyes of others. Indeed, our informants know others see them as anorexics, and some worry about living up to that label. Beyond our sample, Warin (2010: 77) reports "a puzzling desire to belong" to the category, and clinicians know in-patients can compete to outdo other anorexics on the ward (Vandereycken 2011).
6. While most foreground where they are going, some do not. A few (e.g., Amorn) are exploring and do not know where their will is taking them; others (e.g., Francesca) are depressed and do not care.

CHAPTER 7

The Core
Elementary Anorexia

> The search for hidden motivations is the alpha and omega . . . of our modern culture. Our number one principle is that no human phenomenon is really what it seems to be.
> —René Girard, "Eating Disorders and Mimetic Desire"

We agree with Wittgenstein (1953: 108) that "[a]n intention is embedded in its situation, in human customs and institutions." That is why anorexia yields to observation. And that is the finding behind our findings. Other diseases may flourish invisibly, but anorexia is like breaking a leg—it happens in plain sight. Sufferers are eyewitnesses. That is how our informants could readily describe a dynamics of starving (chapter 6) that researchers had never noticed. Their eye-opening knowledge was always there, ready for the asking.

Why has no one thought to ask? Supposedly anorexia has deep causes, secrets that victims will not tell or cannot know. So starving hides some festering trauma, flawed family or cultural pathology, some larger truth about the psyche or gender or power. Here, where symptoms become symbols, some deeper purpose or aim—a *telos*—works itself out as anorexia.

We disagree. Our profession's tradition, ethnography, disputes seeking traumas and flaws behind what everyday evidence can explain. Explaining anorexia takes methodical observation, not interpretive leaps. Anorexia's core—its distinctive pathology—develops midcourse as a byproduct of starving. So there need not always be a prior problem. Hunting up symbolic clues is often a detour, sometimes a fantasy. As an activity, anorexia is in the doing, not the imagining. And, as doing is observable, studying life's surface ethnographically explains anorexia's basics better than ransacking the psyche for secrets.

Getting at Anorexia Ethnographically

No one knows anorexia's variables, much less how to isolate them for experimental control. So at least for now, since we cannot pull anorexia apart under laboratory conditions, we must study it as it comes to us—all mixed into the person's life. Here three strategies can logically isolate what we cannot literally control. One, clinical inference, has typically devoted itself to finding an underlying prior problem—so far without success. Another tool, epidemiology, quantifies. It has narrowed down the "who" of anorexia, but the syndrome is too rare and ambiguous for statistics to isolate "why" and "how" precisely. That leaves ethnography, either by itself or strengthened by comparison.

Our Ethnographic Approach. As anorexia is an observable reality, it should yield to ethnography as a descriptive practice. Describing sounds like a simple matter of collecting facts, but in fact it is a demanding art. Just choosing what to describe presumes a theory that could already presume too much. So good ethnography develops recursively. It is inductive and deductive by turns, adjusting itself to fit the reality it is studying.

Studying anorexia ethnographically posed challenges. One was recovering the past from the present. Another was getting from twenty-two anorexias—one for each interviewee—to a larger picture of the disease. To do that we used frames and methodically mapped both differences and similarities. So when everyone reported exhilaration, we did not stop at settling for the general similarity. Instead we went on to distinguish how some described transcendence, others immanence. We sweated the small stuff because ethnography strives to capture life as people live it. Getting that richly textured surface right reveals why humans do what they do.

Our ethnographic strategy was largely inductive. As we knew anorexia was heavily researched but still poorly understood, we had to suspect pitfalls in getting at the disease. So we made every effort not to presume what we would find, ruling out applying a theory deductively. Instead we worked up all the evidence methodically—piece by piece, perspective by perspective. It yielded many low-level empirical generalizations in clusters of facts like Exhilaration. These paid off threefold. Most obviously, this new knowledge was useful in itself (e.g., grasping Exhilaration should help therapists understand patients). Second, new knowledge supported further discoveries and better questions (e.g., is Exhilaration why anorexics resist treatment?). And lastly these solid yet simple findings disciplined theory by establishing empirical realities needing adequate explanations. Take male anorexia. Working up those cases carefully brought out no justification for excluding men. That uncompromising fact challenged the explanation of anorexia as a woman's disease. The researcher's plaint, "a perfectly good theory killed by a nasty fact," is exactly how nuanced ethnography holds theory accountable to established evidence.

Our chapters arose ethnographically, not logically. We had no preconceived scheme for dividing up anorexia. Instead we found the interviews' naturally occurring patterns and worked them up into the low-level generalizations that organize each chapter. So story-like patterns became chapter 3 ("Stories"), whereas character similarities became chapter 5 ("Bodily Bent"). Each chapter thus stands largely on its own, cross-referenced to the others but not reconciled in content. Taken together, they establish the empirical landscape—the groupings of elements—that any larger theory of anorexia must address. This, then, is how ethnography gets at anorexia.

Comparing Approaches. How does ethnographic analysis compare to clinical inference? While the two traditions overlap, they handle evidence quite differently. Where ethnography works inductively to explain contextually, clinical inference typically deduces an underlying cause, a reductive explanation (Luhrmann 2000). More specifically, where ethnography makes many small empirical steps that progressively constrain its conclusions, clinical inference sorts and re-sorts the evidence, searching for the one insight that organizes the facts. The ethnographer, we might say, plods forward methodically to advance science while the clinician paces restlessly and then leaps intuitively to effect a cure. Each approach has its virtues.

Plodding constructs anorexia quite differently from leaping. As straightforward empiricism, plodding inevitably stays close to describing appearances. Leaving secrets to other methods, it sees an elementary anorexia developed out of the activity of starving, a project that context can explain. Meanwhile, the clinical tradition[1] typically infers anorexia has (1) an underlying cause that acts as (2) *telos* and reveals (3) a prior condition that is (4) pathological. Such leaps are not wrong in themselves, as deducing underlying causes can work brilliantly. But these four jumps naively disregard contrary ethnographic evidence on (1) where anorexia develops, (2) what it is, and (3) why it persists. The following sections take up these discrepancies one by one.

Is Anorexia In or Behind Appearances?

Are anorexia's causes obvious or hidden, in daylight or darkness? That question opens an ancient philosophical debate between Aristotle's empiricism and Plato's logic. Is reality *in* or *behind* appearances? If it is in appearances, then you stress straightforward observation and treat anorexics as eyewitnesses the way we have. On the other hand, if reality is behind appearances, then you deduce anorexia's underlying form—its essential character—to find its cause. Here what anorexics observe becomes derivative, even deluded.

Essentializing Anorexia. While most experts readily agree that anorexia has an underlying cause, they disagree radically on what it is. Where feminists see patriarchy, Freudians find oral impregnation fears. Others attribute self-starvation to attention-getting, malignant mothering, or sexual abuse. For anthropologists it varies culture to culture, from fashioning a heroic self in Israel (Gooldin 2008) to staving off adulthood in Japan (Pike and Borovoy 2004). And for Hilde Bruch, the clinician who popularized body image, the true cause is far removed from appearances: *behind* the syndrome is a distorted body image, *behind* that are conceptual and perceptual errors, *behind* those hides a deficient sense of self, and that goes back to early parenting. Should we worry that Bruch never actually observes that parenting? Is it problematic that she works with her patients and their families long after anorexia has twisted their lives? Not to Bruch: her writing, classic in the field, takes for granted that she can see *through* the present, *penetrate* people's guises, *uncover* the past's hidden truths. And that is not just Bruch or even psychotherapy. From literary critics to social activists, modern sophisticates pride themselves on seeing behind anorexia's supposed veil.

Contextualizing Anorexia. Ethnography says anorexia is a practice, not a veil or symbol. Straightforward description ties that practice tightly to three observable realities that also are as they appear. One is social situation: anorexia is often an ascetic response to stressful conditions (Section II). It relieves that stress literally, not symbolically. No mystery there. A second reality is cultural context: anorexics incarnate surrounding values. That is what normal humans do (chapter 4). No secret there. A third reality is the activity (chapter 6), a practice all can see—nothing hidden there.

What then is *behind* anorexia's appearances? Nothing much. The disease is *in* an activity, not behind it. It does not symbolize anything. What is behind the activity? Often nothing deep or dark: anorexia's starving combines everyday self-denial with virtuous eating, a popular social movement (chapter 10). True, that combination has an insidious inner gravity, and Isolation (chapter 6) allows anything strange to get stranger, but intense involvement characterizes many successful people and is neither bad nor unusual in itself.

Is Anorexia *Telos* or Accident?

Attributing anorexia to an activity rather than a prior abnormality says some cases are accidental. That contradicts a long, deterministic tradition that insists starving is just a symptom of some more fundamental biological, personal, familial, or cultural flaw. Ironically, strong evidence against this argument comes from how its own advocates cannot agree on what that flaw is. One by one they refute each other. What is left—perhaps the only untried possibility—is that anorexia does not signify anything. It is an accident. That sounds naive after Freud, but the long-running failure to find a cure calls the entire interpretive enterprise into question.

Our ethnographic evidence questions prior-problem claims thrice over. First, with perhaps two exceptions, the only clear abnormalities appear *after* sustained starving, not before. Second, our informants' apparently normal and overtly successful prior lives argue against any significant prior problem. How serious could an abnormality be if it did not disrupt their childhood? Third, as our methodical analysis of twenty-two interviews showed, what preceded anorexia was simply too various for a common prior pathology to be plausible. Take motive: the immediate context-apparent impetus for starving ranged from standing out to its exact opposite, fitting in. Or consider character: we interviewed bubbly optimists and melancholy realists, social butterflies and shy workaholics, identifying no common denominator. And though our sample is small, epidemiologists surveying huge populations have also found no single prior pathology. Weighing all this evidence, empiricism demands a simple conclusion: when no preexisting problem is evident and relentless efforts to uncover one fail, there is no prior pathology.

What, then, changes healthy achiever into harrowed anorexic? When what precedes starving explains neither that activity nor what follows it, the likely agent of change is the activity itself. How else could differing people on differing paths with differing motives all become alike? The obvious cause is their one common denominator—the activity of starving.

What Is Anorexia's Core? The Ethnographic Answer

To explain anorexia we need to discern its core. It is not the prior problem that clinical inference has long sought but never found. Judging by ethnography, anorexia develops out of the practice of starving. This activity, the recurring element in all cases, is elementary anorexia. Because this pathology arises *within* the activity, it is endogenous: it is what the activity of starving does in and of itself (Keys et al. 1950; Wonderlich et al. 2005: S69).

Three exogenous influences complicate most and perhaps all activity-created cases. One is situational: many in our sample suffered social stress in school or family (Section II). A second exogenous complication is cultural: in our experience, anorexics get caught up in cultural scripts that energize starving from outside the activity (Section III).

A third complication is any prior or subsequent pathology that gets drawn into anorexia's vortex—or vice versa. Although most cases never enter the clinical system (Lucas et al. 1991), either clearing up on their own or never becoming sufficiently serious, comorbidities typify the ones that do. For example, a sexually abused person may give restricted eating energies that the activity alone cannot explain. Here anorexia acts as an idiom of distress (Kleinman 1986), attracting and expressing other difficulties. In these instances the eating disorder may well be "the co-morbidity rather than the main disorder" (Rosling et al. 2011: 309). No doubt such compounding characterizes serious and protracted cases. Yet epidemiology suggests (Lucas et al. 1991) and ethnography argues that these are exceptions, not the rule.

Anorexia's Second Wind: Why An Accident Persists

Saying elementary anorexia can be accidental creates a new mystery: why is the disease so resistant to healing? Most accidents get repaired, but anorexics cling to their illness tenaciously. Does that prove a deeper pathology? Well it could, but the ethnographic explanation is simple and well-documented: sustained starving changes the person (Keys et al. 1950), and the longer it goes the less likely recovery becomes (Wilson et al. 2007: 202). We explain that change as an emergent system, but however it happens, ethnography tells us restricting comes to feel safe and right while eating turns dangerous and wrong.

Anorexics, Peters (1995: 64) says, "are caught up in a phenomenon they have stumbled upon unexpectedly and found gratifying." A disease that begins accidentally thus persists for its practical payoffs. Here intense self-denial taps three ascetic powers—coping with life, exploring the self, and remaking the person—that pull anorexics down their deadly path.

Coping with Life. Asceticism rejects the modern impulse to multiply our choices. More choice distresses most people (Schwartz 2004). Asceticism tackles this head on: its discipline restricts involvements and defines what *really* matters. Endless little decisions are replaced by one big choice: the discipline or not. Once asceticism battled lust and gluttony, but today's challenge is "cop[ing] with overwrought feelings and satisfy[ing] the need . . . for a less superficial existence" (Allegre 1955: 259). Like centering prayer and meditation techniques, the anorexic's asceticism focuses the person and calms the body.

Had choice overburdened our informants? We did not hear that. Life, they said, felt out of control. Asceticism conquers that feeling by shrinking life to a discipline. All asceticism works this way. It does not put all one's surroundings in order but rather chooses one manageable segment, orders it rigorously, and dismisses all else. That is as true for an anorexic who lives in a regimen as for a monk withdrawing to a cloister. Either shrinks his or her life to fit an ascetic frame. Monks once fled a sinful world; today anorexics flee our chaotic one. Then or now, asceticism is a calming, responsible solution.

Exploring the Self. All ascetics end up exploring the self. An ascetic discipline makes the self "at once self-aware, structured, knowable, and valuable" (Harpham 1987: xiv). How so? Everyday life immerses us in the moment's people, places, and events. To experience yourself as truly separate, you need to restrict how you extend into your surroundings and they extend into you. Asceticism hones that separateness through fasting, solitude, chastity, poverty, vigil, and extreme exertion—activities that concentrate the self and focus life by restricting worldly extensions and intrusions. The one pitfall is pride: self-denial can paradoxically yield the self-celebration we heard in Exhilaration.

Did our interviewees explore the self? All test bodily limits and most feel pride in discovering their world-class willpower (e.g., "*It's amazing. It's like, 'Wow! I can do this.' It's special. You feel like a better person*"—Fred). Earlier Francesca described her fascination with starving and cutting as intensely embodied experiences. Reflecting on her motives, she says, "*I wouldn't say that I just let it happen but I was willing to just fall. For one, I almost felt like I just wanted to see what happened.*" Also exploring, Amorn starts restricting casually, largely out of curiosity, only to get caught up in discovering her limits—"*How far can I go?*" Natalie's "*point of pride*" is "*being able to withstand things.*" "*I was very much, like, 'bring it on,' 'I can take this.*'" Is this anorexia talking? No, it is asceticism—religious adepts likewise suffer heroically.

Remaking the Person. "At the center of ascetical activity," Valantasis (1995: 547) says, "is a self who . . . seeks to become a different person, a new self." How does that happen? An invented ascetic form—the anorexic's discipline—turns a healthy person into an anorexic in the same way St. Benedict's rules transform postulants into Benedictines (cf. Lester 2005). In Greek antiquity these "techniques of the self" were "intentional and voluntary actions by which men not only set themselves rules of conduct, but also [sought] to transform themselves" by establishing "a relationship of domination of oneself" so as not to be "carried away by . . . appetites and pleasures" (Foucault 1990: 10, 70, 31; cf. Lester 1997). In this way our informants bootstrapped themselves into anorexia. As the last chapter described, Discipline, Feedback, and Goading leveraged small changes that Consolidation turned into a new sensibility. That is asceticism's magic: it changes small stuff day by day until one day the big stuff—the whole person—changes too.

Two other anthropologists have studied anorexics' techniques of self. For Lester (1997: 485–486), the "anorexic's rituals . . . have a goal, a purpose, which only peripherally has to do with being thin . . . and has everything to do with changing and modifying the self." The "ultimate 'goal'" of this "project of self-tailoring" is to deny "that, in our culture, a woman *is* first and foremost her body." Gooldin (2008: 290–291), in contrast, stresses how Israeli anorexics' "self-inflicted hunger" functions "as a selfing device," "actively using corporeal experiences to construct a sense of heroic selfhood." One disease, two explanations—who has it right? Lester and Gooldin differ over anorexia's ends, not its means. In our sample the initial goals were too various to explain anything, and the final outcome, as an accident, cannot be an end.

Discipline's Triumph. Discipline gives asceticism these remarkable powers. If nothing else, keeping a discipline molds the body continually and thereby slowly shapes thought and feelings accordingly. Yet there is much else. Thought and feeling are discipline's change agents too. Among our informants, only Susanna glimpses how she might really remake herself. She copies a famous dancer, anorexia and all. Others, like Molly and Melissa, aim to remake their bodies, not themselves. No one fully grasps the powers unleashed.

How does asceticism overpower them? As Cartesians, no one sees it coming. All assume that, if they have enough willpower, they are in control and can do whatever they want with their bodies. To exert that control over themselves, they put eating and exercising rules—their invented discipline—far above other wishes, bodily protests, and doubtful inner voices. That discipline becomes *the* voice that they hear. And the more their bodies resist and lives refuse, the more literal-minded and uncompromising this authority becomes. Day in, day out, they use the discipline to regulate themselves, surrendering their other sides bit by bit until all that is left is their invented discipline.

Why do anorexics not fight this tyrant? Were school or parents to impose such a relentless regimen, they would readily rebel. But how do you resist yourself? They yield to their own heartless creation that, at least in our sample, has adolescent origins (Section II). Then, too, discipline musters an outer ally: moral sentiments. Anorexics create their own rules, but their morals are not just made up: they are enacting what is good and right to their group. Thus the anorexic's invented discipline stood above the self from the start.

Conclusion

Anorexia thrives in plain sight, hidden by Cartesian blinders. Separating mind from body falsely isolates actor from activity, making the syndrome incomprehensible. It excludes what simple observation could explain, setting off today's snipe hunt for secret causes.

Our era made this blindness. Four centuries ago English physicians could explain what now mystifies us. By *observing* their patients *in context* they realized anorexia came from leading an overly pious life (Rubin 1994: 40–41). Nineteenth-century medicine lost that insight. Instead of stressing what healers observed directly, modern medicine increasingly theorized underlying causes, seeking law-like regularities behind life's manifest diversity. Thus the best minds turned to looking through rather than at appearances. Calling a physician an empiricist implied he was a quack, someone who practiced by personal observation rather than scientific theory (Oxford English Dictionary 1989). That usage is outdated, but the disposition lives on: high theory still trumps straightforward observation. Even today's "evidence-based medicine" is not based on what is directly evident—quite the contrary, it uses highly developed statistical tools to test sophisticated theories across large populations. That is many times removed from what is directly observable.

Anorexia's deep, dark secret is that there need be no secret. Some cases definitely manifest a prior problem or tragically damaged life, and protracted cases, if not elementary ones, can certainly develop deep pathologies. So no one should downplay anorexia's seriousness or psychological complexity. Yet everyone should listen to ethnography. It says quite clearly that anorexia is sometimes an accident and never just a symbol; that it traps the person in a new identity, not old traumas; and that it persists by relieving stress literally, not symbolically. That, we argue, is far closer to what the ordinary sufferer experiences than the assumptions built into the disease's treatment today.

Notes

1. Treatment today often manages anorexia with drugs. That said, Platonic interpretation is deeply rooted in medicine and one can still agree with Goffman's (1967: 137) complaint that social acts are not studied for what they are but "called symptoms" and "interpreted or read as . . . communication."

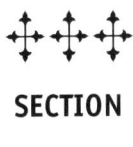

SECTION

II

The Life Cycle
A Developmental Disorder

Section II places anorexia in adolescence, its life-cycle home. Although some cases develop earlier or later, adolescence typifies the syndrome's timing as well as its character in the North American mainstream.

Today's life cycle opens adolescence to mis-development. Children can settle into childhood, but modern youth can and indeed must remake themselves. Yet even as the life cycle expects change, contemporary culture withholds help. Instead of a rite of passage that makes children into adults, coming of age is a risky do-it-yourself project. It is little wonder that some do it wrong.

CHAPTER 8

Youth
How Adolescence Invites Anorexia

> Freedom's just another word for nothin' left to lose
> —Kris Kristofferson, *Me and Bobby McGee*

Anorexia is largely a disease of adolescence. Almost all cases begin then, and as today's adolescence comes ever earlier, so too does anorexia's onset. Yet is age incidental or integral? For Bruch (1979: 35, 1985: 13), it is incidental—adolescence is when damage done in early childhood finally appears. For us, age is integral—adolescence does the damage. Growing up, North American youth face high but conflicting expectations. Torn between societal openness ("you can be whatever you want to be") and local closure ("be like us!"), they worry if they are worthy and doing what is right. When these pressures play out in eating, adolescence provokes eating disorders.

The Adolescent Point of View: Who Am I Becoming?

Vast as the literature on adolescence is, research typically takes an adult point of view (Valsiner 1997: xi). One notable exception is Csikszentmihalyi and Larson's (1984: 8) study of adolescents' everyday lives. Here, amid drama and routine, stands "one central question: what kind of person am I turning out to be?" Is one's "kind" due to nature or nurture? Is success due to luck, or ability, or effort? Youth live in a limbo of pending questions.

Adolescents who ask and answer these questions face conflicting attitudes. Is youth a time to experiment and find what is right for you? That traditional view makes it easy for youth to separate their larger future from adolescent pitfalls. Someone currently doing poorly with school or peers could still succeed later.

This wait-and-see ease contrasts with the pressure anorexics and other driven students feel. Here, the more they accept school's progressive message that each day's deeds decide their future, the more they see themselves—their very self—as in process. Their central question then becomes "What kind of person *am I making myself into*?"—a heavy burden that makes their effort and control life-defining.

Schooling, an inescapable modern condition, obliges all youth to reckon with progress, an Enlightenment tradition. Some, like the anorexic person and other good students, adopt the school's progressive viewpoint and work to better themselves. Others drag their feet or rebel, tapping democratic currents and romantic resistance to Enlightenment reason. Either way, to understand an adolescent viewpoint, we must relate it to surrounding societal and culture-historical conditions.

Society's Disappearing Stage: Adolescence?

Is adolescence real or imagined? The years between childhood and adulthood are so disparate that some scholars doubt adolescence is a useful notion. Others dismiss it altogether as a fabrication. We disagree. Adolescence is real enough, and not just because society says so. Absent a concept of adolescence, youth would still face developmental hurdles and society would still have transitional realities. That said, the idea of adolescence has a history.

Although recognition of a child-to-adult transition is old in the West and perhaps universal (Schlegel and Barry 1991), the contemporary idea of adolescence dates back roughly a century to the same modern cultural crisis that made sports and slimming into passions. Modern life, its critics claimed, was morally lost and heartlessly demanding. It misled youth, taking advantage of their changing bodies and impressionable minds. In response outdoor activities, organized sports, and youth programs arose to guide growing up (Neubauer 1992). A host of professions (counselors, coaches, youth workers) and institutions (scouting, sports leagues, high school) arose to manage youth and meet their special needs.

Now scholars dissolve adolescence, formerly a well-accepted stage, into many lesser transitions (Graber and Brooks-Gunn 1996) with little "storm and strife" (McNamara 2000: 34). Can we then forget adolescence as a dying modern myth? Hardly. However our culture once constructed and now deconstructs adolescence, cultural traditions and societal conditions impact adolescence powerfully. Whether our era marks a child-to-adult passage or not, that transition is part and parcel of anorexia.

This child-to-adult transition, then, is an ecological condition with psychological consequences. It is outside the person as well as within. Our next sections look at the outside, first nationally and then locally.

A Culture-Historical Openness: You Choose!

How does North American society organize adolescence? Or perhaps we should say disorganize: our era has no rite of passage or shared idea that orchestrates coming of age around a single set of coherent values. Instead, adolescents face an array of competing interests and institutions, each with its own values. School, family, church, and friends each can pull in a different direction. Caught in these value-binds, anorexics reject ambiguity and compromise to adopt a single standard of rigorous self-denial.

Anorexia's radical solution is just one niche within an ecology of adolescence. Choices come clustered in complexes or sets. Although these sets overlap and interact, we shall consider five of them one by one. Two are traditions (Protestant and democratic/romantic legacies), another two are conditions (the modern and postmodern), and the fifth, the human life cycle, frames how adolescence unfolds.

The Human Life Cycle: A Hidden Truth. Although not always marked, adolescence is a natural step in the human life cycle (Schlegel and Barry 1991). In many cultures that truth invites youth to reflect on life's wholeness—how birth, growth, and death bind old to young, person to society, humans to nature. But in our era, although some life-cycle awareness can seep into adolescence, perhaps especially for girls because of childbearing, the humbling thought of being just one link in a larger family and human chain need never dawn on today's youth. Real as the life cycle is, its truth gets slighted, if not repressed.

What hides the life cycle? In splitting spirit from matter, Enlightenment thought imagined the person apart from not just body, family, and society, but nature itself. One spin-off, autonomous individuality, was already well established in North America when Tocqueville (1945, 2: 104–106) visited the United States in the 1830s. He found democratic opportunity had created such mobility that "the woof of time is every instant broken and the track of generations effaced. Those who went before are soon forgotten; of those who will come after no one has any idea." Out of this came an individualism that not only makes "every man forget his ancestors, but . . . hides his descendants . . . and threatens in the end to confine him entirely within the solitude of his own heart." That individualism still lives and grows (Bellah et al. 1985). Whether it is me-first materialism or my-identity narcissism, the more today's ruling reality is not family or community but the self, the less life cycle matters.

Another Enlightenment spin-off, the ideology of modernity, also denies the life cycle. Many modern practices alienate the young from the life cycle within their own bodies. A girl's first menstrual period, for example, typically elicits a focus on hygiene, not her changed life-cycle place and promise (Brumberg 1997). Or take modern birth control, which neatly severs sex from procreation. Sex education is no longer the birds and bees, a metaphor that put humans in nature. Instead it is value-free practical knowledge—classroom learning that carefully isolates sexuality from the real-world emotional, ethical, moral, and aesthetic urgings that earthly life tangles within us. In such practices, where modernity celebrates its control over nature and freedom from custom, the life cycle disappears.

Anorexia rejects the life cycle's family motives and meaning. Where meals celebrate life and join generations, the anorexic goes hungry. Where new life requires sexuality and fertility, starving strangles both. Melissa recalls: "*I wanted to adopt kids because I didn't want to get pregnant. I didn't want to gain weight.*" Our informants lost their periods without regrets ("*that's a blessing*"—Lynn). Within anorexia, the life cycle dies.

Of course these two ideologies—individualism and modernity—hardly erase all life-cycle inklings, but they do make family-centered motives less worthy and fulfilling. Our era urges the young to find a larger life-purpose in a wider world. Here modern youth tap two rich traditions—romanticism and Protestantism.

Finding a Larger Purpose: A Protestant Legacy. Our era expects youth to find a larger purpose to life. That, anyway, is what Evangelicals urge as rebirth, other churches await as calling, and society secularizes as career. True, anyone can live an aimless or hedonistic life, but the mainstream expects a worthy life-course, a Reformation tradition.

How can a sixteenth-century legacy—the Protestant call to a Godly life—compete against twenty-first-century consumerism? Oddly enough, the two agree in the seductively powerful idea that every person has a unique inner essence—a soul, a personality, a nature—that should show outwardly. But they differ about outward expressions of the inner, which range from consumerism's pleasures and possessions to Protestantism's high purpose and righteous living. The latter finds its clearest religious expression in the evangelical's direct personal encounter with God; its secular version is careers that act as callings. Whereas once only clergy properly had a calling, the Reformation made any Protestant's worldly work what God called him or her to do. In this wider, eventually modern sense of calling, a person's work became "morally inseparable from his or her life," drawing the good person into a "community of disciplined practice" that served God as well as neighbors (Bellah et al. 1985: 66). Today's best-established professions not only secularize Protestant calling but impose strict ethical standards on members. Practice of, say, medicine or teaching need no longer serve God intentionally, but good professionals always serve the public as well as their profession, never just themselves.

Rebirth, calling, or career—each demands commitment. That, Taylor (1989: 185) shows, is a tenet of modern individualism. "No way of life is truly good," we have come to hold, "unless it is endorsed with the whole will." What way of life is best? Here democracy's openness obliges young people to choose. One cannot drift forever. Sooner or later, the good person must commit to one or another path.

Is anorexia such a path? Although our informants claimed no higher purpose for starving, the syndrome exacts purposeful devotion and engages "the whole will" just as a career, calling, or religious rebirth might do. In that sense anorexia fills a socio-religious niche that our larger traditions create yet leave empty. That emptiness is no accident: it defers to individual choice—a paramount value— whereby youth explore and express their individuality.

Exploring and Expressing the Self: Democracy's Romance. Democracy, Tocqueville (1945, 2: 104–106) found, fosters individualism. Where one's fate is achieved rather than inherited, kin and community have little hold over the individual. In growing up, many leave home and fashion their own identity. Democracy thereby privileges adolescence as a time to explore and express oneself.

Romanticism feeds this explore-and-express impetus. The nineteenth-century literary and artistic movement's spontaneity, emotion, and heroic individualism opposed both Classical styles' rule-driven formality and Enlightenment rationalism. Long eclipsed artistically, romanticism still flourishes in consumerism and youth culture (Baumeister 1997; Campbell 1987; Taylor 1989). Fascinated with the rebel, romanticism leads youth to adopt styles (tattooing, body piercing, cutting) and take risks (drinking, drugs, reckless driving, unprotected sex) that mock mainstream values. As dramatic self-expression, this boundary breaking echoes the way Romanticism's passionate artistic intensity defied the Enlightenment's cold imperial logic.

Anorexia taps these romantic and democratic traditions, drawing upon youth culture as well as the larger society. In all twenty-two cases, austerities become heroic, and in all except six, they are a solitary practice separated from friends and family. Although most of our cases become anorexic accidentally, some develop out of the risk-taking of youthful exploring, either at the start (Lynn and Susanna aim to be anorexic) or along the way (Amorn and Francesca want to see what happens next). Regardless of whether anorexia is intended, almost all fight off interference, defending their values and individuality heroically. And though none sought outside allies, pro-Ana websites now legitimate anorexia as a lifestyle.

Facing Progress: A Modern Challenge. Modernity imposes perpetual progress on all of us, young or old, all the time. Progress, then, is not a matter of choice like Protestant purpose and Romantic exploring. To the contrary, thanks to compulsory schooling, all the young must address the modern injunction to improve.

School ideally serves democracy as well as progress. Mass public education opens opportunities, develops citizenship, and advances knowledge, all for the common good. That mandate gives the school not just legal but moral authority, allowing it to compel attendance and manage its conscripts' lives. Although high school bores and saddens most students and slights its intended lessons (Csikszentmihalyi and

Larson 1984: 224, 217, chap. 10), it does succeed at structuring adolescent life around daily devotions to progress: each class, every assignment, and indeed the entire institution aim at perpetual self-improvement. Is this the source of anorexics' relentless drive? Perpetual progress orders successful students' lives for years before that energy turns to cutting calories and dropping weight.

What end does progress serve? Enlightenment ideals once easily justified education as advancing knowledge and developing the whole person, each for its own sake. But although those values remain, today's economic rationale is simply pragmatic: schooling trains the workforce. Wise or not, these business values change school's place in society and adolescence. As education becomes less intrinsically good than simply necessary to get a job, schooling loses the moral authority that inspires community support and student learning. Meanwhile, yoking education to economic payoffs fights what our traditions urge youth to do. Take Protestant purpose: all who hear that call seek not just a high salary but a higher purpose in labor, and they expect work to express their true character or God's purpose, not the market's roulette. Or consider romanticism: urged to discover their passion, youth find it conflicts with curricula that serve practicality. No wonder high school bores and saddens them.

The more education serves the economy rather than the Enlightenment, the more children and youth become small adults. If you want a competitive child or nation, education cannot start soon enough or go fast enough. Of course such pressure clashes with how Romanticism indulges dreaming and Protestant calling licenses discovery. Adult responsibility thus falls heavily on kids, who become less childlike. Anorexics are nothing if not serious and responsible in managing eating, exercise, and their bodies—all fields for further improvement.

Were we to sort out these competing injunctions to youth, then alongside "commit," "explore," and "progress," modernity would add "control." Carefully built into programs like scouting that arose to help youth cope with modern life, control is methodically tested in team sports, another legacy of that era with the same rationale; further, it pervades modern education: a good student, a good school, and a good course all require control. In explaining their eating disorders as asserting control, our interviewees epitomize a modern value.

Crafting an Identity: A Postmodern Challenge. In recent decades, as modernity's dominance has declined, life has turned postmodern. Facing issues from Hiroshima to global warming, few trust that life improves just because science advances and the economy grows. Even as faith in progress fades, diverse lifeways blossom. Thus a single Western, largely male story of progress yields to the unique tale now told by each group and every person. Here the postmodern revamps adolescence thrice over.

First, the postmodern ends youth's privileged place. To help adolescents grow up, the modern era promoted outdoor, athletic, artistic, and service programs.

Youth, the thinking went, were society's future (McDonald 1999: 3). That privileged education as a national project and gave students a national role to play. As the young progressed, so too would the nation. But once the postmodern edits progress out of those propositions, youth becomes just another interest group competing against poverty, the environment, minorities, and women. In this less privileged place, ambitious adolescents serve themselves, not society's betterment.

Second, the postmodern dissolves adolescence into segmental identities. In the 1950s, the idea of youth was implicitly white, ideally middle-class, and highly gendered. No one doubted youth's actual diversity—that there were class, racial, and ethnic varieties—but the white middle class was, or took itself to be, normative. That is long dead. Today's youth live within a shifting social mosaic, fashioning designer identities to express who they are and who they are not.

Third, the postmodern makes growing up morally confusing. The more the mainstream's authority disappears, the more youth must fashion responsible lives on their own. Whereas copying parents or keeping conventions once carried most into adulthood, now just getting through middle school breaks with what came before. Being good has thus gotten harder (Baumeister 1997; Campbell 1987; Parks 2000). The problem is not growing temptations but shrinking conventions of worth, which being good requires. Once the worthy upheld well-established norms of gender, age, class, race, and locality (Danziger 1997: 145–146). Today such standards are old-fashioned if not discriminatory. So youth must seek self-worth in ever narrower social segments whose values the larger society does not know or even disdains. The result, Danziger (1997: 146) argues, creates anxiety about self-worth even as "the normative pressure . . . to engage in self-assessment is stronger than ever."

These three postmodern shifts in the place, diversity, and morality of adolescence parallel the rise of eating disorders. From anorexia to obesity, all revolve around choices the postmodern opens. How you regulate yourself is increasingly up to you. What happens then to the well-intentioned child, someone who strives to be good in a society that debates goodness? Here anorexia's virtuous regimen replaces what the postmodern removes.

In sum, instead of a single compelling message, youth hear a cacophony of modern and postmodern voices over a chorus of Protestant, democratic, romantic, developmental, and life-cycle urgings. Choosing becomes a practical and indeed moral burden.

Local Closure: Choose Us or Them!

Wherever mass society pushes "you choose!" openness, local life can just as insistently impose us-or-them closure. Indeed, the more tolerant and inclusive society becomes nationally, the more strident and exclusive identity politics becomes locally, promoting "circumscribed, intensely specific, intensely felt, public identities" (Geertz 2000: 176). That battle engulfs adolescence. Where youth once enjoyed wait-and-see looseness during a time for finding themselves rather than asserting their identity, now social class, community, and school force narrower choices.

Social Class. Class shows how the larger society's legacies compete locally. Imagine two teenagers, one working-class and the other upper-middle-class, who flirt with youth culture's rebelliousness (a romantic legacy). The former would hear counterclaims for helping kin or starting a family (life-cycle expectations). The latter would reckon rebellion's cost to be bad grades that cut off careers (modern and Protestant expectations). Of course, to be *really* rebellious, each might adopt the other's class attitudes. The point, then, is not that class dictates choice (it does not), or that individuals choose freely (they do not), or that deciding and then doing what is right is easy (it is not), but that the choosing gets done locally.

Community. How adolescent openness and local closure intersect also varies from place to place. Compare Sewanee, a college town, to neighboring Appalachia. In that rural county folks still call high school "the best years of your life," a time of freedom before settling down to adult responsibilities of work, church, and family. That traditional Protestant view licenses exploration before commitment, lessens progress's pressure on schooling, and works well for those who stay to take a local job. Teens here grow up with clear and authoritative cues about what is right. Although some cues clash, life-cycle awareness makes it easy to see how life adds up. Youth still rebel, but their rule-breaking is itself conventional. All in all, the challenge in growing up is not figuring out what is right but just doing it.

In Sewanee, an upper-middle-class college town, growing up is getting educated to be competitive globally. Middle school's identity hell ushers in years of limbo. Most buckle down to study and sports, serious competitive tasks that prefigure their future. Here too adolescents rebel, but the cost could be their future, not just annoyed adults; and the town's cosmopolitan distrust of social labels makes it even harder not just to rebel but to believe in alternatives. After all, without clear social lines drawn by labels, it is far harder to feel you have been good (Baumeister 1997) or that life adds up. Sewanee, in working honorably to end social wrongs that come with racial, class, sexual, and gender labeling, offers no easy answers to youth's question "Who am I?" So while the Appalachian kids get clear answers, Sewanee's young find such finalities withheld.

School. Schooling forces identity issues. It did not always. A half-century ago high school styles pushed youth to accept mainstream middle-class values or stand out as rebels. After the 1960s, however, mainstream dominance faded. Take Eckert's (1989) study of a suburban Michigan high school. No longer taken for granted, the middle-class style (pro-school jocks) had become a marked category contrasting with rebels (largely lower-class burnouts). At the time most kids still fell between these two clearly marked extremes. Now middle school imposes riotous diversity—goths, potheads, gangstas, agbos, band kids, rednecks, kickers, thugs, and theater kids as well as jocks, preps, geeks, nerds, and ethnic labels galore. Students feel compelled to commit to one or another style in clothes, music, grooming, and decorum. Although most treat these styles lightly—"they're just what people like"—they represent the heavy hand of competing societal values. "Taste" and "choice" thereby set up class, income, political, ethnic, religious, and moral distinctions. Although this is not deterministic—upper-class kids, for instance, readily sport lower-class styles—the vanishing neutral ground takes adolescent latency with it.

School, with its competing identity groups and crosscutting values, creates an intricate, intense social world. Like a rainforest, each group has its own niche in relation to others; no group stands alone. On the contrary, each defines itself not just by who it is (positively and inwardly by shared values) but also by who it is not (negatively and outwardly by what is opposed). The result, then, is a matrix of value-specific adolescences. These conditions of openness yet closure, freedom yet forced choice, make "doing right" and "being good" so worrisome as to invite anorexia's value-laden response.

The Good Person's Dilemma: Choosing Commitments

While societal crosstalk gets sorted out locally, youth still do what they will. So some conform, others rebel, and most mix the two. What none can do, however, is not choose. Sooner or later the ever-more-exclusive identity question "Who am I?" demands a public answer expressing a value-laden choice. Consider how Fred works out his answer:

> *I'm from Jonesville, Georgia, a pseudo small town outside Atlanta. It's a little bit redneck. Public high school—not many people expect to go to college, no stress on academics. My mom was stay-at-home until I got into middle school when she started working. My dad has worked in trucking his whole life. They divorced when I was in sixth grade. They always stayed civil and did a really good job of being nice in front of me and my brother. So it was never very hard on me. They're recently getting back together, which I'm not entirely crazy about. One reason they got divorced—he was cheating on my mom. I have a huge personal problem with cheating. It's a personal thing. It gets to me.*
>
> *I started out a bookworm, bit of a nerd. I tested really high, really, really gifted for my age. Just wanted to read, didn't want to get outside much. Fourth grade I started*

wrestling. Took to it really well. Coming up through middle school—I don't want to toot my own horn—but everybody saw me as a prodigy. I was a natural. I started three years varsity in middle school. So they were really, really looking forward to me coming up. My freshman year—this was great!—I was weighing about 120 and so was a senior who was team captain. We both said we were going to go 112. So there was a conflict. The first week of practice I just toyed with him—technically he wasn't that good. He was just really strong. He tried to throw me around. I just threw some tilts and stuff in and he'd scream and cuss—"I'm losing to a f-ing freshman!" When he went into the locker room, I'd be grinning ear to ear. I ended up qualifying for State that year.

Sophomore year I was as much of a wrestler as I could be. That was when I really, really started cutting a lot of weight. I was walking around at about 130—and I wasn't out of shape. I was going to go 119. Then coach said something about me trying to dodge a guy from our cross-county rival, who was state champ at 112. He always picked at me, prodded me—I was like, "You know, coach, F-you! I'm going to go 112 and I'm going to beat him." So that was probably a bad idea.

Anorexia isn't just not eating. If you overly work out, that's just as bad. That was how I got my weight off. I was cut down to the bone. I was so ripped. Without even making weight, you could see abs, obliques—I was muscle-bound without an ounce of fat on me. I would chug water until I felt sick to keep from being hungry. Since I had no body fat I was always cold. So lunchtime I'd curl up in a locker with a hoodie and a letterman jacket on. I'd pass out and get the weight trainers to wake me for class.

I had it calculated up to where all the calories I'd gotten the day before I'd burn off at wrestling practice. Then I'd eat dinner, do my homework and run to burn off dinner. It got really bad. When I was really, really close—bad on my weight—I'd cut out some of those small meals and replace them with caffeine pills and Metabolife pills—just really, really tore me up. It moved from athletic training to focusing just on weight, not physical condition. It's not even something I noticed. The more weight I sucked, the more my body held on to what I ate. So I'd have to keep killing myself and killing my body. It just happens. I had to lose twenty pounds.

The weight-cutting got to me. I wrestled terribly at State. I lost stock in wrestling. I did everything I could imagine to be the best. And I wasn't. It didn't make sense to me. Like everything I'd been told—you put your effort in in the practice room and it'll pay off on the mat—and it really kind of shook me. After I didn't place at State I expected to be treated different, treated less [well]. Nothing changed. There was a realization, like "Wow! This isn't the most important thing. There's other things to life." My junior year I still cut weight but it wasn't the mental necessity that it had been my sophomore year. I hung out with friends more. And I realized that I don't want to do this in college. I'm going to college on academics. It wasn't life or death after that.

Fred's story revolves around making and keeping commitments. He cannot get into the story without denouncing his father's broken vows and rule-breaking generally. For Fred the good person makes and honors commitments wholeheartedly. So he gives his all ("*I was as much of a wrestler as I could be*"), while his father did not ("*My dad wrestled in high school* [but] *never took it seriously. He was more a pothead than an athlete.*"). We have already seen identity-defining commitments to virtue—Lindsay, for example, drops her boyfriend when he takes up drugs and drops academics—but Fred's devotion to wrestling shows how doing right can become one with competition.

Fred's story also involves finding and following one's gifts. At the start he is a bookworm, a gift that surely pleases parents and teachers. Yet he discovers another talent—he is a natural wrestler. He cultivates it so intensely, makes himself so completely a wrestler, that when he loses at State he expects to be treated as a loser and is surprised that people accept him as a person, not just a wrestler. He continues the sport but returns to the scholarly identity he once had. In answering youth's identity question "Who am I?" Fred makes the value-laden moves evident in all our interviews. Here, by embodying values and rejecting alternatives, our interviewees take a moral stance at once adolescent, modern, and moralistic.

Sometimes anorexia is simply adolescent, not particularly modern or mature. For our interviewees, self-starvation is heroic in itself and, in risking death to be special, updates what the Romantics did.[1] Here, as a life-risking regimen, anorexia commands the prestige of the real, something others get from drugs, sex, or crime. Like many alternate identities, it flouts bourgeois conventions (safety, practicality, moderation). Of course anorexics, having been perfect children, embody virtues in their rebellion (self-discipline, a slim body, healthy eating, vigorous exercise)—even when acting out, they do not act especially bad. Instead they embody a modern morality.

What makes this morality modern? Consider three traits and what they oppose. First, like the modern, anorexics insist on unending progress. Each weight or purity goal is met and surpassed—and then the bar gets raised. Although this drive has its own inner energy, it mocks postmodern alternatives. So just as modern society dislikes the self-satisfied, anorexics shun living for present pleasures or on past accomplishments. Second, like the modern, anorexics obsess over control. The less God rules the cosmos, the more control falls to humans. Here, as Bauman (1991: 12) shows, modernity prides itself on fragmenting the world into practical problems. When these are managed one by one, the big question—Is the world manageable?—disappears altogether. Anorexics do the same: eating becomes the one manageable problem that puts the larger question—Am I in control of my life?—out of the picture. Third, just as the late nineteenth century made sports into a moral microcosm, an arena that rewards effort and virtue, anorexia is a self-contained island that mirrors and yet moralizes the surrounding sea. So just as someone can play tennis and never question its larger worth, an anorexic can shed weight never asking the cost. Whether in sports or anorexia, life adds up: you can quantify the progress, feel the control, validate your worth—all apart from an uncaring world.

What makes these attitudes not just moral but moralistic is their contrast to what others do. Virtuous eating slights the fat and unhealthy. Strength in saying "no" to foods separates one from weak-willed peers who say "yes" to eating freely as well as drugs, drinking, and sex. Rock-steady control sets one off from erratic peers. All of this makes anorexics squeaky clean amid mud-playing peers. Here, caught between societal openness and local closure, anorexia is an escape that expresses one's values and disposition.

Conclusion

The "you choose!" openness that unsettles adolescence is no cultural accident: it expresses democratic and Enlightenment values aimed at freeing the individual from society's constraints. And they would do so, if humans were truly Cartesian creatures. But our species evolved bioculturally. Our spirit is part and parcel of our moral, material, and social surroundings. So today's disorganized adolescence disorganizes youth. The resulting openness benefits some, but it blights those who understand themselves more through than apart from society. For that sort of person—and for that side of everyone—if society's reply to "Who am I?" or "What is right?" is an empty "Whatever," the anomie evokes angst rather than ease. To grow into adulthood, such well-intentioned people need coherent structures to give their lives order and meaning. Anorexia is one such structure. A sense of identity, security, and self-worth that the larger society no longer offers (Giddens 1991: 105–107) now comes from the syndrome's misdirected achieving.

As modern adolescence dies, eating disorders plague more and more lives. The shift is not "either/or" as though one's decline evoked the other's rise; rather, each follows the same societal sea change. Adolescence, a late-nineteenth-century invention, arose with modern life. Now, as that era's homogenizing reverses into diversifying, disordered eating looks like just another postmodern spin-off. Yet what actually links the two? How does a societal shift evoke a personal pathology? Consider how Falk (1994: 25) puts body and society in dialogue: "the erosion of rigid social structures—from social hierarchies to cultural categorizations . . . in the larger world goes hand in hand with the elaboration of boundaries of body and self in the personal world." In consequence "the body becomes more 'closed' in its relationship to . . . the outside world" and strengthens "control over the flows in and out of the body." That describes anorexics perfectly, places them dead center in a societal trend, and spotlights their "success" versus bulimics' and binge eaters' failure. Various as these syndromes are, all echo the same chaotic conditions. These struggles are societal, not just personal.

Do these pathogenic conditions afflict only adolescents? Obviously not, but radical openness hits people harder at that age. No longer sheltered as children, they are not yet constrained as adults are. Adult commitments—earning a living, making a marriage, raising children, pursuing a career—bring relative closure. Life's larger questions do not go away but just get anchored in practical activities and local regimens. Until that anchoring, anorexia brings closure amid the wild openness of adolescence.

Notes

1. Although Gooldin (2008: 290) does not address adolescence, she finds Israeli anorexics used hunger "to construct a sense of heroic selfhood."

CHAPTER 9

Coming of Age
Meeting an Imagined Real World

> It [anorexia] is not a scramble to get back *into* the nest. It's a flying leap *out*.
>
> —Marya Hornbacher, *Wasted*

Coming of age drives anorexia. Although the pathology can arise at other times over other issues, the child-to-adult shift frames and fuels all our cases. None cling to childhood. A few court death as Francesca does, but most, like Megan, are just eager to grow up. All face the same dilemma: our era has no authoritative rite of passage that changes child into adult. Left in limbo, youth must decide—does adulthood come willy-nilly or willfully? The anorexic person chooses willful change.

In choosing to change, our informants prepare for an imagined real world. Using eating and exercise, they humble its toughest standards. Yet these earnest efforts go awry. Instead of mastering adulthood as it actually is, anorexics incarnate society's unending improvement and implicit asceticisms. A relentless modern logic—ruthless, exacting, unquenchable—seizes their body and being. What began as a bid to grow up becomes a prison.

While anorexia develops its own inner character (chapter 6), coming of age initiates and energizes the activity from outside. We explore these developmental, social, cultural, and religious energies in turn.

Developmental Energies: Taking a Good Thing Too Far

To grow up, children reorganize themselves psychologically to become adults. That happens in adolescence, anorexia's primetime. Is anorexia then a developmental disorder? Our informants say no. In their stories anorexia is just a mistake, a dead end. Surely that is true as far as it goes, but in three developmental tasks—establishing autonomy, identity, and purposeful patterns—our informants are not odd but overzealous. Their abnormality is taking the normal too far.

Autonomy through Achieving. Anna Freud thought youth met adolescence with sublimation, intellectualism, or asceticism (Austrian 2002: 128–130). The ascetic strategy counters "more urgent desires with more stringent prohibitions." That dynamic could end in anorexia, but most adolescents "swing-over from asceticism to instinctual excess," producing a "spontaneous recovery." Only those with strong egos succeed in relentlessly repudiating their instincts (Mogul 1980)—as anorexics in fact do.

Mogul finds Anna Freud's assessment apt for anorexics: "In many ways their responses are similar to those of other adolescents, but the reliance on asceticism as the answer to all of their conflicts . . . becomes more and more extreme" (160). Yet instead of instinctual drives, Mogul finds autonomy and achieving whenever fasting established their "sense of strength and freedom from dependence on parents" (170, 158). To succeed, therapy has to recognize the anorexic's "wish to be a strong person with lofty ideals, to be clearly distinguished from the 'petty materialistic' people around her" (171)—all typical adolescent sentiments.

Identity. A healthy adolescence, Erikson (1971: 259) writes, involved "some serious struggle" and a "search for new values." Instead of instincts (Freud) or autonomy (Mogul), Erikson (1964: 91–92) sees identity. As a developmental project, identity establishes continuity over time (between what the child was and the adult to come) and consistency in the present (between how others see you and how you see yourself).

As a life-defining task, identity can end in wholeness or totality. Wholeness kept "a sound, organic, progressive mutuality" with open boundaries. In contrast, totality forged "an absolute boundary" where "nothing that belongs inside must be left outside, nothing that must be outside can be tolerated inside"—a closure that was "as absolutely inclusive as it [was] utterly exclusive" (Erikson 1964: 92). That describes anorexic eating perfectly: defining yourself rigidly around fat, calories, or food that you let in or keep out. You *really* are what you eat!

Does feeling uprooted or endangered—as Erikson explains totality—cause anorexia? Anorexics say their regimen feels centered and safe. Moreover, if identity aligns the inner with the outer person as Erikson says, then anorexics succeed dramatically by making their body express their will directly. They also master Erikson's other identity task: by creating continuity between passing child and emerging adult, they translate their "good child" into the disciplined person an adult should be. To be sure, Erikson would qualify this as precocious moral rigor, saying it forecloses a healthy adolescence because one virtue, disciplined eating, cuts off exploring other paths.

Purposeful Patterns. To become adults, adolescents must develop "purposeful patterns" (Csikszentmihalyi and Larson 1984: 4). Whereas pattern hones practical, life-structuring routines (when to sleep, eat, work, play), purpose establishes moral, life-orienting values. Separately or together, they have two developmental payoffs. One is that youth develop the capacity to get absorbed in activities that become intrinsically rewarding. The other is that adolescents gain greater control over their inner states (Csikszentmihalyi and Rochberg-Halton 1981: 117–118). So although anyone can be blindsided by feelings of loneliness or worthlessness, purposeful patterns make youth manage the internal response more adeptly. Acting cool helps. So do externals that one can control physically: objects like "stereos, television and musical instruments" act as "tools [that] allow teenagers to modulate their emotions" (Csikszentmihalyi and Rochberg-Halton 1981: 118), as do clothes, food, and privacy. Overall the "ability to take disorder and turn it into order is perhaps the major skill adolescents perfect as they grow into adulthood" (Csikszentmihalyi and Larson 1984: 278).

Anorexics master that chaos-into-order skill. Using their chosen tools—food, exercise, eating—they develop an increasingly complex, rewarding life-structuring activity. Creating its own world, the regimen controls their feelings and isolates them from friends and meals, giving them the privacy that other teens get in other ways (headphones, closed doors, cynicism, hostility). If adulthood's challenge is to fashion purposeful patterns that manage emotions and enact values, anorexics succeed dramatically in meeting it.

Overdoing Development. In these three developmental tasks (developing autonomy, identity, and purposeful patterns), anorexics overshoot the mark. Why? Once the explanation was a distorted body image: anorexics could not actually *see* they had gone too far. Yet research has shown even healthy people to be similarly perceptually and cognitively impaired (Hsu and Sobkiewicz 1991). So the mystery remains. We propose that anorexics go too far because humans are biocultural hybrids, not rational minds overseeing emotional bodies. What we see in the mirror or say to clinicians actualizes lived traditions of seeing and saying. Knowing anorexics have constituted themselves around superior performance, we would expect these overachievers to overdo development. What is surprising, however, is the energy they put into coming of age. To understand why, we return to the anorexic's point of view.

Social Energies: Grappling with the Real World

Whereas development reorganizes the person's psyche invisibly, our informants reorganize their social life consciously. None accept adolescent limbo passively. Eager to prove their competence, they instead tackle the so-called real world.

Facing the Real World. The "real world" is a modern myth. Supposedly a hard reality, it is the fuzzy fiction that civilization is a sham—"it's a jungle out there," where "only the strong survive." It likens growing up to leaving a bubble. Our informants wrestle this imagined real world in one or more of three overlapping spheres—family, friends, and a competitive arena (sports, dance, academics). Take Melissa, whose childhood happily interwove friends, family, and academic success. All that collapses in adolescence. Suddenly she decides that to compete socially, she has to be slim. Only later, after putting herself through anorexic hell, does she realize her friends were not that shallow.

Our informants' sphere-specific struggles vary. Although each sphere addresses all three developmental tasks, autonomy bedevils the family sphere, identity struggles play out among friends, and purposeful patterning dominates the competitive arena. We consider each in turn.

The Family Sphere: A Failed Haven. Is the family a haven or hard-knocks schooling? We see both extremes. Half our sample (11) praise their families as supportive, and nearly a quarter (5) treat family as irrelevant. But just over a quarter (6) describe families beset by real-world troubles. Their difficulties vary—divorce, putting work before family, criticizing a child's weight or grades—yet the result is the same: our informants feel unsupported yet pressured to succeed.

Having heard from three of these six—Francesca, Lindsay, and Natalie—we now consider two more. Jane grew up in a *"very Jewish suburb"* of Toronto with her Israeli parents.

> *I was always a little bit overweight, chubby, you know? Not ridiculously overweight—maybe ten or fifteen pounds. It bothered me. My mother grew up in Israel where everyone's like crazy, like size zero, like minus five. So she started dieting at fourteen and went through anorexic periods. She'd say things like "I'm cleansing my system" and survive on orange juice and water for three days. Most of my friends were really thin. I did Weight Watchers at eleven. It was so embarrassing. Like I didn't tell anyone I was there. So that was the first time I dieted. I'd go and my mom would sit with me. It was encouraging. Like, "Oh my mom is doing this with me. It's easier."*
>
> *He* [her father] *always, always used to say things about my weight. That's what affected me the most. He used to call me names or comment on my weight. And my family in Israel, oh my God they were the worst! You know what they would call me? Soofgania* [doughnut in Hebrew]*! And I was like "Thank you. Thanks a lot."*
>
> *I just decided one day that I was going to lose weight. It was in July and I went to a concert with a friend. I hadn't eaten all day. I realized "Wow, I can not eat and I'm fine." In the beginning it was just, like, I'd have orange juice in the morning. I knew I was starving myself. I'd have a really small lunch. Then I'd have like half dinner. Then, like, I started making the portions smaller and smaller and smaller*

and smaller. They [her family] *all knew. They saw that I wasn't eating. That's what bothers me until today—they knew!* [Crying]. *They didn't stop it.*

The first week I lost five pounds; the first month fifteen; in two months twenty-five. I think of that now and I have no idea how I had the will to do that. But it was so motivating when people would compliment me, like, "You look good" and I was like, "Oh my God, I can lose another five pounds and I'd look even better." After three, four weeks, I'd faint maybe like two or three times a day. But I got really good at it. So I'd know like this is the feeling I get before I faint. So I'd sit down and close my eyes. I remember once I was knocking on my mother's washroom door and I fainted, just dropped to the floor.

My mom would encourage me to exercise. So we used to go walking every day for an hour. Then my mom would tell me an hour of speed walking burns 300 calories and I thought, "Wow, if I only eat 300 calories and then I go walking, it could be like nothing." I started counting [calories] *obsessively. It took over my life* [crying].

So by the time I got back to school, I'd lost twenty-five pounds. For some reason, I grew like maybe four or five inches in that one summer. So when I went back to school everyone was like "Oh my gosh what happened to you?" And that was even more motivating. When the really pretty, really thin and popular girls were like, "Oh my God, you look great," I was like, "Oh wow, I could do this for so long, I could keep going." Another few months and I lost another ten pounds. The worst was grade ten and eleven. My teachers were saying things [crying]. *"You are way too thin," and they were like, "Is something wrong?" and they'd try to get me to talk about it. I have no idea how I performed so well in school without eating. I was so focused. Like the top of my class and I wasn't eating at all, at all.*

Friends in high school were also [dieting]. *Two friends, one was anorexic and the other bulimic. So I had that support. Like, "Let's not eat together." And then another of my close friends, she was anorexic and bulimic. It was like a very cool thing to do in high school, like starve yourself. I was really close with those girls. We all did really well, at the top of our class. We were motivating each other more than competing. But at times we were, you know, "I want to look as good as her." We'd push each other, like, "Don't eat that. It's bad." And I'd exercise more with my friend. But I was never big on exercising.*

First year at York I started gaining a little bit of weight. Then last year, I was in Israel for the year. I went to Tel Aviv University. Being in Israel away from like where I lived—my parents, my home, everything—and just being on my own and doing everything for myself was a major event in my life. At the beginning it was really hard. I'd call my parents crying every day. Then I went on this organized trip and became close with this group of girls. I didn't even call home once. I really really really enjoyed myself.

I was dating this guy. I was like, "Oh wow, someone likes me" [crying]. *I don't even know why this is happening* [about crying]. *So we'd go out to eat and I was* like, "This isn't part of my routine. What do I do now?" Then I just thought I was going to start eating whatever I want. I realized [crying] he liked me for me and not the way I looked. And it was my first real relationship, my first relationship period. It was the biggest confidence boost of my life. I realized, I could eat whatever I want and he'd be fine. It [dieting] was never pleasing people physically. I never wanted to impress people with the way I looked.

Pursuing autonomy gets Jane into and then out of anorexia. Her entry, self-starvation, gives her adult competence in her family's eyes, suggesting Mogul's autonomy through achieving. In Israel friends and romance give her a new, healthier autonomy.

Family pressure pushes Jane into anorexia. We have seen this before, felt directly (Lindsay) or sympathetically (Becca preempting her sister's freshman fifteen). Asked why excess weight upsets her father, Jane speculates:

It's a good question. Umm, I don't know. It's important to him that my mom is also a size, like, negative five. I know that he doesn't like overweight people. He's like, "Overweight—they're all lazy." Like it's gross. But he's not a superficial person. He doesn't care about materials. He's very modest. So it's interesting that weight is so important to him. He's really tall and really really thin. Getting older and gaining a bit, he's like, "Oh it bothers me." And I'm like, "Do something about it!"

Apparently her father leads an ascetic life. He wants to see that in his own and his daughter's body. Yet neither he nor Jane can articulate that principle, making his value-driven sentiments appear quite arbitrary.

Unlike Jane, Elizabeth sees parental slimming pressure as well intentioned even as she blames it for her own and her older sister's anorexia:

My mother was very weight conscious. We were never given sugar. We were fed all health food. I think my mom hated that my sister was just this naturally chubby little kid. Hated it. To this day my sister will accuse my mom for calling her fat. But my mom says "Your sister would—I mean she just—she came home and she watched TV. It was the wrong way to handle it, but I wanted to change her habits." I remember my mother's angst, her fear that my sister's life was going to be harder if she was overweight.

Does Elizabeth have her mother's intentions right? Slim women have advantages, but that is not what her mother says. She complains about TV-watching and bad habits, pressuring her chubby daughter to lead a more active, disciplined life. Does she nag over values or looks? We cannot say. As long as a slim body signifies virtue *and* serves success, neither we nor our informants can easily separate moral sentiments from practical motives. What we can say, however, is that adapting to an imagined real world shapes these families.

Janet attributes her anorexia to maternal neglect, not parental nagging.

I grew up in St. Johns, Florida, lovely town. My parents separated when I was in second grade. My sister sided with my mom and I sided with my dad. Living with my mom, I didn't get a lot of attention from her. She knew something was going on [the eating disorder] and never said anything. She even admitted that the first time we talked about it. "Well, oh, I assumed something was going on." "You're a nurse!" What was she thinking, not to say anything? I was looking for attention. I wanted her to notice it.

Schooling was good. I got tested twice to get into the gifted program. It's really the only good thing about the public schools but it's really good. My first time I didn't make it in. It was a big bummer. My sister had gotten in in second grade and so I felt pretty bad when I didn't make it. A year later we tried again and I made it. It was amazing. From third to eighth grade I was with the same group of kids in the same class.

Sixth grade I was on top of the world. In gymnastics, leotards and mirrors, but it never occurred to me to be concerned about the way I looked. Because I was doing so good in gymnastics and everything was great. My sister was always the really good one academically. We had this Future Problem Solvers, which was this academic, creative writing thing. It's a huge deal. She went to Internationals twice. I never even made it to State. My mom was the coach. I always felt she was the star and sixth grade was when I really found my group of girls. I got sick of competitions every weekend so I quit gymnastics. Then it was, 'What do I have now?' There was nothing I did that my sister couldn't do. It doesn't matter that she's three years older. When we were younger, we'd do sports together and Connie would always back out because I'd get better than her. I was always the athletic type and she was the brain. But I quit that and I didn't have anything I was better at. That was a huge part of it [anorexia].

With my mom away at work we didn't have a lot of family meals. Dinner was just whatever you made it. For me that meant, "What sounds good?" I could eat that half-gallon of ice cream! I became a huge binge-eater. It was like, "I'm going to sit in front of the TV because nobody's here and nobody cares and I'm going to eat whatever I want, as much as I want." That was the way meals went at my house.

In eighth grade we got our gym membership. That's where calorie counting got intense. They've got machines that say you've burned this many calories. So I'd be running and I'd say, "Well, all I had was ninety calories at breakfast and I'm already in the negatives. This is great!" I kept a little food journal and I wrote down every single thing. If I ate a two-calorie breath mint, it was on there. It was like I was getting affirmation for myself because I wasn't getting it from my mom. I'd circle the calories at the end of the day—usually negative. Sometimes I'd put stickers on the page or write notes saying, "This is great." Or if I gave in, I'd write things like, "You're a fat ass." Horrible things! It was like the physical me and the mental me were completely different. The mental me was talking to the physical me via this journal.

Eating disorder things got really bad. I wasn't a very happy person. I went to five different high schools. I started in a school for the arts, a dance major. I've already got this image in my head of how I want to look and I feel like complete crap about myself. All the highest-level dancers were so thin. My freshman year two got hospitalized. It was like "Wow! They really did it." It seemed like success to me. The different arts departments had parties. Theater had pizza and soda. You could smell it down the hall. And the dance party, carrots, celery sticks and fat-free dressing. I started losing a lot of weight and supplementing anorexia with bulimia when I'd have to eat. We didn't talk about it, but when all the dancers sit together and don't eat—it's what's not being said. Also in ninth grade I started smoking to suppress my appetite. I was like "Cool! Awesome!"

My older sister and I were very close and the end of ninth grade I found out she had been throwing up too—which brought things to a whole new level. We'd spend the days not eating, doing anything not to eat—bike rides, the gym, whatever it took. We started doing this apple-a-day thing. We'd cut it into four pieces and she said to me, "You have one slice for breakfast, one for lunch, one for dinner, and throw the last one away." She was, "That is success!" Which is what it was all about to me—succeeding at something.

I spent a semester at St. Johns High—hated every moment! For the first time in my life I wasn't doing accelerated programs. I didn't have a lot of friends. Then I went to the Wilderness School—an amazing place. My sister had been there, my cousin had been there. Very close community—twenty-six kids and about an equal number of faculty. Eating at the school blew my mind. We were very environmentally conscious. We didn't waste food. If you put it on your plate, you eat it. If you don't, people nag you. Meals were huge. Our cook made the best food. Three meals a day. Never in my life had I sat down for three FULL meals a day. I started freaking out pretty soon. I'd sneak away to this bathroom and throw up my food. My bunkmate told one of the faculty.

I remember being called into the Director's office in tears. They made me call my mom, right there, at work, and tell her. At work my mom is always stressed out. She was being very short with me, very "I'm busy, I'm busy, I'm busy." I said, "Mom I've been having some problems with eating." "Her reply was, "Oh, yeah I know you've been losing a lot of weight. I was pretty sure you'd been throwing up." I was sitting there—there's the Director and the President of the foundation with me, and my jaw just drops. "What, you knew?" And I started a huge thing with my mom. To stay at the school, I had to start therapy.

Janet exemplifies autonomy-through-achieving anorexia. Achieving orders her life—it is her family ethos and how she sees herself. Like Jane's, her home is demanding, not a haven. If she fails, there is no retreat, no shelter where she can recoup. Her story says her mother wants a successful achiever, not the less-than-perfect Janet who does not always win. Her "*nobody's here and nobody cares*" feelings crystallize into self-starvation as "*succeeding at something,*" "*getting affirmation for myself because I wasn't getting it from my mom.*" Of course we do not know her mother's side or what actually happened, but if anorexia develops within the anorexic's point of view, then Janet's lived reality is what matters most. Here she embodies yet resists autonomy: she expects to achieve as an autonomous individual but she wants backup at home.

Francesca tells a similar story. She feels she had no childhood: "*when I was a kid I was absolutely, all the time, expected to be an adult.*" Academic pressure was intense:

> When I got a B—to this day my mother does this—she thinks it's a joke but it's not funny. She says, "God, Fran, you only got a B?" And she laughs. But it really undermined me as a kid. When I got Cs—which I rarely did—I was bombarded about how disappointed they were in me.

Like Janet, parental love feels contingent on performance. Both suffer depression that, at least for Francesca, "*totally came out of the fact that I felt so abandoned by them throughout my life.*" Angered that her parents ignore her emotional needs, she becomes self-destructive, showing them that if they will not nurture her, she will not nurture herself.

The Friends Sphere: Preserving Identity. Other parents try but fail to keep their children from internalizing outside pressures. When this means pleasing peers (the friends sphere), the developmental issue is more identity than autonomy. Such cases are the fitting-in anorexia described earlier. Consider Melissa:

> I'm from Peters, Alabama, a small town. I love my parents. They're perfect. I have a really tight-knit family. Everybody—my cousins, second cousins, aunts, uncles—we all get together almost every weekend. It's wonderful. I'm very close to my mom. She's really into my life. I grew up a very heavy child. My mom never made it an issue. I had overweight friends whose moms would get onto them. My mom always said, "You're beautiful blah blah blah." So when I was younger I didn't think anything of it.
>
> I went to St. Mary Catholic kindergarten through eighth grade, a wonderful school. All the teachers were so supportive. I grew up with the same thirteen kids. But then I had to go to public school for high school. That was awful. My freshman year was horrible, completely horrible. I didn't know anybody. That's when I became anorexic.

When I hit puberty I made this plan: "I've got to lose weight before I go to high school." So Christmas in the seventh grade I said to my mom, "I'm going on a diet and I'm going to exercise." She said, "Oh, okay, I'll support you but you don't have to." It was puberty and I started realizing how people saw me.

So I went on a diet and was really successful with it. By end of eighth grade, I had gotten down to maybe 140. According to the doctors that was the ideal healthy weight. I was happy with the way I looked. Actually I've never been happy with the way I looked, but I was like, "I've come a long way. This is fine. I'll stop here." I was still eating 1,000 calories a day, and every Friday I'd eat whatever I wanted.

Then I went to high school. First thing—this is what always happens to me first thing—I thought: "No one likes me because I'm so fat." Even now—if anything happens, if I make a bad grade, it's because I'm fat. So, I thought, "OK, I've got to lose more weight." My mom even took me to a psychologist about it. I have this ability to make people think I'm fine. So the psychologist was like, "Oh you're fine but if you want to lose weight, just quit your free Friday." I was like, "Okay." And I quit.

Over the summer, I thought, "I'm going to lose a lot. When I go back, I'll have friends." I got fanatic about exercising. I got down to 120 sophomore year. Feeling better about myself, I had the confidence to talk to people. Freshman year I didn't talk to anyone. People would tell me later, "We thought you were just stuck up because you didn't talk to anyone." I said, "No, I was just scared. I didn't know anyone." Anyway I got a lot of friends. I associated it with losing weight, not greater confidence. I was like, "If I lose more weight, I'll have more friends."

Sophomore year was awful. After school, I'd run for an hour. Then I'd do 800 jumping jacks, an aerobics tape, arm weights and sit-ups. After that I'd work out at the gym for two hours. I was exercising four hours a day. I was eating, like, nothing. My mom worried about me but she was so close to me that I could fool her too. I'd tell her, "I'm fine, I'm being healthy." Other family were like, "She's not healthy, this is bad." Mom's like, "She's my daughter. She's not doing anything I don't—she's not throwing up. She's fine, she's healthy." By the end of sophomore year I was like ninety pounds.

Junior year my aunt was diagnosed with ovarian cancer, and my dad had a heart attack. The way I dealt with that was to exercise more. I got down to eighty-five pounds. I don't think I could've gotten any lower than that. Even I knew I was unhealthy—my bowel movements had blood, my heart would skip, sometimes I'd black out—but I didn't tell anybody because I was like, "I can't gain weight. Don't make me gain weight."

Then I started having heart problems. I went from someone who could exercise five hours a day to someone who couldn't get out of bed. If I walked from my room to the kitchen I'd be out of breath. I started gaining weight because I couldn't exercise. I got back up to 120 pounds in a month. I was freaking out. I was like, "This isn't fair. I've worked too hard for this." I took a bunch of pills to kill myself. I cut myself. It was awful.

Anyway, it's a long story. My senior year I got diagnosed with a central nervous system problem. Being anorexic caused it. I got medicine and then I was a completely different person. It's hard for me to explain how my anorexia went away because it just went away. That's where my story's kind of unclear. Family caring about me didn't work. Psychologists didn't work. The only thing—and I really believe this—God works in mysterious ways.

Identity drives Melissa's anorexia. Popular and successful through the early grades, she wants that in upper school too. As a seventh grader, still cocooned by caring family and small school, she diets to prepare for high school, where an overweight girl has no place. Or so she assumed. In fact Melissa preempts criticism. She mentions no mocking peers and later, heavy again, she has plenty of friends.

Unlike Melissa's self-inflicted struggle, peers initiate anorexia in Mary, a Russian-Lithuanian immigrant whose Canadian schoolmates pressure her to slim up.

I came to Canada when I was twelve. As a kid I was like troublemaker. I didn't care for the marks. I had my friends. We did the craziest things. My mom was a teacher. She'd switch schools and I'd come along. In every school I made friends, every school. After two or three days I'd have friends calling.

So we came here and I couldn't make friends. Kids used to tease me for being an immigrant and an earlier developer. Like I had the biggest breasts of all the girls. I already felt out of place because I had no friends. At recess the girls were completely ignoring me. I felt like it was a problem with me.

In grade eight [starts to cry] *this girl called me "fat ass." So I thought I was fat. And I wasn't. I was at most 115–120 pounds. I started skipping lunches. The summer between grade eight and nine my parents let me join the gym. I'd go five, six times a week two hours every time. And I took out all the library books about nutrition. So I knew calorie intake for every single food. Every morning I'd write down I can have this and this and add up the calories. I dropped to about 100 pounds. I stopped having my period. My mother took me to the doctor and she said "Well, maybe she is anorexic." My parents didn't even know what it is and neither did I* [crying]. *We were like "What is it?" She's like "How often do you eat?" I was like, "Well I eat regularly, but they just don't see it." But I stopped eating any food that we used to eat back home. It was the fat—butter or oil, I'd never touch anything like that. Then Halloween my sister went trick-or-treating. She brought lots of candy. I just couldn't stop looking. I binged, like I ate whatever there was. The next day I counted all the calories, and I didn't eat for the next two days and I had to go work out* [sniffling].

> *The end of grade ten my friend introduced me to her cousin. So I started dating him and I kind of like stopped. I don't know, I just stopped. We'd go out for dinner. So I couldn't say, "No I'm sorry but I can't eat." I'd choose the lighter choices, but sometimes he'd make me eat. Then one day I just started crying and told him. He was really supportive. Like so I started eating kind of normal.*

Like Melissa's, Mary's anorexia develops out of an identity struggle for continuity. She starves to regain her childhood popularity. Her rescuing boyfriend is also an Eastern European immigrant. Once she gets friends, starving recedes—only to return with academic pressure.

> *In high school I got really high marks. I wanted to be doctor and worked hard. I went to university and first semester was ok, but second I had chemistry. I studied so hard and I just couldn't get the grade I wanted. I stressed out. So I kind of started not eating again. But not to be skinny. So I, like, started, again around March. In August I took summer school and got a B+. My first B+. I felt so bad. But then October I just said, "Forget it, I don't care." I just started eating like normal again. So I go back and forth. Second time around, I didn't eat because I had no appetite.*

Once peer pressure starts anorexia, academic pressure brings relapse. First it is to be slim, then successful. How can one syndrome serve such different ends? If anorexia is just slimming, then the second bout remains a mystery. But if anorexia is achieving's self-denial, then the two are alike in meeting competitive conditions. Yet her achieving is not just self-serving:

> *My parents give up their careers to bring me here. My mom used to be a teacher and here she's a cleaner. Same with my dad. He was like—not vice dean—but, you know, of a university. Here he had to take whatever was offered, and it wasn't much. So I got to feel really guilty. I wanted to achieve to make my parents proud and make sure I could support them at the end.*

The Competitive Arena: Anorexia's Gateway. The third sphere, the competitive arena, is the real world writ small and made safe. Here you win at soccer as in life because you have what it takes; and you succeed at school as in work because you give your all—no exceptions, no excuses. To meet these tough standards, everyone develops purposeful patterns.

Take Megan. Secure in the other two spheres (family and friends), she willfully breaks that bubble and starts running competitively to establish an independent identity. No longer a child, she celebrates the freedom to make running as much of her life as she wants and to treat her body as ruthlessly as she likes. That purposeful pattern fast-tracks her into anorexia.

Or consider Fred. He has a natural gift for wrestling but knows that is not enough. So he methodically patterns his life for the purpose of wrestling. Rejecting all laxity, he imagines competitors to push himself harder ("*The guy across the street, the guy at the next high school—he's working harder. What are you going to do about it?*"). He is not just preparing to compete; he is living competitively 24/7, only to wrestle "*terribly at State.*" He is disillusioned:

> *I lost stock in wrestling. I did everything I could imagine to be the best. And I wasn't. It didn't make sense to me. Like everything I'd been told—you put your effort in in the practice room and it'll pay off on the mat—and it really kind of shook me.*

Succeeding competitively requires purposeful patterns that epitomize the so-called real world. While Fred takes the gospel of competition (hard work will be rewarded) too literally, our other interviewees all take the challenge of sports, dance, and school to heart. Is that not the way the world really works? After all, it is in these symbolic arenas that children glimpse real-world competition, see winners and losers, and learn to redouble effort and tough out pain. All this schools them for anorexia.

Ritual Energies: Living in the Real World

Is anorexia religious? Early on we distinguished the syndrome's diffuse religiosity from its quite specific morality. Since then we have focused on that morality's essentially secular ascetic practice. Yet coming of age inevitability raises religious questions.

How does our informants' adolescent religiosity unfold? No one develops a new church involvement or intensifies a prior one. Some drift away from institutional religion and others persist mechanically, but no one finds church especially relevant. Indeed, mainstream denominations downplay asceticism, keeping in tune with laxer times. In three areas—coming of age, loss of faith or direction, and daily practice—anorexia's asceticism either fills a religious void or offers a secular ritual alternative to conventional religiosity.

Coming of Age: Seeking Intensity. Modern life treats coming of age pragmatically rather than religiously. Instead of bundling adulthood's start into a single rite that addresses ultimates, our era splits the transition into many proximate practicalities—everything from getting a driver's license to choosing a career. Apparently that works well enough for most people.

Anorexics are not most people. Clinicians describe a need to be special (e.g., Bruch 1979: 22), and certainly our informants' achieving distinguishes them. So too does their intense ascetic religiosity, which renders conventional religion entirely too easy and ethereal. Listen to Elizabeth:

> You have all these people who, you know, say "I'm Catholic" and they choose the things. It's like they're menu-Catholic, designing their own [religion]. "Well, I don't really like no pre-marital sex but I like confession. I'll take that." People end up doing that. That's been my turn-off from religion.

Is she then an atheist? Not at all!—"*I definitely believe in religion and am glad I've had it in my life.*" For top-notch performers like Elizabeth, contemporary religion is simply too warm and fuzzy. Church neither urges greatness nor commands obedience nor measures one's mettle. Anorexia does, as self-starvation demands serious sacrifice and complete devotion.

How does this rogue religiosity arise? For some, this expanding cult of purity or control crowds out an already full, happy life. Others experience a prior religious break—a loss of faith or direction—creating an emptiness that anorexia fills.

Filling a Hole: Loss of Faith or Direction. Some informants remember a malaise that invites anorexia. Earlier Francesca described her parents' abrupt departure. Here she places that trauma in her religious life:

> I used to be intensely religious. I went to church every week and sat in the front pew with my parents. My father was—is—very, very religious. Everything he does is for God. I modeled my faith after my father. A couple of times he used Jesus on the cross to justify my mother's abuse. So that image isn't one I connect with. Also God-the-Father imagery. I'm not a big fan of that. My issues with the church came to a head when I wasn't eating. If you'd asked me then if they were related, I might've said yes in that I felt spiritually displaced. Massively displaced. To this day I don't fit anywhere religiously.

Somewhere between the front pew and the psychiatric ward, Francesca loses faith in both religion and her parents. Religion once ordered her life, but anorexia offers a compelling alternative. Sarah suspects a similar link. Confirmed at thirteen, she was "*pretty religious*" at that age. Anorexia then develops "*around the time I stopped believing in God.*" Although she had never connected the two until our interview, it now makes sense to her. Anorexia, she realizes, "*has a lot of the same aspects of religion*" in that both urge one "*to be a better person.*"

Where Francesca uses a religious vocabulary, Amorn taps secular psychology. Dropping gymnastics leaves her with "*a great big void inside*" that anorexia eventually fills. Although this "*emptiness*" in "*the larger scheme of my life*" is not openly religious, she seeks the grace and purpose she once got from gymnastics: "*I tried different sports*" but to no avail. "*I wasn't particularly good at any one of them. I guess I wanted to be good like I was at gymnastics.*" Indeed, training and trophies once gave her purpose and pride. In their absence a crisis of self-worth, "*low self-esteem,*" invites anorexia.

Whereas Amorn felt empty, Megan had it all but felt like it was not hers. In the shadow of her elder sister, suddenly she *"wanted to be something completely different."*

> *It's so vivid in my memory, this breaking point. I remember thinking, "I have nothing to be unhappy about. I have friends, I'm doing the things I want, I'm lucky beyond belief. Why pity myself like this?" I'd say this breaking point was only eased by these gradual invisible steps* [into anorexia]. *Just this weird, indescribable thrill of controlling, of not eating at all. I was being defeated by unhappiness but liberated by this strength and power that I had to go and run.*

Megan's privilege felt unearned (*"I'm completely taken care of"*), but with anorexia every gain—each ounce lost, every second shed—took sweat and pain. Recovery comes from realizing "*I need to be doing something better* [with my life]." Still morally driven, she now has "*a huge drive to reform education*" and says "*I was raised to do humanitarian work.*" Indeed, her parents pursue socially redeeming careers; one grandfather is even a national religious leader. A thirst for higher purpose haunts her life. Recovery comes once she makes her own way in the world and lives responsibly.

Where others struggle to grasp a religious crisis in the secular language of disease and practicality, Susanna casts her anorexia as a rite of passage into adulthood:

> *I've been thinking lately about loss of innocence. We get broken at some point. That's how we grow. There's lots about that crazy* [anorexic] *discipline that has served me very well. It has given me windows into a more compassionate life. It's having to go the hard way. Like, you know, I've never experienced poverty, or enforced starvation. A lot of doors have opened for me. I have a lot of support and a lot of love around me. So my battles have been more internal. They make me who I am, and I'm starting to like who I am.*

Again, privilege burdens, but where Megan would repay her good fortune by improving society, Susanna suffers directly, as if to balance life's books. Moreover, for her anorexia is not entirely bad. Where it is a detour for Amorn and Megan, as a rite of passage it is Susanna's way forward.

> *There was a clean ritual beauty to a lot of what I created for myself* [in anorexia]. *Something about the structure and the discipline and the container of it, something about me becoming a woman. I was creating my own rituals. It comes out a lot now in the performance work I create. It's very much about ritual and rites of passage and transformation.*

For Susanna, anorexia's ritual fills a religious void. It is ritual that externalizes an inner crisis, that yokes the body to what the soul seeks, that calms larger, deeper religious worries.

Living in the Real World: Secular Asceticism. Only some cases begin in religious crises, but all move toward a secular asceticism that satisfies religious needs. Although the anorexic's regimen has neither church nor God nor theology, it provides a worldview, a daily liturgy, and a moral code. Its tangible righteousness humbles airy ideals. One frets over fat at lunch, not loving thy neighbor. Its asceticism lets youth explore self, remake life, feel righteous, sense grace, keep control, sacrifice meaningfully, and cope with everyday life.

If asceticism attracts youth, why do churches not embrace it? For over a century mainstream religion has favored inner meaning over outward ritual, feeling over authority, ethical debate over moral rigor, attracting members over enjoining sacrifice (A. Douglas 1977: 143–196; M. Douglas 1973; Wolfe 2003). Saying "God is love," today's religion would revive the soul, not discipline the body. So fasting is not just pointless but actively opposed (Bolster and de Lange 2002: 7; Dugan 1995: 542; Vogüé 1989: 34; Wimbush and Valantasis 1995: xx).

As churches shed religious asceticism, "secularized asceticism" enjoys a "resurgence" (Winkler 1994: 244). Lindt (1995: 595–596) sees a "pluralization and secularization of . . . [the] ascetic impulse in American culture" fostering "a free-floating market in ascetic ideas and practices." Here "deliberate strategies of withdrawal" counter "a consumerist ethos manipulated by powerful institutions" (Van Ness 1995: 592) and help one "cope with over-wrought feelings" and live "a less superficial existence" (Allegre 1955: 259). Secular asceticism fills a religious hole.

Jill, a fifty-two-year-old nun, has a specifically religious asceticism. Her anorexia dates to her senior year in high school, well before she took vows. She now lives two ascetic lives—anorexia's secular one and the religious asceticism she chose later in life. Although she struggles to keep weight on, she shows how anorexia can settle into a relatively stable ascetic lifestyle.

I grew up in the Midwest. My Dad's both a college professor and a minister and Mom ended up a college professor. Wonderful childhood. I went to a Catholic school with nuns. My sister and I were one and a half years apart. We were friends. Wonderful memories! I was on the swim team. I did well in school so I felt good about school, felt good about church.

Two things weren't fairy book. I did have lots of fears. I was a little afraid of Mom. Mom tells it like it is. You couldn't bring a friend up and say, "Mom could she spend the night?" If it weren't convenient, Mom would just say "No." So there were those fears—and just fears about life, I would imagine. I remember imagining someone coming in the house and being frozen with fear. And the other thing that my parents tell me now, I was very bossy and very controlling of my little brothers. I wasn't aware of it but they were.

Then seventh grade Dad decided he'd like to go back to teaching. He'd had a church for a while. We moved to Seattle, Washington. Good schools, still continued hiking as a family, did well in school. They were good years. That was the time of the Vietnam War, President Kennedy saying, "Don't ask what your country can do for you, ask what you can do for your country." Being in high school at that time has shaped the way I look at the world, very much. Mom and Dad said, "Find something you love to do but also make a positive contribution to the world." We never had lots of money—you know, professors—but we had enough to live on and we had family and we had friends. That was good. Then they called from South Carolina and asked father to head Political Science. So they moved south. I stayed for senior year. Then came south for college.

It [anorexia] began when I was seventeen. I was out in Seattle living with a family. I had two very, very close friends. My closest friend moved. And my other really close friend was gone most weekends. Those things, just before it happened. Never had difficulty with weight. The summer before senior year I gained twenty pounds. I decided I'd lose weight, and I'm a very disciplined person. Going from 148, by Christmas to 118, down to 102 by end of senior year. The lowest was ninety-eight. So it was like fifty pounds in a year.

So I started college. Even on steak night, I'd eat, like, four or five bowls of vegetables. Exercise every day, usually alone. Some running but also a lot of biking, a compulsion for exercise. Being serious about my faith [I had] this thing with fasting. During my college days I didn't gain any weight, didn't try to gain any weight. I went to grad school. Started teaching school, still weighing 102 pounds, not worried at all that I didn't have a period. I'd decided I was going to be a Sister. So having kids—there's no reason to do that. I was teaching, very active in church.

At the age of twenty-seven, I realized—and it really bothered me—I believed in God but food was my god. Even though I didn't want food to be the most important thing in my life, it was. The other crazy thinking was I'd see the news and I couldn't do anything to help. So I felt I had to fast, I had to give up dessert. It got crazy, denying myself. I remember crying and saying, "God, something has to change. I don't know what it is, but help me." Then that summer I found a twelve-step program—Overeaters Anonymous. They welcomed me with open arms. They combined food with God, the spiritual aspect with the disease. I thought, "This is an answer." I went to counseling, I committed myself to eating three meals. Like an alcoholic has to say "I just don't drink."

So that's what helped me. At thirty-six I was the happiest I'd ever been. Loved my work. I was teaching special ed in the prison system, enjoying my nieces and nephews and just enjoying life. But I'd always thought of becoming a Sister. So decided to test my vocation. After six months, it was like a change in the disease. I started *wanting to purge. I'd lost weight. So I was hospitalized in the psychiatric unit for two weeks. They diagnosed depression. The community* [religious order] *supported me through it. Then I went out to California for a decade and worked in the inner city. I continued twelve-step meetings.* [But] *the weight would come off. I developed bulimic tendencies. After five years out there, I started my new depression. I started back in counseling.*

So here I am at fifty-two. I've never been able to get up to a healthy weight. In looking back I wonder if it was that time when I was having to make decisions about college, take the SATs. I didn't have my parents or my two closest friends. I wonder if when everything else was so out of control if it [losing weight] *was the one thing that made me feel good about myself.*

Here asceticism copes with stress, and in echoing certain Christian and modern values, self-restraint might well feel virtuous. With friends and family gone, Jill faces coming-of-age autonomy alone. Here restricting asserts autonomy both literally and metaphorically. A secular asceticism begins, fits her religiosity, and makes adulthood feel manageable.

Goal-oriented like our other informants, Jill sets religious goals. She works on her faith. Besides fasting,

I used to make myself stay up until 11:30, 12:00, 1:00—just in case God was going to ask me to—though I was exhausted. If God is ever going to ask me to do that, I'd need to practice, so I can. I'd turn the heat off to practice. I nearly killed myself thinking I was doing this for God.

Sound familiar? Jill trains for God's call, just as Jim gives his all for running. Religious or secular, asceticism pulls differing people with differing goals into the same deadly trap.

Conclusion

Contemporary youth face three culturally constructed challenges. One is the cultural crosstalk, a cacophony (chapter 8) that directs them every which way, scattering the sympathetic and befuddling the well-intended. When growing up, how can the virtuous "be good" and "do right" when the larger society debates what is worthy? Amid this anomie, anorexia's single-minded voice gives clarity while its regimen incarnates virtue.

Another challenge is the absence of an authoritative rite of passage. Many peoples orchestrate the child-to-adult passage ritually, but our era has no such collective ceremony. In its absence, it is no wonder that anorexics make their own by ballooning dieting and training into tests of toughness and virtue where they prove their worth.

The last challenge is controlling the modern metaphors that overload our lives. Today your body is no longer just a body or even entirely your own. Instead your physical being now represents you, the social and moral person. Moreover, the two of you—body and person—represent society and nation even as they represent you. In this hall of mirrors, eating, weight, and appearance play out a cultural crisis of discipline and control. Anorexia grows in this fertile ground. The next three chapters trace how these symbols came to rule our lives.

SECTION

III

Modern Traditions

Cultural Paths into Anorexia

Culture now takes center stage. Given that anorexia slims, contemporary culture looks like a smoking gun. Yet looking closer, there is no telltale bullet, no one-to-one causal link. Indeed, culture does not cause anorexia directly. Culture does, however, shepherd people to the disorder's gateway practices, where it energizes the syndrome's deadly logic. That logic feeds and follows from three cultural scripts pervading modern life—virtuous eating (chapter 10), the good body (chapter 11), and the attractive person (chapter 12). Living these scripts creates the "local biologies" (Lock 1998) that feed anorexia, solidify the syndrome, impede recovery, and invite relapse.

CHAPTER 10

Virtuous Eating
A Modern Morality

> Every individual should . . . restrain himself to the smallest quantity which . . . will fully meet the alimentary wants of . . . his system, knowing that whatsoever is more than this is evil.
> —Sylvester Graham, nineteenth-century health reformer[1]

Anorexia taps outer as well as inner energies. The inner energies (Part I, "The Disease") are universal: in any place or day, starving can take on a life of its own. The outer energies are unique to place and day. In our era, externals that energize anorexia are conditions like adolescence (Part II) and modern traditions of eating, body and appearance (Part III), which we now consider.

Today's anorexia gets its ascetic discipline and moral conviction from a Gilded Age cultural crisis. By the late nineteenth century, immigration, urbanization, industrialization, and robber baron capitalism had shredded North America's social fabric. An old middle class—shopkeepers, artisans, yeoman farmers—found their livelihoods dying and virtues mocked. As global markets ruined local entrepreneurs, corporate giants ruled like kings. Suddenly, getting ahead took trickery or influence, not effort or ability. As modern life derided decency, a malaise befell the middle class. Then, as some gave up, others got going. Embracing modernity energetically, a new middle class arose around faith in progress and perpetual self-improvement. Inspired by health and fitness movements, this progressive middle class lauds the slim body as well as eating and exercise ideals that we now take for granted.

Is Healthy Eating Behind Anorexia?

A survey of anorexics' parents found "healthy eating . . . was . . . a contributing factor in the development of eating disorders" (MacDonald 2000: 15). That stressing health brings disease is paradoxical, yet nearly three-quarters of our informants mention healthy eating as either a major family concern (9) or basic to their lifestyle (7). Whatever their initial attitude, all emerge from anorexia as health-oriented eaters. After months or years reading food labels and calculating fat and calories, no one is come-what-may about eating. So although their eating is freer, it is still controlled. Now, if Melissa wants a chocolate drop, she eats one—just one.

Megan remembers healthy eating and living during anorexia.

> *I really enjoyed being this ultimate healthy being. I'd wake up on a Saturday, go swimming, go for a ride, take a shower, get worked on. I went on this big kick of "Americans think wrong about food." I enjoyed knowing exactly what was in my body, always fresh fruit, all these wonderful things.*

On a completely organic diet, she sees what most eat as "*all junk.*"

Healthy eating typically builds on family patterns. Take Lindsay:

> *My mom was a health fanatic. I knew about omega 3 and fiber when I was seven. Mom used to put health articles on my desk and I read them. We always had skim milk, always tons of vegetables. We never had any junk food in the house. My sister hated it. In high school she'd eat like twenty doughnuts after school. Rebelling, you know?*

Lindsay, the perfect child, doing what is right, builds anorexia out of healthy eating. In Natalie's family, healthy eating is a fugitive ideal. Her mom made "*some honest attempts*" to improve.

> *My mom went through a couple really shocking phases. Like she bought only healthy food: "We are going to eat right from now on." That meant gross bread and not fun stuff. My dad's a junk food fiend. He grew up on Pink Elephant popcorn and Pepsi. His French Canadian background—lots of gravy, lots of sugar. So she tried, she tried. She would do her best. We were like, "We want something to eat." She'd say, "There's fruit." We'd be like, "I'm not THAT hungry!"*

Sheena's mother is health conscious, but a friend intensifies it:

> *There was this shift with turning vegetarian, of being really conscious of what I was eating, reading labels, starting to really understand what was in food. My best friend was the same. We fed off each other. If she was really at it, then I was really going at it.*

Jill's healthy eating impetus was "*not in my family as much* [as] *in the society. The natural foods thing was big in Washington State and we'd go to the U* [University] *District and get all healthy things.*"
Healthy eating comes to express virtue. It is not just what is good for you; it is you being good. Our informants repeatedly treat restricting as a way to feel good about themselves or even be a good person. Susanna remembers,

> *I'm getting a flash of moments in church and that particular kind of spirituality. You know I did really think that being thinner was being more virtuous. Things like fat* [I] *associated with base humanness or weakness or sex and sin.*

Many describe judging others by what and how they ate. Is this moralizing how anorexia distorts their thinking? To answer, we need to examine what ordinary people say and do.

Reports from the Field: Is Eating Moralized?

Our informants' moralizing is not just anorexia talking. Healthy people have similar attitudes. Consider four in-depth field studies that show this discourse across regions and groups:

- A three-year study of junior high girls in the American Southwest found the plaint "I'm so fat!" was highly conventionalized. As self-criticism it preempted others' judgment, recognized shared values (a thin body, watching what one ate), and depicted oneself as properly valuing appearance. Expressing guilt and distress, it sought—and usually got—reassurance and absolution from peers (Nichter 2000).
- A two-year study of a Cincinnati weight-loss group found women used religious vocabulary (temptation, sin, guilt, confession, ritual, magic) to capture their experience. The "slim body unequivocally communicate[d] . . . 'I take care of myself,' 'I live right,' 'I make smart choices,' 'I'm healthy,' and 'I'm in charge'"—all virtues of contemporary individualism (Stinson 2001: 202–207).
- Student food diaries at two mid-Atlantic colleges showed men and women judged others by the food they ate and bought. Eating often expressed "the tension between the pleasures of consumption and the moral superiority deriving from abstention." Whereas "splurging on sweets or other special foods [was] sanctioned as a crutch for dealing with emotional distress," standing on one's own was better (Counihan 1999: 114–120).
- Christian devotional dieting groups arose in the 1950s, began spreading in the 1970s, grew rapidly in the 1990s, and are now quite common. Dieting is not for

looks but "to cultivate self-control and obedience in order to defeat Satan and please God" (Griffith 2004: 192).

Competing Lifestyles: Where Does Virtuous Eating Fit?

While this moralizing is everywhere, so is obesity. In fact, few follow Virtuous Eating rigorously, many only dabble in it, and still others reject it, either hedonistically or to follow other customs. Yet Virtuous Eating holds the high ground. Few argue back. Unredeemed, they just eat in other ways. Men, more than women, typically resist Virtuous Eating, as do various regional, minority, and lower-class lifestyles that keep other customs. Against this backdrop, eating virtuously is a disproportionately female practice that characterizes WASP upper classes and their wannabes.

How WASPish is this? A meta-study of dieting—analyzing fifty studies covering over a quarter million people—finds dieting is significantly more likely among White women than non-White (Black, Hispanic, and Asian) minority women (Crago and Shisslak 2003). Or look at size: the National Health Interview Survey finds obesity nearly twice as likely for Black women as White (National Center for Health Statistics 1997). Or listen to Megan, a White Southerner who went to a 97 percent Black high school:

> *I had a lot of friends who are very large girls. They were comfortable and beautiful and happy—just happy in their own skin. It's such a different thing to work for. Instead of changing my size, it's even harder to go, "How can I like myself? Let's work on that."*

Ironically, her "let's work on that" activism denies the bodily acceptance she seeks.

Does Virtuous Eating also typify the upper more than lower classes? Income tracks class. Here Hsu (1996: 694) finds a "reversal of fatness" by income: "adolescent females in high-income families start out being fatter but end up being leaner than those of lower income families." Another class marker is education: the National Health Interview Survey finds 61 percent of adult women with less than a ninth grade education are overweight; that number drops as education rises, falling to 29 percent for women with graduate degrees. Obesity shows that pattern: 10 percent for the best educated, 27 percent for the least. This is not new: in 1954, a massive door-to-door Manhattan survey established that the higher the socioeconomic status, the thinner women were and the lower obesity's incidence for both men and women (Goldblatt et al. 1965). For female adherents of Episcopalianism, the quintessential WASP religion, obesity was 3 percent, versus 27 percent among Italian women.[2]

Virtuous Eating anchors a healthy lifestyle widely promoted by the progressive middle class.[3] Other than eating nutritiously and moderately, it requires regular exercise, weight control, and avoiding all health risks (smoking, food contaminants, etc.). Anyone who takes it too seriously risks becoming a joyless orthorexic, obsessively pursuing proper foods and practices to ensure the healthiest life (Bratman 2000). In fact, although Virtuous Living is a lifestyle, the attitude is less about how people actually live than how self-discipline and health orient their living. In this view conscientious effort and a strong will earn health (Scheper-Hughes and Lock 1987), and responsible people do the best they can. Such attitudes treat "'health' as the New Morality by which character and moral worth are judged" (M. Becker 1986: 19).

What allows this lifestyle of a few to lord it over the many? Virtuous Living taps faith in progress. From restricted eating to regular exercise, a healthy lifestyle that follows what science says comes across as more advanced than the alternatives. True, we now say "practical" or "realistic" rather than "advanced," but the older word captures how this attitude got going and why so few argue back. For over a century now, North Americans have used progress to organize—and judge—difference. As Schudson (1984: 79) observes: "In modern societies, people mark themselves not only in social space but in social time.... They display their modernity or their resistance to modernity. They mark their allegiance to groups that embrace social change or to groups that hold to tradition." In the 1920s, when progress meant flouting Victorian standards, smoking marked the new woman as modern. Of course today, as health progresses, smoking is an outdated public affront. Always changing, the one constant is that modernity measures us against the new. That then gives restricted eating its moral authority: Virtuous Living, a modern and progressive lifestyle, purports to be the wave of the future.

A Successful Lifestyle: What Makes Virtuous Living Meaningful?

Like any modern lifestyle, Virtuous Living's devotees justify their practices rationally: eating right and staying fit promises a long, healthy life and pays off almost immediately ("it feels good"). Yet reason is a hard master. So while everyone knows the "oughts" of staying slim, fit, and healthy, not everyone succeeds. Indeed, given today's temptations, living responsibly takes great will and effort. In lauding these values, Virtuous Living goes beyond the true—its charter in reason—to claim the good and the beautiful. Like any lifestyle, it affirms values that it cannot otherwise explain.

Is Virtuous Living Applied Science? Virtuous Living claims scientific authority. Although science has yet to explain a value like responsibility, devotees do indeed align eating and lifestyle with all the latest scientific findings. They are, however, using selective science selectively. Research targets lifestyle choices, not health holistically. Then, out of many mixed findings, only a few get popularized. So the cure-all is bran one month, broccoli the next. Undaunted by how one finding overturns another, this ever hopeful discourse puts health in our hands, right where will and effort matter—or so it seems.

A more realistic science would be less encouraging. Reconciling shifting and piecemeal findings, it would likely support Marshall Becker's (1986: 21, 20) conclusion that the "domain of personal health over which the individual has direct control is *very* small when compared to heredity, culture, environment, and chance." Despite this, health has become "a new religion, in which we worship ourselves, attribute good health to our devoutness, and view illness as just punishment for those who have not yet seen the Way."

Is Virtuous Living Religious? Health raises religious questions. Established religions offer thoughtful answers as well as practical rites to cure the sick, ward off illness, and strengthen wellness—or they did. As faith shifts to science, mainstream churches have less to offer. So when the good die young, faulting cancer or blaming genes neither soothes the ache nor rights the wrong. Virtuous Living fights that void. A cult of will and effort, it pits hope against despair.

Dubbing healthism a religion, Becker uses an analogy: devotees of healthy living follow their regimen with the same faith, fervor, and surety of virtue as religious enthusiasts. Indeed, as the healthy proselytize the lax, keeping their brother's body the way Evangelicals save souls, dieters use a religious vocabulary (sin, guilt, ritual) in slimming down to become a better person (Stinson 2001). In venerating "willpower" that eases up "only under certain culturally sanctioned conditions" (Counihan 1999: 118), today's eating sounds like Puritanism.

Yet what religion neither believes in a god nor has a church? In fact, many religious cultures lack one or both. If we define religion by the way it works, not recent Western conventions like sermons and prayers, then Virtuous Living functions as an embodied spirituality. Certainly keeping one's daily practice takes the same faith, commitment, and ritual that religion once required. Moreover, as that regimen progressively defines its practitioners in their own and others' eyes, science can guide a modern life just as God once did. Although it is best to describe Virtuous Living as religious rather than an actual religion, its embodied spirituality reclaims hope and power that mainstream denominations ceded to science long ago.

Is Virtuous Living Effective? Skeptics need not believe in Virtuous Living to find that it works. The more affluent we are, the more choices we have and want; and the less custom rules our lives, the more we can and must choose. The catch is that too many choices can complicate life and make us unhappy or even depressed (B. Schwartz 2004). Adhering to almost any daily regimen might be better than suffering excessive choice.

Yet Virtuous Living today is not just any regimen but a lifestyle descended from progressives' fight against modernity's malaise. It meets a spiraling need to self-regulate as society deregulates (Bauman 1997: 2), and it counters the shallow modern notion that humans are only self-interested creatures who crave freedom, possessions, and pleasure endlessly. Against that facile idea, Virtuous Living's ascetic practice makes restraint and simplicity feel rewarding. Indeed, given that many cultures find purity, power, and transcendence in voluntary austerities (chapter 1), saying a restrained lifestyle feels better than excess is perfectly reasonable.

Virtuous Living also meets identity needs. Valorizing restraint amid abundance stakes a countercultural stance. Any such clear contrast strengthens identity and promises a moral coherence that consumerism lacks—all quite apart from broccoli's real or imagined benefits. As Mintz (1993: 269) says, "contemporary American society, even while consuming material goods at an unprecedented pace, remains noticeably preoccupied by the moral arena. . . . We consume; but we are not, all of us and always, by any means altogether happy about it. . . . The feeling that in self-denial lies virtue, and in consumption sin, is still powerfully present."

In sum, restricted eating's healthy, progressive lifestyle meets practical, religious, and ethical needs created by modern life. Yet what makes Virtuous Living—as but one of many responses to modernity (alienation, anti-modernism, political activism, societal reform, etc.)—so popular and successful? The answer, we argue, is largely historical.

Meeting a Modern Crisis: How Did Virtuous Living Arise?

Today we adapt to Virtuous Living even as it adapts to us. Thus we cannot explain this lifestyle by the needs it currently meets but must also consider how, as a living tradition, it shapes and creates those needs. That takes us back over a century.

Modernity's Midlife Crisis. By the late nineteenth century, massive industrialization, urbanization, and migration threatened the customs and verities that organized civil society and democratic states. Although the crisis was transatlantic (Higham 2001: 183; Lears 1981), on the American side a deep "cultural pessimism" (Green 1988: xi) arose as brutal factories, corrupting cities, and an arrogant commercial aristocracy profaned republican values (Dyreson 1997: 121; Higham 1955: 36, 68). By the 1890s the once-triumphant "cult of progress and materialism" had lost its luster, as it seemed to have no rational solution to the problems of industrial civilization (Higham 2001: 185). Was modern life worth living? An epidemic of neurasthenia, an "immobilizing, self-punishing depression," plagued the middle class and "epitomized the crisis of cultural authority" (Lears 1981: 47, 56; Park 1989: 148; Whorton 1989).

Early Health and Fitness Movements: Rejecting the Changes. Popular responses to modern conditions predate that cultural crisis. One early response—the Second Great Awakening, an early nineteenth-century Evangelical religious revival—swept North America and revitalized Christianity. Yet that did not satisfy everyone. As Rubin (1994: 200) says, "When evangelical pastoral care failed to remedy religious melancholy . . . afflicted persons sought alternative healing ideas: homeopathic medicine, water cure, Grahamism, spiritualism, and later mind cure, Christian Science and mesmerism, to name a few." So health and fitness movements begun early in the nineteenth century met the cultural crisis at its end. Supposedly secular and scientific, they had an evangelical air (Green 1988: 319), gave practical answers to life's larger questions, and spread like religious cults. The influential reformer Sylvester Graham prescribed a regimen of whole-meal bread, exercise, and sexual abstinence to "purge the souls of his generation by cleansing their debauched bodies" (Nissenbaum 1980: 3). In these movements one's health was an individual responsibility, not God's doing.

These save-yourself movements had save-society ambitions. By mid-century, writing about health "linked the health of the body with that of the body politic and . . . the spirit" (Green 1989: 8). One influential reformer, Catherine Beecher, blamed modern jobs for no longer letting people work with their hands. That put the ambitious in a bind: adapting to this new economy endangered not just your health but your soul and society. So even as North America prospered, economic upheavals regularly summoned "a serpent in the garden of economic, political and technological delights" (Green 1989: 8). Little wonder that Graham's movement arose when it did. His regimen promised health through ascetic withdrawal from the marketplace, right when impersonal, unregulated markets were ravaging trustworthy local exchange and household production (Nissenbaum 1980).

Vigorous Living: Engaging the Changes. In the late nineteenth century, as society's changes sank some into depression, others embraced an active, upbeat lifestyle. The strenuous life—a "master impulse" of the era (Higham 2001: 173–197) popularized by Teddy Roosevelt—fought modern comforts that weakened the once hardy individual. Like earlier health and fitness movements, the self-help cure of vigor would save the person as well as the nation: societal problems were the individual's failings writ large (Green 1988: 322). Yet where earlier movements turned back the clock, vigorous living welcomed the future optimistically and aggressively.

One lasting legacy is today's passion for sports. Entering the nineteenth century, the middle class disdained sports as wasteful, dangerous and corrupting. At century's end athletes were national heroes, and athletics were middle-class. Meantime a "veritable craze for physical training and athletics" had swept the country (Park 1989: 123). What explains this reversal? Sports re-masculinized a country that felt weakened by modern ways and feminine influences (A. Douglas 1977). While manual labor kept the working class fit and manly, middle-class work rewarded intelligence and people-pleasing rather than honest effort and masculine candor. Now that the workplace no longer taught upstanding values, the mainstream saw sports as building character and community in youth and creating "a virtuous citizenry" (Dyreson 1997: 126–127, 23). Analogies between sports and nation "connected the well-ordered body to the well-ordered body politic" (Dyreson 1997: 136–137), and by the 1896 Olympics, rhetoric described nations as physical bodies with human properties, and human bodies like political systems (Budd 1997: x).

Another lasting legacy is the idealized slim body. Between 1890 and 1910, "middle-class America began its ongoing battle against body fat," a "moral mobilization" like today's revulsion at smoking (Stearns 1997: 3–4, 23). That meant appetite control for women and muscle development for men. Why suddenly attack fat? Stearns (1997: 59) sees a societal reaction against consumerism: "The widespread association of fat with laziness . . . directly translated the desire to use disciplined eating as a moral tool in a society where . . . consumer tastes and . . . abundant leisure time seemed to contradict the work ethic of the Victorian middle class." Hillel Schwartz (1986: 95, 88) sees the same shift at the same time but attributes it to a "cultural pincher movement" between a new economics attacking needless excess and "a new kinesthetic ideal" of a light, balanced, efficiently controlled body—witness cartoons where fat people gum up the streetcars, elevators, and turnstiles of modern life. For Schwartz (1986: 28) the "culture of slimming collaborates with capitalism to adapt the body shapes of workers to machines that cannot abide loose flesh or imbalanced forms." Was the slim body modeling modern life (Schwartz) or repudiating modern ease and laxity (Stearns)? Apparently both: as the slim body incarnated a modern aesthetic, it rejected modern indulgence. A slim person was stylistically up-to-date yet morally traditional.

Weighing oneself illustrates this acceptance-yet-rejection blend. On the one hand, as an everyday regimen, weighing brought scientific measurability and the factory's mass-produced scales into the home. On the other hand, watching one's weight updated an old Protestant passion for monitoring one's will and measuring self-improvement. Similar conforming-yet-controlling appeared in how sports epitomized modernity's measured competitive performance while also celebrating traditional virtues of will, effort, and ascetic self-denial.

Indulgence with Discipline: Managing Modern Change. What sports and slimming shared—a disciplined body displaying will and effort—came to define a culture-wide response to modernity. Although moralists decried growing laxity, Stearns (1999: x) shows the actual change went in two opposite directions: "a new delight in personal gratification" was yoked to "a new insistence on self-restraint." Tradeoffs developed. By the mid-1890s, when dieting could "compensate for prior excess," people followed a balancing-accounts logic (Stearns 1999: chap. 4, 24, 100). Take sexual freedom: as immigrant and working-class sexualities loosened middle-class Victorianism (D'Emilio and Freedman 1997: 173), standards of bodily cleanliness and emotional control tightened. In Stearns's (1999: 194) words, "Greater sexual interests and opportunity were matched by new regulations and restrictions" that "applied to both genders." That meant "control of the figure (and also body hair)" for women and "greater anxiety about homosexual leanings" for men. To enjoy modern pleasures, you had to pay a price.

Tracing these trade-offs from the late nineteenth century to the verge of the twenty-first, Stearns (323) concludes that the relaxing of Victorian societal standards was largely offset by greater pressure for individual self-discipline. What brought relaxation on the one hand and increased pressure on the other? On relaxation, Stearns (13) sees science overturning Victorian beliefs, art critiquing bourgeois values, and economic change (a service economy, consumerism) easing restraint. On increased pressure for self-discipline, Stearns (324) assumes that Americans are collectively "uncomfortable with the increase in license and permissiveness and have deliberately, if often implicitly, formed compensatory disciplinary categories." How did this actually happen? We suspect competing groups: a nativistic reaction against immigrants and a rising progressive middle class both made self-discipline a virtue and laxity a vice.

The Progressive Middle Class: Agents of Moralizing Change. Once largely self-employed, the middle class changed as the economy did. Their jobs moved from local enterprises to national conglomerates. From 1880 to 1980, as the self-employed fell from 36.9 percent to 8.6 percent of the U.S. workforce (Szymanski 1983: 164), the middle class changed from independent entrepreneurs running substantial farms or small businesses to salaried employees in larger organizations. Whereas the old middle class put its faith in established practices and local citizenship, the new middle class valued progress (keeping up with latest) and national citizenship (joining a professional organization). By taking pride in their technical expertise, these progressives hitched their worth to keeping up with a profession's ever-changing knowledge. As this class emerges some complain of mental exhaustion, but the new middle class comes to embrace education optimistically and develops into the typically upper-middle-class carriers of Virtuous Eating.[4]

Competing Groups: The Immigrant Threat. Immigration fueled the cultural crisis. Unlike earlier immigrants, Southern and Eastern Europeans contrasted sharply with the country's Anglo-Saxon heritage. WASP attitudes toward pleasure, savings, work, and gender became status markers (Wagner 1997: 108). Food, eating, and the body all marked native-born/immigrant differences.

A slim body came to symbolize long-established Americans and their values. Although Europeans had long characterized Americans as lean (H. Schwartz 1986: 40), only in the late nineteenth century did a fleshy Lady Liberty yield to a tall, lean Uncle Sam. He contrasted with his old rival, England's corpulent John Bull, as well as the shorter, stockier immigrants (Higham 2001: 41; H. Schwartz 1986: 143).

Food also marked the contrast. The newcomers had cereal-based diets that were oilier than longtime Americans'. As first-generation immigrants kept their Old World foodways (Gabaccia 1998: 51), New World abundance added weight. On the old-timers' side, American food reformers often took the abstemious New England diet as particularly natural and healthy. Nutritional science developed "with an essentially nativist disapproval of migrant cuisine" (Mennell et al. 1992: 26).

Health and fitness movements allied with political efforts to restrict immigration (Green 1989). As newcomers often did manual labor, worries that the better-off Anglo-Saxon male had become effete led to the middle-class emphasis on vigorous physical activity (Pope 1997: 14). The rise of sports thus "reflected the need of established mainline bourgeois culture to define parameters and isolate itself from alien 'others'" (Green 1989: 14). Like diet, athletics marked ethnicity because first generation immigrants were generally uninterested in American sports (Pope 1997: 14).

Although sports and diet eventually faded as ethnic markers, becoming bridges to assimilation rather than barriers, the slim body lives on as an achieved American status. A 1954 Manhattan survey (Goldblatt et al. 1965) found the longer the women's lineage in the U.S., the lower the obesity percentage, which went from 22 percent for foreign-born to 4 or 5 percent by the fourth generation. Male obesity rates fell almost as sharply, dropping two-thirds in four generations.

Conclusion

How does modern culture impact anorexia? The media seems a poison, Virtuous Eating an antidote. But we found otherwise: our informants rejected media influences flatly and embraced Virtuous Eating enthusiastically. Its supposedly healthy lifestyle pervaded their lives: most grew up around healthy eating, all exaggerate its logic into anorexic regimens, and in recovery all respect its tenets. As a gateway to anorexia, it not only restricts just as the disease does, but it gives anorexics the sense of superior virtue they relish. In the culture/disease connection, Virtuous Eating is a missing link.

Virtuous Eating strands its devotees on an embattled moral island ready-made for anorexia. In itself island-making is neither odd nor pathological. It is in sports, professions, and today's burgeoning lifestyle involvements—all little islands of sense and satisfaction in a societal sea that feels neither fair nor reasonable. Is this how a "sectoral form of organization" came to distinguish American society (Bellah et al. 1985: 43–44)? Certainly this is thoroughly modern: the "overall thrust of modern institutions is to create settings . . . ordered in terms of modernity's own dynamics and severed from 'external criteria'" (Giddens 1991: 7). Anorexia epitomizes that: its relentless quantified progress orders the syndrome and mimics modern dynamics, all cut off from what health and reason allow.

Notes

1. From *Lectures on the Science of Human Life*, 1839. Quoted in Rubin (1994: 189–190).
2. Presumably the Italians were Catholic. Do Catholics really differ from the Protestant 'P' in WASP? Griffith (2004: 197–199), who could not find a single Catholic devotional dieting book comparable to the dozens of Protestant best-sellers, suggests that "Catholic bodily obsessions have typically focused on matters other than food."
3. "Progressive" marks the Progressive Era origins of a faith in education and progress that typifies upper-middle-class professionals. This segment plays "an overweening role in defining 'America,' its moods, political direction and moral tone" (Ehrenreich 1989: 6). It is "a model to members of other classes, who often come to emulate it or to define their identities against it" (Lamont 1992: 4).
4. Although this new middle class built on the old by incorporating classically defining values like self-control, asceticism, achievement, and diligence (Hunt 1999: 21; Wagner 1997: 49–50, 104), as early as the 1850s "habits of self-discipline, physical fitness, dietary control, temperance and sexual restraint" (Bledstein 1976: 26) were developing the grounds for Virtuous Eating that health and fitness movements spread evangelically.

CHAPTER 11

The Conflicted Body
Sympathy and Control as Competing Virtues

> We get our thoughts entangled in metaphors and act fatally on the strength of them.
>
> —George Eliot, *Middlemarch*

Again and again, our informants explain anorexia as control. It is their way of controlling their lives, they say. Oddly, their lives are not necessarily out of control—they just feel that way. Equally odd is that restrictive eating and excessive exercise calm those feelings. Those actions do not actually control their lives but just two bodily aspects. How can that be all it takes for life to feel controlled? The person *is* the body and the body *is* its eating and exercise. Collapsing large into little shrinks an out-of-control world to a few controllable parts. Control moves metaphorically, not literally.

Anorexic people feel out of control in the first place because they sympathize too widely and try to control too much. Not only do they tie inner feelings to outer realities (people, events, situations) outside their control, but their sympathizing tries to make their surroundings resemble them. Here anorexics embody two powerful, competing traditions. One, person/world oneness, puts humans in sympathy with their surroundings. It moves metaphorically and counsels harmony. The other tradition, mind/body dualism, separates humanity (spirit) from its environs (matter) and thereby allows us to act on environs that need not act on us. In experiencing these opposite pulls, anorexics embody a cultural conflict between sympathy and control.

Control: Our Informants' Explanations

Well before we could ask, most informants related their anorexia to control. Eighteen out of twenty-two see control as *a* or *the* key factor. For Jill this is so obvious that it is a perfunctory aside ("*I couldn't control anything else in my life. It was the one thing I could control*") that barely interrupts her story. Others explain:

> *I was emotionally all over the place. I hated my boyfriend but was too scared to do anything about it. The weight and the food was all I could control by myself.*—Sarah.

> *It* [eating] *was something I could control. I studied so hard. I just couldn't get the chemistry grade. I was just so shaky. I hate it when it's unpredictable and, you know, shaky situations.*—Mary.

> *My senior year all my friends applied to college early. I ended up not applying early. My friends knew where they were going and I didn't. There was for the first time in my life a lot of uncertainty. I felt like my future was in the hands of these random colleges. And running was something I had control over.*—Elizabeth.

These statements highlight three facts. First, control means managing emotions. Where they elaborate, it is about being or feeling powerless to change some situation. Here acting ascetically or metaphorically relieves stress—they do feel better—although no one explains why.

Second, all give situational explanations. Take Elizabeth. To ease her college uncertainty, an outcome she cannot control, she intensifies her running, an activity she does control. Of course uncertainty plagues many lives but few people become anorexic. So what is decisive is less the situation than how our informants respond to it. Arguably that is constitutional—performative, ascetic and virtuous dispositions all stress control.

Third, their statements take the need for control for granted. None wonder at this response. It is like a thirsty person taking a drink—what is to explain? But of course their control thirst is hardly self-explanatory. How starving manages, say, romance or grades requires much explaining. None try beyond saying it felt better. No one says why one should feel better when the problems are no better.

They feel better for three interconnected reasons. The first, asceticism, detaches them from the troubling situation. The second, physical action, gives bodily relief to an embodied worry. The third, metaphor, changes how they experience the situation. Arguably their distress arose metaphorically in the first place: they took the negative situation (a part) not for what it was (bad luck, incidental) but as a negative judgment on themselves (the whole). Be that as it may, acting metaphorically externalizes their intents. Take Sarah: restricting does with food what she wants to do with her boyfriend. Or Mary: if studying hard entails self-denial, then studying still harder means more self-denial. She does not just say this to herself but also acts, striving vigilantly to align herself with what the reality she would master demands. Although Sarah's and Mary's aims differ, controlling one part (eating) that represents the whole (the person) makes both feel "in control."

Is this madness? To Cartesians, yes; in person/world oneness, no—acting on yourself acts on your situation: if the person is one part of a larger interdependent whole, changing any part (oneself in this instance) changes the rest (the situation one wants changed). That ecological truth turns the tables on Descartes: mind/body dualism, in separating humans (spirit) from nature (matter), is too ontologically simplistic to ever recognize biocultural realities. Our informants intuitively grasp what Cartesians obtusely miss: changing yourself *does* change your immediate world.

Modernity's Control Imperative

Most informants found their control worries too obvious to explain. And they are in contemporary North America. Yet expecting such thoroughgoing control would strike many cultures as foolish or even offensive. In Fiji, where kin take responsibility for one's bodily state (Becker 1995), modern controlling would question local arrangements. Or take Upland Southeast Asia, where each person reckons with inner and outer spirits as well as the authority of elders and custom. There, to exert control, the individual negotiates compromises. Here, in North America, the individual implements unilateral personal plans that assume he or she is a discrete, autonomous whole. This increasingly sacred modern precept (Carrither 1996) makes individual self-control vital for personal and societal well-being.

Today's concern about control is relatively new and distinctively modern. For Europeans in the sixteenth century, when "self, society, and the cosmos" had the "interdependence" of a single organism (Merchant 1980: 1, xvii), only God exercised the control that modern individuals now expect. Yet once the Enlightenment split mind (spirit) from body (matter), human consciousness stood apart from a material world, which we could now act on freely. In that shift, our own body and all of nature became objects for us to use and control as we liked.

How did this abstract possibility become today's obsessive controlling? In the late nineteenth century the middle class felt, as anorexics do today, that life was spinning out of control. Indeed, in the past century national markets had ravaged small towns while science questioned God's controlling hand. By mid-century, the decline of small communities and religious unity brought a "new emphasis on the individual" that shifted "moral teaching" from inculcating deference for authority to emphasizing personal self-control (Bellah et al. 1985: 222). By century's end, Victorian social codes were dead or dying. Many felt society was out of control. This cultural crisis spawned Virtuous Eating as well as the bodily attitudes and control issues that today's eating disorders exaggerate.

Are our bodies stuck in that past? Virtuous Eating and the slim body may well be historical accidents, but without them we would just have to invent another way to live coherently under modern conditions. After all, the less custom, kin, church, and community regulate our individual lives, the more we must self-regulate, and the easier it gets for the sympathetic and virtuous to over-regulate as anorexics do.

Society and Sympathy

Modern life widens one's sympathies. As early as the 1830s Tocqueville (1945, 2: 105) saw democracy erasing social barriers that once kept caring close to home. Today, as local, racial, cultural, and other social barriers fall, we become more compassionate toward once distant or alien people (Sznaider 2001).

A sympathetic attitude has now become a social marker. Today, sympathy-giving, "a key ingredient in 'niceness,'" is institutionalized "in the social role of the 'good person'" (Clark 1997: 11). Valuing niceness is yet another late-nineteenth-century legacy. As robber baron capitalism brutalized society, popular culture "seemed bent on establishing a perpetual Mother's Day" of saccharine sweetness (A. Douglas 1977: 5, 11). In this sentimentalism, kindness compensates for a cold, cruel world. One spin-off, today's gendered division of emotional labor, expects women to be more sympathetic than men (Clark 1997: 187). Another spin-off, save-the-world caring, stands against the realist's toughness. In coming of age and having to decide how good and nice to be, anorexics withdraw into their own virtuous rituals.

Competing Traditions: Dualism and Oneness

In expecting both greater sympathy and stricter personal control, our era taps two competing traditions. To trace their logics, we liken each to a language.

Two Languages. Our bodies feel and function in two quasi-languages, each with its own life-organizing grammar. To become modern adults, we learn to hear and honor one language—conscious reason—and ignore the other as myth or intuition. The voice we hear consciously echoes the Enlightenment. Droning "control" and "reason," it divides mind from body, isolating individuals from social sympathies that we feel but cannot explain. The other voice, loud in infancy and quieter later, is in the resonance between self and society, where body and nature echo each other. Here little-to-large metaphors liken body, person, society, and nation. So the person can be society writ small or society can be the person writ large. Similarly, moral sentiments pull the virtuous person into embodying society's values and conflicts.

How language-like are these patterns? They *approach* the learned, shared, inherited, freestanding coherence of a language, but they never get there. Instead, like everyday speech, they remain open and negotiated. That said, to live a balanced modern life, we must become the cultural equivalent of bilingual,[1] moving between two logics.

Mind/Body Dualism. Modern folk live mind/body dualism, a contemporary twist on the soul/body dualism that is ancient to Western civilization and rather common globally (Lincoln 1986a). Today we experience this spirit/matter split as the conflict between home and work, love and sex, serving others or just oneself. Here the slim body rejects modern indulgence while incarnating its real-world discipline. Anorexia embodies this logic.

In separating our species from nature, mind/body duality assumes humans can exert great control over their lives. Historically that dualism broke the West out of an enchanted existence, freeing society from capricious spirits, magical powers, and finally God. Meanwhile, as Enlightenment Reason, this duality attacked custom as unreason, weakening groups and freeing individuals to regulate themselves. Lastly, in separating mind from body within the person, it freed the conscious will to rule its bodily home. The body then became mere matter, an object for us to shape and use as we like. So whenever some "higher" goal seizes heart or mind, we take pride in pushing ourselves, denying our "lowly" body food, sleep, or rest. In anorexia that free will turns tyrant.

Person/World Oneness. Unlike mind-body struggles, everyday life favors little/large metaphors. In this idiom, waging an inner mind-against-body battle forgets life's oneness. The body is a whole. So too is the person. Opposing one to the other therefore misunderstands that one is not only within but miniaturizes the other. To say you "push your body" is utter nonsense; if anything, you push yourself, the whole package. And if you push yourself, you push nature and indeed the cosmos because the person is in and miniaturizes nature/cosmos just as the body is in and miniaturizes the person. Like a set of Russian dolls, all in the same image, little fits within larger, but none divide along dualism's battle lines (spirit/matter, good/evil, moral/practical). To the contrary, little or large, each properly functions as an undivided whole. Undivided does not mean uniform—indeed, each whole holds all the world's diversity—but as a bounded system, each internally diverse whole is not just similar but equivalent to all the others. In this scheme, the person is not powerless but prospers by harmonizing with nature's inevitabilities. To live well within their body, family, and environs, the wise sympathize with their surroundings.

Strange as this thinking sounds, body- or person-centered metaphors are universal (Lakoff and Johnson 1999; O'Neill 1985: 37, 36), and the little/larger set just sketched pervades Indo-European thought (Lincoln 1986b). Saying man is made in God's image says the microcosmic human echoes the divine cosmos. Such thinking pervades the Bible (Marmorstein 1968, vol. 2), was commonplace in medieval days (Bakhtin 1968) and the Renaissance (Barkan 1975), still flourishes in poetry and intuition, and survives in immunologists' description of the immune response (Martin 1994).

Today person/world oneness patterns our lives quietly. Enlightenment science banished such thinking from the field of reason, rearranging "the entire *episteme* of Western culture" (Foucault 1970: 54). Yet once science had vanquished little/large metaphors, nationalism revived them with revolutionary passion. Now taken for granted, the person/nation homology works both ways. Large to little, the nation defines each person as its national from birth to death. Saying "I'm Canadian" does not distinguish mind from body in the person any more than it separates spirit from matter in the nation. Little to large, "the figure of the human body is fundamental to our understanding of the American nation" (Holland 2001: xxv). Indeed, in having will, mind, and body like a person, the nation is a collective individual (Dumont 1970), a person writ large. Culturally, person/nation equivalence crosses intervening loyalties—family, kin, locality, religion—to give patriotism its remarkable intensity (Anderson 1998: 360–368) and make today's autonomous individual not just plausible but proper.

Mixing Modes. Can one person follow both dualism and oneness? In fact most of us do, moving between the mind/body dualism that rules public discourse and the person/world ways that apply at home. Mixing and matching the two may set up today's eating disorders. Certainly without person/world oneness, collapsing the person into the body (Lester 1997: 486) and the body into eating or hygiene (Warin 2003a) would be just a quirky thought, not a life-crippling passion. And without mind/body dualism to implement those metaphors, the poetry could not become a pathology. Yet anorexics, in mixing these symbolic modes, create a deadly combination. That said, this particular mix is not any odder than today's health and fitness movements.

Mixing Traditions: Health and Fitness Movements

Exercise is almost the national pastime. Why do so many work out so seriously? Off-the-cuff answers—"for my health," "to keep in shape," "to lose weight," "it feels good"—either exalt the body or justify exercise as a means to a better life. All of these rationales are straightforward mind/body discourse, justifying what we do by individual self-interested choice. That is part of the story.

Then there is the rest of the story: fitness is a sweeping social movement fighting modern ease. It is not as if science discovered the benefits of exercise and then people followed compliantly: to the contrary, medical research followed the fad (M. Becker 1986: 19; Gillick 1984: 375). By the late 1970s, fitness had coupled personal with social redemption—improving oneself improved America (Gillick 1984: 381). President Kennedy said as much: "young Americans . . . are neglecting their bodies . . . [and] getting soft. And such softness on the part of individual citizens can . . . destroy the vitality of a nation" (quoted in Gillick 1984: 381–382). We might object that national strength rests on institutions, not individuals, or that vitality comes from purpose, not pushups, but the president was just voicing a nineteenth-century cliché (Green 1989: 8; Park 1989). Popular thought had long equated polity with society, society with the person, and the person with his or her body—all accepted homologies.

Fitness bespeaks the body's rise. An unmentionable in Victorian America, the body has become a veritable icon of the individual. Yet in the nineteenth century, Brumberg (1997: xxi) remarks, young women who sought to improve themselves "almost always focused on their internal character and how it was reflected in outward behavior." They "rarely mentioned their bodies in terms of strategies for self-improvement." Today, however, "the shape and appearance of their bodies" is "a primary expression of their individual identity." And not just women's identities: an ongoing culture-wide shift is making the body an ever larger part of any individual's personal and social life. This shift assumes the same person/world oneness that pervaded nineteenth-century health and fitness movements. Consider four areas where these movements evoke oneness and defy dualism.

First, health and fitness movements have a holistic worldview and counsel harmony with nature. Instead of a fallen world, we find the opposite: nature "is absolutely good" (Whorton 1982: 5), and "human maladies . . . are a result of people's inability to live within that system without being victimized by their own passions" (Green 1988: x). Here the person is one autonomous whole, nature is another, and harmony between the two ensures health and happiness. Although mind/body discourse plays a part (human sinfulness explains the fall from grace), unless one first assumes each human is a microcosm in a harmonious cosmos, these reforming "religions of physical perfection" (Whorton 1982: 5) are impossible.

Second, these movements see nature and person or body as transformations of each other, and society as upsetting their natural harmony. Some reformers attack society directly, but health and fitness movements more typically aim to change individuals, reasoning that society is only the person writ large. This may sound conservative today, but in the nineteenth century it was not. Even today the liberal view (blame society!—the person is society writ small) and the conservative rejoinder (blame individuals!—society is the person writ large) both rely on person/world reasoning that makes the person's body a battleground for "foreign" wars (societal struggles like abortion and homosexuality) as well as "domestic" strife (fighting fat, aging, and laziness in oneself). Only thus could we arrive at "'health' as the New Morality by which character and moral worth are judged" (M. Becker 1986: 19).

Third, these movements put harmonizing with nature in the person's own hands (M. Becker 1986; Green 1988: x). "Individual responsibility for health through clean and upright living," Gillick (1984: 369) observes, "is part of a venerable American tradition. The fundamental tenet of this . . . physical hygienism, dating at least to John Wesley . . . is that health results from living in accord with 'the laws of nature.'"

Fourth, the person is unitary, not divided. Today's fitness denies dualities, insisting that "[t]hrough fitness, selves are truly *embodied*" (Glassner 1990: 222–223). That is not new—in his aptly titled history of American health reform, *Crusaders for Fitness*, Whorton (1982: 348) finds that hygienic ideologies appeal to "our primitive intuition that the body and soul are intimately wed." One late-nineteenth-century spin-off was the rise of sports, an activity that fused spirit with body. In sports, Mrozek (1983: 228) writes, "turn-of-the-century Americans betrayed the primacy of the material world in their own minds. Yet, at the same time, they reached toward a reintegration of mind with body and of spirit with matter. The sense of unity that had been part of the Puritan gift had been jeopardized . . . by the Enlightenment." So sports reclaimed person/world oneness right when industrialization tore spirit and matter apart.

Returning to the question of why so many—anorexics included—work out so religiously, the larger answer is that a person/world tradition powerfully influences how they reason, what they feel, and the bodies they want.

Anorexia's Embodied Conflict

Like health and fitness activists, anorexics are reformers. What anorexics would reform is their body or eating or indeed their life (Lester 1997). In reforming, a mind/body discourse, they stand apart from the world to objectify it. That is the genius of the dualism that science uses so brilliantly. It is also the fallacy that eating disorders exaggerate so disastrously: you cannot actually stand apart from your body (Bateson 2000). A mind cannot disembody itself. If it could, then anorexia's activity could never seize the person as it does. That is, bodily actions could not control consciousness as they do.

Also like health and fitness activists, anorexics mix modes of thinking. What allows both parties to start reforming is the assumption that a society, life, or body is just a machine to rebuild as they like. At the same time, little/large metaphors direct this reform-minded dualism to its target, going for the body to better the person or society.

Arguably, if anorexics pursued only a mind/body discourse, it would free them from their disease. Were they dualists only, they would be too self-interested and too detached from their bodies to invest any more than that mere object would return. Indeed, were the self that autonomous, a person could take a cynical view of any metaphoric societal scheme seizing the sympathetic body. Why improve, such skeptics might ask? We glimpse this when some informants suddenly, mysteriously stop caring about their ascetic discipline. Mary, for example, says, "*I was feeling like I had no control. So I kind of got control through what I* [would] *eat.*" Then, "*I just said, 'Forget it. I don't care.*" Yet for anorexics who are constitutionally pro-social, it is hard not to care, and Mary later resumes her self-sacrificing achieving.

How does anorexia resolve control worries? The features discussed in chapter 6 suggest two steps. Anorexics initially experience Exhilaration, a sense of control that religious ascetics also report. Once that fades, Isolation cuts off overextended sympathies and reorients anorexics to their regimen, that is, their Discipline, which makes the body a closed moral arena. Keeping one's regimen replaces the self-worth anorexics once got socially and sympathetically, resolving the control-or-sympathy struggle.

Conclusion

Anorexia controls by collapsing. A whole person collapses into a physical part; that part, the body, collapses into one active part, its regimen; that regimen collapses into ideals of order and purity (cf. Warin 2003a); and those ideals can be kept or lost only in their entirety. Leap by metaphoric leap, a many-sided life shrinks to a single facet: the strength or will or control it takes to keep one's discipline.

Is this madness? No, the anorexic person follows a well-trodden path. Is it "the secret language of eating disorders"? That phrasing—from a title by Claude-Pierre (1997)—suggests Freudian thought, where symptoms reveal repressed secrets. We find otherwise (chapter 7). Anorexia's metaphors are implicit, not repressed. They hide nothing but their own arbitrary world-creating powers.

A powerful metaphor, person/world oneness gives the body its remarkable modern salience. It paves a way to anorexia, often via its close cousin, Virtuous Eating. Our next chapter takes up a third tradition: an appearance ethic that also leads people into anorexia. In all three traditions, modern life energizes anorexia from outside, fueling what the activity itself sets up within the person.

Notes

1. Other scholars argue for two languages (Bellah et al. 1985), voices (Gilligan 1982) or worlds (Habermas 1975), or for an intrinsic dualism of modernity (Hewitt 1989). Whether languages number one, two, or many—or are even not language-like at all—the point is that metaphors mediate embodiment in discernible and contrasting patterns.

CHAPTER 12

The Attractive Person
A Modern Appearance Ethic

What part does appearance play in anorexia? Once starving begins to show, appearance complicates every case. Unlike bulimics, anorexics cannot hide their affliction forever. Sooner or later, *outside* attention shapes anorexia's course. Yet what is the *inner* involvement? How much looks initially mattered varies widely for our informants. Some were highly appearance-involved, others hardly at all.

Appearance is not beauty. Beauty is an ideal. Some have more beauty than others, but everyone has to look one way or another, so no one has more appearance than another. Beauty ranks, separating people, whereas appearance joins them in a showing/watching exchange. Appearance highlights difference, not rank: how we look is an individualizing display for others to see, just as we see their individuality. This sociability ensnares anorexics.

Today's appearance practices descend from the same late-nineteenth-century cultural crisis that shaped our current eating and body attitudes. Like Virtuous Eating, an appearance ethic adapts to modern life. Unlike healthy eating and living, however, it has no moralizing activists, no missionaries urging better looks for the good of all. What promotes today's appearance involvement is not a group at all but the rising tides of consumerism and identity politics. Swept along by these currents, our era frets that appearances matter too much and scapegoats anorexics to avoid the truth.

Misplacing Anorexia: Beauty and Body Image Associations

Attributing anorexia to a woman's quest for beauty should strike us as odd. After all, beauty is not just weight. Even if it were, anorexic weight loss looks ghastly. Starvers lose eye sparkle and skin tone; hard bony lines replace feminine curves and sculpted muscles. They look wan, develop dark circles under their eyes, grow extra body hair, and start losing head hair. In the end, shriveled limbs set off an outsized head. That skeletal look is not beautiful today and was no more so when nineteenth-century physicians first isolated anorexia. Not surprisingly, then, they did not find beauty explained it, nor did several successive generations.

How did a beauty explanation become popular? Three independent forces converge: activists feminize the disease, social critics seize upon it to skewer media influence, and body image catches on out of all proportion to its utility and validity. Beauty and body image confusions are part of this explanation.

The Beauty Confusion. The beauty explanation is so influential that we need to detail just how wantonly it defies evidence and reason. First, the theory excludes cases to save itself. Attributing anorexia to feminine beauty ideals arbitrarily dismisses the male anorexics making up perhaps 19 percent of the full-syndrome and 40 percent of the partial-syndrome population (Woodside et al. 2001). This theory-saving exclusion has no accepted theoretical or empirical justification. It is the same disease, male or female. Meanwhile, attributing anorexia to thin-as-beautiful arbitrarily dismisses anorexia among African Americans and in cultures that esteem fleshier bodies. And notably, many well-documented cases lack the fear of fat and distorted body image cited by the beauty argument (Katzman and Lee 1997; Palmer 1993).

Moreover, this theory dismisses the anorexic's point of view. Recovered anorexics do not typically attribute their disease to desire for greater beauty. In Garrett's (1998: 61) interviews with Australian anorexics, none "thought it had anything to do with 'vanity.'" Our interviews support that finding. All subordinated beauty to more fundamental causes. Several knew they looked ghastly, and some enjoyed that. Further, no major study shows anorexics were inordinately concerned with beauty prior to their disease. Practicing anorexics meticulously regulate eating, not beauty (Warin 2003b).

Finally, the theory holds only when beauty is defined selectively. Beauty has changed over the past century, but anorexia has not. Some fashions have glorified an anorexic appearance (e.g., the 1960s' little-girl look; cocaine chic) and others have not (e.g., the busty 1950s; today's buff body), but anorexia's incidence has not varied accordingly. Modern beauty stresses a person's overall look (face, grooming, clothes, demeanor), not just weight. Ignoring these other dimensions to reduce the whole to a slim body radically misrepresents beauty.

How did such a mistaken idea gain such acceptance? The beauty explanation required Bruch's (1962) influential idea that anorexics could not see their body as it actually was.

The Body Image Confusion. Our informants cast doubt on Bruch's body image explanation. A few took pains to say that they knew exactly how their body looked. More tellingly, no one's initial story invoked body image dysmorphia to explain particulars. In follow-up questions, only two interviewees made a distorted body image basic to their illness. Our sample suggests a distorted body image is neither especially common nor essential to the disease.

Although it officially typifies today's disease, body image distortion was identified only in the 1960s, nearly a century after medicine first isolated the syndrome. Could clinicians have missed such an obvious symptom for so long? Finding that implausible, Russell (1985) concluded that anorexia had "changed in its manifestations" because experimental evidence confirmed what clinicians now saw. He spoke too soon: by the 1990s meta-studies seeking to reconcile conflicting findings could no longer support any strong or consistent claim that anorexics have distorted body images (Haworth-Hoeppner 1999; Hsu and Sobkiewicz 1991). Some do and some do not, but that is not distinctive—healthy people are roughly the same. "Despite extensive research over the past 30 years," Szymanski and Seime (1997) conclude, "body image distortion and its role in the eating disorders remain ill-defined and equivocal." Hsu and Sobkiewicz (1991) urge abandoning the concept altogether.

Was body image a bad idea from the start, or has anorexia changed yet again? We do not know. Worse, using current research, we cannot know. Although body image was initially invoked to understand the person as a whole (Schilder 1935), Bruch's Cartesian discourse split mind from body. Since then research has relentlessly taken an abstract image out of the anorexic's concrete experience. In one meta-study combining 222 separate studies covering 140,836 different people (Feingold and Mazzella 1998), the authors talk readily about body image but never mention any real bodies or even go beyond testing others' tests. To get this far from an actual person's experience, the research has to *assume* that one can separate a body image from the whole person. We dispute that.

The origins of body image research lie in two features highlighted by Bruch (1962: 189). One is her patients' "delusional disturbance in self-concept and body image," judged so because they "defended as normal and right" their emaciated state. The other is "a disturbance in the accuracy of perception or cognitive interpretation of stimuli arising in the body" such that "[a]wareness of hunger and appetite in the ordinary sense seems to be absent." She attributes these problems to their early upbringing. Our explanation is simpler and surer: asceticism. Ascetics defend their discipline rigorously because it is all or none—you keep the rules or you do not. Keeping your discipline strictly changes how you experience your body—a change we documented and called Consolidation (chapter 6). As for Bruch's particular illustration, the feeling of hunger, it is well established that fasting monks can calm or even lose this urge (Bushell 1995: 556, 559; Vogüé 1989: 10). Anorexics are no different.

Thus, neither beauty nor body image reveals much about anorexia. In our sample, neither is integral to the disease. A distorted body image is at best a complication of anorexia, not a cause; and although beauty is sometimes relevant at the start, it ceases to matter once an ascetic discipline establishes itself. Together, beauty and body image misplace anorexia in women coping with gender expectations. Our research situates anorexia amidst everyday moral struggles to be a good person. Here, although appearance is not central, it can factor in, as we find when exploring what our informants can teach us.

Grounding Appearance: Our Informants' Involvements

Just over a third (8) of our twenty-two interviewees phrase anorexia visually. Fred states: "*I got into the vanity because I realized, 'Wow, I'm ripped.' I'm that guy who when I take my shirt off in a room, people look twice.*" Experiencing himself in the eyes of others energizes him. Another group (5) is also visual but phrases their experience more neutrally than Fred's group. The remainder (9), not quite half, either do not describe their experience visually or deny that appearance matters. Considering the visual half, four features merit comment.

Mirror Gazing. Our informants vary widely on the importance of mirrors. Jill says, "*I didn't do mirrors much,*" and they have no place in Melissa's regimen ("*I never looked at myself in the mirror.*" "*I always looked awful, so it didn't matter.*"). Molly went to the other extreme:

> *I liked the way I looked. Loved mirrors. My sister would be like, "Molly! What are you doing?" Because I'd walk past a mirror and turn and look. Even if I wasn't planning on looking in a mirror, if I saw one* [I'd look].

Well aware of media stereotypes, she adds: "*I wasn't comparing myself to people on TV. I was comparing myself to girls in my high school and to my sister.*"

Mirror gazing is less admiration of beauty than a technique of self for feedback. Sarah, for example, talks of starving's "*visual payoff.*" Mirrors also serve Goading, another mid-course feature. Lindsay remembers, "*I'd stand naked in front of the mirror and be disgusted with myself and pinch fat where I could and be like, 'Oh I'm disgusting.'*" Whereas Lindsay's looking makes her goals concrete—she can pinch the spot—Jim sees his body's athletic potential ("*This is awful, this is terrible, you look bad. You're not going to be able to run well*").

Does mirror-oriented anorexia develop differently? As feedback, numbers (calorie counting, weight watching) track restricting overall, while the visual highlights single body parts. For Beth, "*You see your trouble areas. You see the places that you're the least satisfied with and you zone in on those.*" Similarly, Janet recalls how, during dance, *in the mirror, my tights made this little indentation on my waist. I looked at that all the time. I couldn't stop looking at that.*" Going to a wilderness school gives temporary relief ("*I wasn't dancing that I needed to be concerned about the way I looked,"* and *"the only mirrors that I saw were from here up* [mid-torso]"), but after a week or two she panics (*"I started freaking"*), suggesting other feedback kicks in. In that sense a mirror is just one tool among others. Although such feedback can serve asceticism ("How am I doing with my discipline?") or a social purpose ("How do I look to others?"), it is solitary self-monitoring. Compared with mirror gazing—an individual visual practice—the other three visual features are distinctly social.

Appearance as Valued. At least three informants treat how they look as a visual statement of who they are personally. None mention beauty, but all stress virtue, especially Megan:

> *I definitely have this need to be this all-around, very well put together person. My parents instilled in me if you're going to do something, do it well. You can subscribe to whatever philosophy you want. But if there's no proof in your life* [it is pointless]. *I am doing productive things with my life and I want it to show.*

Her idiom is secular, but manifesting inner convictions outwardly has deep religious roots. For Becca one's appearance must live up to a valued social image (*"this image of Becca,"* *"I wanted every little thing about me to just—I guess—be an example"*). Like Megan, Becca implies a slim body is just part of the package. Sheena is more explicit:

> *I always wanted to be the good kid who does everything right. I felt a need to keep this kind of body type. Not perfect, but the good-kid-personal kind of thing—for lack of a better word. I wanted to be very good at the athletics I did, or dance and stuff. And I wanted to look like a dancer, look like I was in sports. I wanted my body to reflect the activities I was doing. I wanted to have something to show for it and for other people to recognize that.*

Whereas Megan, Becca, and Sheena *want* to show who they are, as adolescents they *have to* do so.

Appearance as Integral to Adolescence. In adolescent identity politics, each person gets measured by where he or she fits. Here physical attractiveness is just part of how clothes, grooming, demeanor, and possessions all place each person visually. *"When you're a kid,"* Melissa says, *"you don't really care about appearances. But when you hit a certain age you kind of worry what people think about you."* For Jesse this happens in junior high, when *"boys and girls are taking particular notice of each other"* and she becomes *"very uncomfortable,"* *"super conscious of what I looked like and how I should look."* It is a sharp change for Janet: *"Sixth grade I was on top of the world. In gymnastics, leotards and mirrors but it never occurred to me to be concerned about the way I looked."* Later, though, at arts school, she gets *"this image in my head of how I want to look,"* but feels *"like complete crap about myself"* because she does not match it. In public school, where Isabel grew up with everyone else, she felt *"completely comfortable,"* partly because at day's end *"you go home and you can get away from everything."* Boarding school, however, is around-the-clock; *"everyone knows everything about everyone and everyone's always looking at each other."* In this fishbowl, her main concern is not how her body looks (she is slim) but how she looks as a eater (what is on her plate).

Appearance as Exchange. Isabel hides her anorexia, but some want others to know. Lynn needed an audience:

> *It* [anorexia] *was very, very self-centered but I needed everybody. I needed the external input. It was for me but I needed all that in order to make it real. It wasn't enough. Like the numbers weren't just enough, and the exercise wasn't enough.*

Where Lynn makes a bodily statement for others to recognize, Sheena mirrors others' expectations:

> *Anytime that my dad or my mom said, "Oh you're looking especially muscley" or "Your legs are looking thin" or something like that, it put pressure on me to keep that up. Whether it was a good comment or bad comment, I wanted to keep that up.*

A wrestler, Fred remembers people's reaction to his well-defined muscles when he took his shirt off:

> *I'll be honest, I liked that. That was cool. It's almost like, you link that weight and what you're doing in your mind to that reaction from people and you don't realize there's another way you can get that. You don't have to not eat or overwork yourself, but that's linked in your mind. 'I'm doing this. People are doing this. Okay.' And people ask you how your weight is going. So you feel if you lose that your social life is going to dwindle. If you get it in your mind that everybody is looking at you, you're going to look at yourself, scrutinizing yourself ten times more than anybody* [else] *ever would. Once you get it into your head, "Okay, this is how they see me. I have to be this," you're going to kill yourself to fit within this mold for them to accept you.*

What Fred describes is universal—that is, basic to all social life. Yet others express culture-specific appearance values (e.g., Megan wanting her actions to testify to her beliefs). The next section sorts out these differing appearance involvements.

Appearance Traditions

The importance of appearance is a human constant, but what is valued varies culturally and locally. Three frames can organize this variety: human, Western, and local.

Human Practices. As social primates, humans rely heavily on visual communication. How we look shapes face-to-face interactions that enculturate infants, sustain small groups, and allow even strangers to work together. The intricate musculature of the face, a highly evolved social organ, can communicate with nuance and speed that humble stumbling words. Less subtle but no less relevant, the body's posture, demeanor, grooming, clothes, and decoration all visually convey information ranging from gender and status to attitudes and occupation. This is all so basic to social life that well-functioning people everywhere attend to their own and others' appearance via traditions that vary widely.

Competing Appearance Traditions. Within this human heritage, the West's many traditions offer two opposite takes on the truth of appearance. In literalism, appearances are real. The world is how it appears—or, given that we judge by what we see, it might as well be. In interpretivism, however, appearances are false: the world is illusory or, judging from what little the surface shows, might as well be. Neither view is new. The Iliad's transparent characters directly manifest their inner life; the Bible, in contrast, leaves its characters' motives and God's plan opaque, giving only clues for interpretation (Auerbach 1968). Despite their great age, these opposites are as current as the debate over cosmetic surgery ("a new you" vs. "it can't change who you really are").

Quite separate from debating what is real (whether you can judge a person by appearances, an epistemological question) and what is done (how much we judge others by appearance, an empirical question) is the issue of what is right (whether we should judge others by appearances, a moral question). Here the public position is clear: judging by appearance is wrong. It offends democracy to make beauty, race, gender, wealth, and class decisive. Ability and deeds, not looks, are the criteria we *should* judge by. What we do falls far short of that ideal, not just because of prejudice but because no person or society can live blindly. In large-scale societies we can neither live comfortably nor work together smoothly unless we type people and situations. Caught in this contradiction, our insistently visual modernity at once blesses appearances and curses their implications—we dote on celebrities yet decry their superficiality, celebrate consumerism yet dismiss possessions.

Local Appearance Practices. How real people manage these appearance complexities is always a local reality. Consider Beausoleil's (1994: 34, 46) research on women's makeup. On the one hand, seen abstractly, societal appearance norms discriminate against women, expecting them to give more time, money, and attention to looks than men do. Here Beausoleil says feminists cast women as victims: "Appearance, 'beauty,' and more generally 'femininity' are seen as nothing more than media images imposed externally on women." On the other hand, considered concretely, women use makeup as a tool of self-expression, and media images are less ideals to emulate than points to reference in crafting one's own distinctive look. As a daily practice that requires artistic skill and social awareness, "women may experience pleasure and creativity as well as satisfaction in . . . doing appearance work."

Clothes are similar. Using focus groups, Crane (2000: 226, 231–232) found "women did not often wish to emulate [fashion models'] appearance." They were not intimidated by the models' beauty, their bodily perfection, or their clothes. Instead, Crane's subjects "evaluated fashionable clothing with a strong sense of stable personal identities." Listen to Lynn:

> *I had posters. They weren't up in my room; they were in a box. I'd get them out and look at them all the time. Like Kate Moss—skinny skinny skinny supermodels. But then athletes too—not thin but muscular. I couldn't see myself at all. It was on a standard that wasn't me. It was a "What do I see as beautiful in other people?" I never wanted to look like Kate Moss.*

Is this pick-and-choose attitude new? Expecting women to idealize models assumes how "nineteenth century fashion consisted of a well-defined standard . . . that was widely adapted." That is decades out of date: women today negotiate between conflicting style norms. As society segments into ever narrower lifestyle niches, high fashion has become visual entertainment, a sometimes bizarre niche most women watch and use selectively but few emulate (Crane 2000: 6, 18, 211–212). As with makeup, supposedly oppressive expectations turn out to be—or get turned into—tools of self-expression. Take British girls' magazines: "practices and rituals of femininity which were once carried out in order to attract boys and to secure a future based on being a wife and mother are now done on behalf of the self" (McRobbie 1991: 183). In the end, manipulating externals like appearance is a powerful and perhaps necessary strategy for cultivating the self that develops one's sensibility, autonomy, and inner control (Csikszentmihalyi and Rochberg-Halton 1981)—even as one also meets society's expectations.

Like anorexia, makeup and fashion are widely misunderstood and subtly maligned, as if all women were rabid competitors in a national beauty contest. Yet actual practices suggest contemporary women do not pursue a single beauty ideal, an *absolute*, but create distinctive appearances *relative* to each other. All this redefines appearance work radically. Now neither simple conformity nor raw ambition can explain such grooming. Instead, thanks to the irony that self-expression is now virtually obligatory, attending to one's appearance becomes a matter of self-respect, perhaps even an obligation to place oneself amid today's diversity. The more social life watches these salient surfaces, the more we live in an appearance society.

Appearance Society: "You Are How You Look"

Today's appearance society obliges people to display their individuality. While women typically attend to their looks more than men do, no one escapes how appearance marks lifestyle differences that either were not displayed or did not exist just a few generations ago.

The Rise of Appearance. In the seventeenth century, when European urban life flourished around well-accepted conventions, appearances masked motives and marginalized individuality (Sennett 1977: chaps. 3–6). Clothing marked only a few broad social categories. Then nineteenth-century industrialization democratized dress (Crane 2000: 3). As clothing became more affordable, appearances became more ambiguous—dress could deceive or display ambition, not actual social place. Since then, as the broad categories that dress once marked have lost relevance, appearances display an ever more various individuality.

Explaining appearance involvement today invokes that same brutal encounter with modern conditions that spawned our current eating and body attitudes. When the nineteenth century began, most North Americans lived in small towns where you could know another person's character. By century's end, huge corporations ruled the landscape, and you had to work with strangers and rely on appearances. Modern life managed this risk in two opposite ways. On the one hand, rather than trust appearances, people sought hard data. Scientific and especially statistical measures replaced trust once put in character. On the other hand, appearances began to carry more weight. The modern ethos, as empirical, visual, and ahistoric, took life literally as it presented itself. It was an "age of simultaneity" where "sweeping changes in technology and culture created distinctive new modes of thinking about and experiencing space and time" (Kern 1983: 278, 1, 182). These changes broke down conventional art, music, literature, and social life, undoing not just the convention of character but the past's relevance for the present. Appearance seized this void. Going by how a person looked not only captured these new realities but also harnessed the visual emphases of modern life to create a flexible yet inescapable social order. Social life began trusting what surfaces said.

Consumerism also made appearances matter more. When what you have defines who you are (your identity) and where you fit (your status), appearances drive society. As industrialization began to meet basic needs, expanding meant creating new needs by inventing ever newer and more distinctive products. As business began manufacturing not just products but distinctions (Sahlins 1976), marketers hyped appearances. That put the economy on its present path, where by the late 1970s, computer-controlled production and niche marketing allowed the faster, finer distinctions that give contemporary social life its appearance-rich diversity.

Should we celebrate or curse the rise of appearance? Like it or not, the more social life centers on surfaces, the more visual we become in how we understand ourselves and others. Once inferior to character, appearance now holds a larger and decidedly more social part of ourselves.

The New Sociability: New Freedom or New Worries? Attending to one's appearance can make social life into visual exchange: you present yourself to others who present themselves to you. That makes our growing individualism more sociable than solitary. It is an appearance ethic, what you owe to others as well as yourself. That is, not caring how you look to others shows you lack self-respect. So say the appearance-involved, at least—not everyone agrees. But the more vibrant this display-and-watch social exchange becomes, the less anyone can ignore appearances.

The more visual modern society becomes, the less it engages the whole person and the tighter it grips our lives. A half-century ago, racial, gender, sexual, and class stereotypes obscured much about the actual person. A lot was—and could be—kept "in the closet." But today authenticity urges everyone "out of the closet" even as enclosing walls come down around us. In other words, the more our expressive individualism means openly living out who we are and baring the heart's every secret, the more social control grips our inner lives.

Appearance and Eating Disorders

Newly rigorous societal expectations for display are perhaps why many now worry about their body in others' eyes. The more who we are socially is how we look physically, the more the body does in fact matter. Moreover, as the body's salience grows, the standards for its management in weight, diet, health, and cleanliness grow stricter (Stearns 1999). That one-two punch—greater salience and stricter standards—incites today's eating disorders.

Appearance society changes anorexia's context and creates new complications. Once self-starvation begins to show, the anorexic's body becomes an identity statement. Now that it is an established role, getting into anorexia is easier and getting out requires a new identity, not just weight gain. Moreover, pro-ana websites suggest self-starvation's morbid lifestyle now attracts its own following, mocking bourgeois beauty as tattooing and body piercing do. That contentious twist was not in our sample, but seeking a grotesque appearance can now inspire anorexia just as Virtuous Eating does.

Where today's anorexia relives the late nineteenth century's encounter with modernity, newer eating disorders like bulimia suggest the late twentieth century's postmodern struggles. Ever slimmer anorexics live modernity's unending progress by endlessly deferring gratification for future good. Bulimics, however, bypass modernity's progressive world absorbing all others and reach a postmodern pluralism oscillating between separate worlds—from out-of-control excess (gorging) to scarcity (dieting) or moderation (control). And instead of joining modernity's relentless march forward, bulimics reverse time (purging undoes what was eaten). Unlike anorexics, whose heroic dieting eventually stands out, bulimics hope to fit in, hiding that they live by contradictory principles. Anorexics' modern morality (self-denial and a slim body as virtues) invents an ethic (dieting procedures that implement their values) and makes them proud, whereas bulimics' postmodern ethic (an established if irregular procedure that leaves contradictory values unresolved) lacks a higher morality. Bulimia, a secret vice, simply expresses rather than resolves inner conflict, and causes shame.

The latter 1960s set the stage for today's postmodern eating disorders. That social revolution crested long ago, but its democratizing attack on prejudices of class, race, gender, disability, and sexual orientation is ongoing. Once these stereotypes tied the person rather tightly to how others typed his or her body. As these constraints loosen, possibilities multiply. Today's challenge is less coping with a stereotypic category (e.g., reckoning with gender prejudice) than creating a distinctive identity (e.g., deciding what gender aspects to accent). Developmental distress shifts accordingly. Instead of coping with authority, today's challenge is to control oneself and create order out of openness. Here, the more the appearance society makes identity body-based, the more eating and exercise become new pathologies for a new day.

Conclusion

Anorexia develops out of an ascetic practice, not a beauty quest. It focuses inwardly on self-control, not outwardly on appearance. Its always visceral grip is only sometimes visual too. Beauty and body image-based explanations are misunderstandings whose only consistent relationship with anorexia is to stereotype and stigmatize it. They are relevant in some cases, but they are not integral to this particular eating disorder.

Seeing anorexia as ascetic suggests why some experience it visually: asceticism externalizes. Unlike reflection, it is an activity that all can see. As a way of managing oneself, "ascetic discipline erects the ideal of a self" that is "wholly externalized, utterly conscious, all surface with no reservoirs of the unknown, the unconquered, or the unpredictable" (Harpham 1987: 25). Asceticism is discipline incarnate—which makes it visible.

SECTION

IV

Recovery

Finding Balance

That there is no cure for anorexia is no one's fault. We state that flatly. Blaming families harms anorexics, and pointing fingers at therapists hurts therapy. Then everyone loses. "Distrust," Cassell (1991: 214–215) says, "interferes with care—and with caring. It is difficult for doctors to care for distrustful patients, and still more to care *about* them. Yet such caring may foster healing and cure." The bottom line is we are all in this together.

Section IV explores how anorexia responds to intervention. Here the syndrome is an elusive adversary known only by its replies. Section I's functionally coherent whole and its contextualization in Sections II and III are no longer at issue. Now we examine piecemeal responses to particular probes. Here our informants discover anorexia much as diagnosticians do: seeing what helps, their illness becomes whatever fights back.

What fights back? Everyone faces two challenges: to get well they must break the activity's grip over their life; and to stay well they must re-channel longstanding ascetic inclinations into healthier activities. Recovery's uncontrolled "experiments" thereby confirm our earlier findings: as sufferers tease out what works, everyone's anorexia responds like an activity disorder that taps constitutional roots.

CHAPTER 13

Getting Out
Undoing Anorexia

No one knows for sure how to escape anorexia. So anorexics often get spectrum-of-care treatment, a grab-bag gamble that something will work. Perhaps 50 percent recover and another 25 to 30 percent improve, but no one knows why. Even leading experts summoned to a National Institutes of Health (NIH) workshop could not say what role treatment plays in recovery: some patients get well on their own, others drop out, and those who complete treatment "often show only modest benefits." No wonder there is "pervasive pessimism" (Agras et al. 2004).

To do better, health care must listen to anorexics. Taking their point of view builds rapport, engages patients in their own treatment, and lets them teach us about recovery. Obviously that is difficult—they do not always know what worked, and what they do know often defies words—but their piecemeal knowledge is far better than what NIH found, namely, caregivers "dismissing patients . . . as nonadherent and difficult to treat" rather than developing "strategies for enhancing motivation to change" (Agras et al. 2004: 517).

What can our informants teach us about recovery? In one word, it would be "negotiate" or even just "listen." But rather than settle for a watchword, we have organized their thoughts naturalistically into heroic, environmental, and intervention therapies. First, however, we need to apply what we have learned about anorexia and relate it to recovery.

The Challenge of Recovery

Recovery is not—or not just—a healthy weight. That is a worthy goal, but low weight is only a symptom. Recovery is when eating is just eating, a relatively autonomous act governed loosely by hunger, pleasure, sociability, and reason. Of course eating will always carry many meanings, but only when it is free of obsessive add-ons is the anorexic fully recovered.

To lighten the overload on eating, anorexics must (1) defy anorexia's inner energy—the loop whereby extreme self-denial creates feelings about food, eating, and self-worth that only self-denial can satisfy; (2) redirect the constitutional bents and momentum that serve the syndrome; and (3) give up collateral payoffs—the sense of identity, control, achievement, superiority, and autonomy that anorexia develops. What makes this so challenging is that these entanglements are not just distorted ideas that reason can vanquish. Worse, they are living biocultural systems that rebound when upset. Worse still, a modern mindset hides what is happening. By dividing mind from body, our cultural tools delay awareness and misdirect self-help. On average, nearly five years elapse before sufferers in the U.K. get medical help (Newton et al. 1993), six years in Norway (Rosenvinge and Klusmeier 2000).

Getting Help and What Is Helpful

Getting medical help brings a powerful institution into one's life. Will it be a gentle giant or a bull in a china shop? Anorexia's character—frustrating, ambiguous, deadly—can bring out the bull. Medicine needs markers, which anorexia befuddles. No one knows when dieting crosses from healthy into deadly. How far is too far in adolescent exploring? The more anorexia is an adolescent strategy, the more we should nurture maturing rather than impose curing.[1] At least five of our interviewees spontaneously said they had grown out of anorexia, and perhaps every case had adolescent complications. That could favor "wait it out" approaches—but then again, the longer the practice goes, the less likely recovery becomes (Wilson et al. 2007). There are no easy answers.

The available help is not always helpful. Judging by a large U.K. survey, nearly half the eating disordered had a negative experience with the family doctor and inpatient treatment (Newton et al. 1993); the ratio was only slightly better in Norway (Rosenvinge and Klusmeier 2000). A large, two-year trial found that full recovery rates were poor (33 percent) and no tested therapy was better than any other (Gowers et al. 2007). Another even longer-term follow-up on three treatments found that only half of cases had had good outcomes and no technique was superior to another (Carter et al. 2011). And there is "no empirical basis for the widespread use of antidepressants" that characterizes treatment in the U.S. (Wilson et al. 2007). That is the bad news.

The good news is that when the right patient finds the right clinician, treatment can work (Clinton 2010). Research demonstrates there is no *generic* cure, but our sample says there is no generic person, purpose, or situation involved.

To be sure, once begun, the syndrome takes a generic course, so at this point it is reasonable to speak of *a* disease; however, each case carries a distinctive past. Vanderlinden (2010: 161) says as much, making "a plea for a more flexible therapeutic approach . . . that adapts its focus depending . . . on the psychopathological pathway which has led to the development of the eating disorder." Different ways in require different ways out—exactly what we found. Here, if research is to serve the clinic, it must reclaim the diversity that universalizing loses. Only then can we fruitfully match therapist, therapy, and patient.

Approaching an Anorexic

When we asked interviewees how they might help a practicing anorexic, no one answered confidently. Some say they have struggled with that question but have no answer. A few express frustration or embarrassment that they cannot do better. As Susanna said, *"sometimes I feel a little bit ashamed that having gone through all of that I still do not have a clear answer."*

All fear a direct approach would be pointless or even harmful. They have heard and ignored cautions themselves. As Jane says, *"I heard the people saying things to me—like, 'You need to end this,' 'You look like a skeleton'—but it didn't affect me until I just came out of it on my own."* Some saw waiting it out as the only recourse.

Wait It Out. Some said one could not help: the disease runs its own course and differs individually.

> *I've had friends who have had sisters or daughters who had anorexia and they always want to know, "What I can do?" I really don't know. It's an individual* [thing]. *It's like alcoholism or drug addiction—you can't make someone* [change]. *It has to take its course. They have to get there on their own.*—Jesse

> *Having gone through it myself I think I could help somebody. And then I can't because it's so relative to what their experience of it is, and where they are coming from and what happens alongside it for them. It's almost in the cards for you or it isn't. You just have to live through it and get to the other side.*—Natalie

This advice fits several of our findings: anorexics' motives indeed differ greatly; their experiences differ, although perhaps not greatly; as an activity the disease follows an inner logic that is hard to fight; and, as coming of age, it follows a course.

Waiting it out works well if the anorexic will outgrow the disease anyway—if recovery is *"maturing, growing up, being on my own"* as Jane says. Yet some never recover. They grow into rather than out of it. Should one still say nothing? Some think trying does more harm than good:

> *Other people's validation kind of feeds it. So if I were to talk to family or friends of someone who had an eating disorder, I'd want them to know that it's almost better to ignore it. Don't give them that feedback, don't comment because that feeds it.* —Sheena

> *When people were trying to help they would tell me things like "You look bad." Maybe this is just my experience, but that's not going to help anybody. They're going to see that as a compliment.* [It] *made me feel like I needed to keep doing it. I'm like, "I must look good and they're just jealous."* —Melissa

Our findings largely support these worries. Although we cannot reduce anorexia to attention-getting—which is rarely if ever *the* motive—the fact that anorexia does get attention entangles everyone in discourses of virtue, appearance, and identity that feed the disease. The direct approach—talking about weight and food—unwittingly validates the anorexic's obsessions.

A further reason to doubt directness is that it attacks a symptom rather than the root cause. Natalie explains:

> *It's not that one thing* [anorexia] *that you have to fix—it's everything else. It's like, in order to stop doing heroin, it wasn't the heroin that I needed to attack. It was my feelings in general, my lifestyle. I needed to stop being scared. I needed to stop living in a dark hole. And it was kind of the same thing for this* [anorexia]. *I needed to be happy in order to stop doing this, but how do you tell someone to be happy?*

Act Indirectly. Some suggest indirection. Jim describes helping an anorexic runner:

> *I tried to indirectly talk to her about it. Just come up and reveal pieces of my personal history. I didn't want to come on too strong—one of the things that really repelled me. So I thought if I just got a word in there, it'd help her in the long-run. For me it was lots and lots of little pieces that came together. She got to the point where she got help.*

Jim coaxes awareness instead of confronting unreason. Saying "I've been there" builds rapport. Lindsay takes a similar strategy and, like Natalie, doubts the relevance of food and weight:

> [I'd say] *I know where your head is. I'd probably want to talk to them about them, and about how they were feeling. And not be like "Eat! Eat!" because it's not so much about that, usually, I think. Let them know that they're a really good person and that they don't have to be perfect and that they're beautiful and that everything is going to be fine.*

Overall the "how to help" answers make access key. They assume if you can reach the anorexic, the rest can be worked out. Reaching means overcoming resistance to recovery.

Resisting Recovery

Anorexics typically resist treatment. One reason is the stigma. Megan says, "*For a long time I was really embarrassed about anyone knowing I went to a psychologist.*" Janet describes being singled out: "*It was so horrible. Nobody else ever left campus. Except me. The only thing separating me was the fact that I was crazy.*" Clinicians can find themselves treating bright and determined adversaries whose "moral certitude" leads to "denial of illness, difficulty establishing trust, and lack of motivation to change" (Agras et al. 2004: 516). One reason is that anorexics are loath to lose what they have achieved (a slim body, a sense of accomplishment, collateral payoffs). Then, too, caregivers lack credibility: patients sense the experts misunderstand anorexia and anorexics. No one puts it that bluntly, but skepticism is palpable.

Some feel treatment means they have lost their minds. Molly cannot get over this: "*I know I'm not a crazy person. I know I'm not crazy*"—and refuses therapy. Indeed, restricted eating is often healthy, not crazy. Aware this is not odd, Jane wants less medicalizing: "*I don't like using the term disease. You don't want to be treated as if, like, there is something wrong with you. You want to be treated as if it's just a sickness.*" Francesca sees labeling's cost:

> *I felt slightly patronized when they called me "ill" and "diseased." I do realize that it's not healthy to be anorexic but I internalized that in a way that wasn't healthy at all. I could just blame it on the fact that I was diseased.* [That] *was not conducive to getting out of* [anorexia].

Having studied medical ethics, Francesca grasps how medicalizing can complicate rather than cure. She evokes youth's assertion of autonomy ("It's my life!") and dismissal of elders' overblown worries. That generational gap haunts the interviews. Indeed, adolescent identity and coming of age interfere with getting anorexics to commit to recovery.

Yet resistance is not inevitable. Consider Lynn's ambivalence when her mother intervenes: "*I didn't want to stop, really. I mean I did—kind of—because I really wanted to eat the chicken sandwich, but I didn't.*" Or how Lindsay also did and did not want to stop:

> *I didn't want her* [mother] *to know. I didn't want her to worry about me, you know? And I didn't want to stop, I guess. But basically at the time my mom said,*

"You want to see someone?"—I was really ready to not do that anymore. So I just was like, "Okay."

Their mixed emotions suggest Lynn and Lindsay could have gone either way, depending on the approach.

Earlier we heard our interviewees recommend indirection. Here is how this works with Lindsay:

My mom actually never said "I think you have an eating disorder." She's like, "I think you might need to talk to someone about some things you're going through." By then I was exhausted. I don't know if at the time I thought it was for an eating disorder. I thought it was Jason [ex-boyfriend].

The *"eating thing did come up with the therapist,"* and *"I started eating more and becoming less focused on that and more focused on myself, my happiness and health."* Reflecting on her therapy, she says,

The focus on weight needs to be, I think, the last thing. It has to be more distraction. Listen, you're not going to be starving yourself if you're really happy and if you're okay with yourself. So any kind of pressure of "You need to gain weight," I think, is a bad idea. If someone said "You have to eat this," I'd have been like, "Fuck you!," you know?

Knowingly or not, Lindsay's mother worked around her daughter's blindness. She did not talk weight and raise resistance. Elizabeth was less fortunate. Her mother got her to a therapist much as Lindsay's mom did—saying, in effect, "You've suffered a trauma"—but then the specialist talked weight right off. Feeling *"ambushed,"* Elizabeth walked out.

With or without resistance, how do actual recoveries unfold? Our interviewees describe three sorts: heroic, environmental, and interventional. Some stress one sort, others mix two or three. Actual recoveries likely mix modes. We label these cur*ing*, a process, rather than cures.

Heroic Curing

Wholehearted starving is a foolish but heroic act. Do anorexics harness that courage for recovery? Nearly every case taps heroic effort, but no one recovers by it alone. We found several scenarios.

Coming to Care. Recalling her recovery, Sarah says, *"I think I started it within myself, by myself, and just managed to work it out by myself—I don't think anyone else could've helped me."* Casting herself as the agent of her own recovery, she tells a tale of rugged individualism. No doubt most and perhaps all recovery takes some such heroic effort to overcome anorexia's momentum.

Heroic curing dismisses therapy. For Sarah, going to a nutritionist "*hurt, it felt so condescending,*" and counseling is useless:

> *They ask the same questions all the time and I never really feel like talking to them. That sounds bitter. They're nice people. I like my psychiatrist a lot. She's a nice lady, but I felt so put on when I'd go there and talk about nothing that really matters. It was more to make my parents feel better. I really hated bringing them into it. I love my parents. I hated to hurt them like that.*

How does the heroic individual turn anorexia around single-handedly? Is it, as Sarah says, "*just a matter of realizing what I was doing to myself*"? No; apparently it is also *feeling* how she is hurting others: hearing Sarah might be hospitalized, "*my mom started crying. It was so painful. That's when I tried to pull myself together for everyone else's sake.*" Is that emotional blackmail—what Sarah calls "*guilting me*"? Arguably Sarah's inward turn is incomplete—she is still accessible. Or perhaps her emotional side—her sympathetic sensibility—is rebelling against anorexia's executive self. Either way, by splitting a once unitary anorexic self, guilting initiates her recovery.

Using a Divided Self. Others attribute recovery to an already divided self: "*I had something in me that ultimately wanted to survive and be healthy*" (Susanna); "*There was a part of me that didn't really want to be doing this from the beginning*" (Lindsay); "*I didn't see it wrong in my eyes. Up front I didn't, but in the back of my mind I knew there was something not right*" (Becca). Jesse's resistance is constitutional: she always "*liked being happy,*" and anorexia makes her life "*this miserable obsession. I just got sick of it and didn't want to be unhappy.*" This other, older sense of self bootstraps her recovery.

Realizing It Is a Problem. Where some describe prior back-of-the-mind doubts, others depict a more unitary self that comes to realize the danger. Jim, for example, runs passionately until he starts passing out and realizes anorexia is "*negatively impacting performance.*" Earlier he shouted down his parents' worries, but now he listens. At the other extreme, Molly says, "*I don't know what triggered it, me getting better and actually making an effort.*" Even as she yields to parental pressure, she says, "*I'd put my defenses up.*" So deciding "*to get better was a very gradual process. It took three years.*"

Jim has a clear realization and Molly never does, but Beth falls in between. Instead of a divided self, she has awareness that comes and goes before it finally sticks. Sent to an eating disorders specialist, she pretends compliance—"*I played little games with him.*" Only later, as she starts college,

> *I slowly came round to where I realized I needed to take steps to fix this. I had these revelations a little bit along the way where I'd look at myself and say, "This is bad"*

and *"You're killing yourself,"* but while thinking all this, I didn't know how severe my problem was. It took me going home [from college] with a friend I'd just started dating and a comment he made about how *"You've just got to gain weight"* that scared me. And at that point, it was like, *"I want to change this right now."*

Jill describes step-like realizations. When her parents say *"I looked like I was from a concentration camp,"* she is untroubled. Then,

> I became good friends with a minister. I went to him and said, "I'm thinking about food all the time." He said, "You know, I think that's not the real issue." That was the first time I recognized there might be something else. During the next two years my sister and mom would give me articles on anorexia. I looked at them but wouldn't acknowledge anything. [Later] one of my closest friends from college days [and I] decided we'd take a trip across country. We started in Tennessee, Yellowstone, Glacier, all the way out to Seattle, down to California and Arizona. I had a wonderful time. She said to me at the end, "You're very difficult to travel with." I was completely oblivious. She said, "You know, if I woke up in the morning and thought, 'Wouldn't it be fun to have pancakes?' I knew that you were so rigid." Her parents were medical doctors and she said, "You know, you should talk to Dad when we get back." We ended up at her house in Kansas. That probably was the first time I said I may have this disease. He encouraged me to get help.

Her friend speaks about anorexia's social consequences, not weight. Reflecting on how she listened to a friend but not family, Jill observes: *"With my sister and my mother, I was more on the defense. When my friend had me talk with her father, it was more a relief."*

Bootstrapping Recovery. In describing her divided self, Jesse says, *"I just had to get sick of it enough"* to take the initial steps toward recovery. Once she decides to gain weight, *"eating became an exercise. It was very difficult to eat. I didn't want to but that part of myself that wanted to get better, wanted to be different, would take over and say, 'Ok, it's all right, you can eat this."* Apparently this reverses a unitary voice's seizure of the anorexic's consciousness. Amorn describes a technique to leverage that change.

> As a part of my therapy, we had a name for anorexia: The Negative Mind. That was a way to try and get me to see it as something separate from myself. I think I understood that but I still wasn't fully separate from it in consciousness.

Did that separate her from her anorexia enough for Amorn to bootstrap her recovery as an inpatient? She remembers the critical shift as a narrative and then a poem:

The first night I stopped purging, I tucked myself in my room. I surrounded myself with tokens of love from family and friends. Little unsuspected gifts, letters, and words became my shield. I broke the pattern of returning to my room and immediately purging by putting my headphones on and listening to a mixed tape my sister made, just for me. I changed into the pajamas my mom bought me, and scattered letters and postcards of love and support all around me. I held a teddy bear in my arms—a gift from my brother. And I let myself fall asleep. Falling asleep, I won. I resisted the urge. I broke the pattern with tokens of love.

From that point on, the positive choice became a little bit easier. My survivor voice gained just enough power through my victory that night to tip the scales towards recovery. Little by little, choice by choice, a thousand choices a day. One more bite when I could have left it on my plate, one less look in the mirror, one less sit-up. I could now see with clarity the positive voice and the eating disorder's negative voice inside me. Distinguishing the two brought an awareness that allowed me to choose the positive. Two positive choices, one negative; three positives, one negative; four positives, one negative. And the scales shifted. The positive gained more power than the negative for the first time in my whole illness. That was beginning the way back out.

Her step-by-step style of change echoes her gymnastics training and perhaps reverses how anorexia developed incrementally in the first place. In verse:

The Way Back Up

The way back up,
out of darkness,
I kept it down.
The first night voices tore at my insides to purge,
to get it out.
But I had my tools, my shield of Love surrounding me.
I had tokens to hold onto—
Letters and songs—words of Life and
Love flying through time and space,
Tokens of others' Belief in Me.
And a little tiny voice inside asking me to please just breathe, please just lie here and
 receive this shield of love.
The way back up,
I kept it down.
I fell asleep with my shield of love around me,
and woke up,
that little voice
a little bit stronger.

Environmental Curing

Anorexia is an island of restricted eating and rigorous exercise. What we call environmental curing counters that isolation in perhaps three ways: reconnecting the anorexic to a wider world, shifting the focus to other activities, and effecting a rite of passage.

Wider-World Curing. Earlier we heard how Elizabeth's anorexia takes off when the underwear-thief affair breaks up a romance and friendships. She is left with running, which takes over her life. Friends try to help.

> *I got tricked into going to a psychiatrist. Two best friends from boarding school came to visit and told my mom. They were like, "Listen! She has a real problem. She never eats." My mom was like, "I know. What am I supposed to do?" And they're like, "You need to get her help. We came here this weekend to tell you this." Of course I didn't know any of this. So, my mom's like, "Well, before you go to college, traumatic things happened in high school* [referring to the underwear thief] *and I think it's important to pack those up. I just want you to talk to this lady and get them all out." And I was like, "Okay, okay, if this will make you happy." And I went to the psychiatrist. I walk in and sit down and the first question the woman asks is how tall I am and how much I weigh. Obviously I realized it was an eating disorder specialist. I was very angry that I'd been ambushed. She was like, "This will only work if you want it to, and if you never want to come in here again, you don't have to." I was like, "Duh!" So that definitely was not what helped me.*

Refusing therapy, Elizabeth graduates and starts freshman year at Sewanee:

> *Southern girls—it really impresses me—I feel it's* [disordered eating] *much less of a problem here. I feel as if up North every girl has a problem with her weight. Coming here I really felt like it wasn't as big an issue. It made me feel abnormal. It wasn't okay. I remember girls used to come up to me and they'd be like, "Sweetie, I always see you running. You're not fat." I'm like, "It's a sport. I'm on the cross-country team." And they're like, "Oh, okay." They really were concerned. They thought I was this crazy girl. I think it took changing environments and maybe just maturing. It was my own self-healing. It just happened naturally.*

Suddenly Elizabeth's obsessive running stands out. We cannot say eating disorders are less common in the South, but a close-knit campus that values a well-rounded life did help Elizabeth normalize her lifestyle.

A radical change in surroundings also cures Natalie. Whereas Elizabeth is privileged, Natalie's family scrapes by. Ill, overworked, overwhelmed, and single, her mother is no help. Yet Natalie recovers by leaving ballet's *"culture of not eating*" to live with street people who savor every morsel—an environmental cure.

Activity-Shift Curing. Elizabeth and Natalie recover by living in a wider world. By contrast, Susanna and Sheena shuttle between activities, going from anorexia to less harmful involvements. Already a vegetarian, Sheena becomes anorexic and has been "*really going at it*" for perhaps two years when she refocuses on relationships. Easing up to get curvier, she spends long hours grooming, attending to fashion, makeup, and hair. After high school she starts college, where academic pressure brings anorexia back. Once again she gets out by getting into another activity—this time, fitness. She joins the campus dance team, where "*there was a lot more focus on being fit versus just being thin. We were always practicing in the gym. That kind of helped me shift from getting thin by restricting to getting thin by working out.*" Sheena repeatedly mentions focusing. Over five years her focus goes from restricting to grooming, back to restricting, and on to exercising. It changes as her environment changes.

Susanna stays within dance, but her attitude changes. Growing up she copies a famous anorexic ballerina. When she wins admission to a famous ballet school, her anorexia "*started to erode a bit.*" Later on at this school she takes another step back upon realizing that in modern dance she does not need to starve into a ballerina's body. "*I felt like in modern dance, and in making my own work, there was an opportunity for me to be myself.*" She leaves the school, moves to Toronto, and begins her career. Previously convinced her eating disorder "*was something I was going to carry the rest of my life,*" at twenty-five she discovers she is free of it.

> *About ten years ago I started working freelance and creating my own work—a really massive shift in my life. I moved out of being in a completely structured environment that I'd been in forever. I stopped dancing for a year because I was injured. I fell in love with a woman and ended up in a six-year relationship. And she wasn't involved in dance at all. I stepped back from the dance community altogether. And although it's been a hard road I've been making this shift, being more myself. Food is not an issue.*

Stepping back from dance—and perhaps getting away from other eating-disordered dancers—let Susanna put her life-defining activity in perspective. Like Sheena, she has made step-by-step transitions into healthier activities.

Rite of Passage Curing. Earlier we heard how Megan escapes anorexia only to become bulimic. Senior year she is "*completely unhappy again.*" This time, making "*a better choice,*" she hikes 500 miles on the Appalachian Trail and is cured by the experience—an unplanned rite of passage. Isabel's recovery is similar. We previously saw how her prior asceticism intensifies in a boarding school environment. What cures her is living abroad:

> On the summer abroad trip to Spain each person lives with a family for five weeks. My family didn't speak English at all and what they serve you have to eat and they're very strict. They yell at their children if they don't eat. They'd like scream. I went on the trip with about thirty-six people and we were all really close. We went to school and met up at little cafes and went shopping together. I just began to eat. I'd eat normally. Everyone noticed and they were just sort of applauding—"Gosh, you're eating now."

Megan and Isabel fall between activity-shift and wider-world curing. Like Sheena and Susanna, they get intensely engaged in another activity, but theirs is a one-time event, a temporary involvement. It does, however, transition them into a wider world, as Elizabeth's and Natalie's more generalized environmental curing does. Springing from an intense one-time event, such curing acts like a rite of passage.

Intervention Curing

We asked what interventions did and did not work. Some gave quite thoughtful answers, and everyone tried to sort out how they recovered. Of course patients and even clinicians cannot always know what works, and without medical records and better controls, neither can researchers. We cannot, then, evaluate treatments. What we can do, however, is convey how our informants remember feeling and reacting. Here intervention's major downside is resistance.

Developed Readiness. No interviewees enter therapy as readily as one might get treated for the flu, but Becca comes close after breaking down in a restaurant. She remembers, "*I sat down with my mom and we realized that there was something wrong, that we needed to go get some help.*" This sounds straightforward, and perhaps it was. In our reading, she got carried away by virtuous eating. It is apt then that what she recalls as effective therapy corrects her distorted view of food.

> I started going to a psychologist once a week. We would talk about my eating patterns and why I thought that way. Then I started going to two people. In the end they decided I should take an anti-depressant. So I started Paxil and going to a lady—I'm not sure what she was—I guess psychologist. I wasn't very comfortable with this lady. Sometimes she'd have my parents come in. One time my dad sat in and she somewhat blamed my eating problems on my dad. That wasn't the case at all!

Treatment exposes one's family to blame. Does that cause resistance? Becca continues:

> What really helped was my psychiatrist because she was so blunt. We're very different personalities. She'd be, "Well why did you think that way?"—questions that put me

> on the spot. And for some reason I loved the way she did it. But the psychologist—I don't know. What made it even harder was that she was a little pudgy.
> Also what helped was just my family and friends. They were so patient. The two people that helped the most were my mom and my best friend. They would listen to me. When I'd get anxious about food or something, we'd talk about, "Well, why are you anxious about this? You don't get fat from one meal." My faith also helped. Definitely my mom, my best friend and my faith are what helped bring me out of this darkness.

Liking one therapist or therapy but not another decides several stories. Francesca, for example, says one counselor "*I honestly feel saved my life*," whereas she feels "*patronized*" by clinicians who, thinking "*it could be fixed with chemicals*," undercut the will she needs to help herself.

Like Becca, Jesse was ready for help. She was exhausted—"*Just sick of not sleeping, being cold all the time. I had a headache all the time. I couldn't think. I was angry, you know. Miserable. Life sucked.*" At friends' urging she sees a high school counselor who gets her to talk to her parents and see the family doctor. Referred to an eating disorders clinic, she has second thoughts.

> I went to the initial visit, and they said "This is what the process is." Then I decided, "No, no, I don't want to do this." And then few months later went back. You went to group therapy and then family went to another group therapy at the same time. I had this big fear that people would laugh at me because they'd think that I was too fat to be an anorexic. That held me back initially, but there was no other way to go through this program. You just had to start up with group therapy. So I finally got up the nerve.

Developing Readiness. Whereas Becca and Jesse want therapy before it starts, Beth illustrates readiness developing along the way. Her father, a physician, refers her to an eating disorder specialist. She acts ready by not openly resisting therapy, but keeps her practices and uses tricks to make weight.

> I did what they told me to do but I manipulated it however I wanted. I knew exactly how to manipulate the scale and tell people exactly what they wanted to hear. So I played that game almost a year without knowing how bad shape I was really in.

Starting college, she visits Counseling Services "*a few times to see a psychologist. I was really good at shooting the bull with people. So I went in with her a couple times and really didn't talk about anything relevant to my problem.*" Then her parents call the school

> about getting somebody set up here to monitor me. First I was really upset, going on about "Why have you done this?" And then I kind of warmed up to the idea and thought, "Well maybe this will help me. This'll be fun. I'll give it a shot."

On her own, Beth went to counseling. Apparently she did not talk about her eating disorder, and the counselor respected that. In her story this sets the stage for progress.

> *And I slowly came round to where I realized I needed to fix this. I got back here and started seeing Alice* [campus nurse] *about once a week to get weighed and Dr. James once a week for counseling. I was still playing games,* [but] *being more open as far as counseling things go.*

Then, as we heard, a peer succeeds where family and professionals have not. His concern "*scared*" her, and she wants "*to change this right now.*" Re-interviewed two years later, she is graduating with honors and headed to medical school.

In our reading, the larger issue was her intense self-denying drive to achieve. If that is so, then the direct approach—stressing food and eating—was off target. It dealt only with symptoms; meanwhile, the general counseling she freely sought may have been pivotal.

Coercing Change. Although not ideal, coercion can also work. When Lynn's parents insist on watching her eat, she secretly resists ("*for a while I still threw up*") and then gives in ("*It was so much harder. They just paid attention so much it wasn't worth the trouble*"). Then, after they think she is well, she tries again, only to find her passion gone ("*I never could get back like it was*").

Where Lynn's mother stays cool ("*She definitely didn't cry—no emotion*"), Molly's gets emotional when her daughter resists:

> *She'd yell at me for not eating, for being anorexic. I'm sure she was so frustrated. We fought all the time. I'm stubborn too. Then the therapy—oof! That would make me not want to eat. I hated it! I don't know if it was her* [the therapist] *in particular. I was mad at my mom for making me go. I was not crazy. I knew I wasn't crazy. The therapist did not help. People forcing food on me—NO! I'd put my defenses up and be like, "Well, you're just jealous. I'm not going to do what you say because I'm eighteen!" Arguing was not good and therapy was not good.*

She was finally moved, she says, by threats (she could not play soccer or go away to college until she gained weight) combined with her mom's tears and parental distress ("*it was more like me seeing how upset my parents were rather than them telling me*"). Though Molly fights to keep her autonomy and resists her therapist ("*She'd ask me a question and I'd just cry*"), she gains weight to go to college and recovers ("*I like to eat now*").

Coercion also cured Amorn. This approach sometimes fails, but fifteen healthy years indicate she has recovered completely:

I don't know if I can really define what [therapies] *worked and what didn't. I see it all as a process. There wasn't one thing that I feel absolutely didn't work. I guess there's two stages in my recovery. My mom—my parents—intervened, and then my mom took over as my caretaker. But my anorexia continued beyond that, even when she was feeding me. We—my mother and I—were so close. She was my lifeline and it was really taking a toll on her. That didn't really work, although it probably kept me alive.*

After a good year of all of this, I ended up in the hospital for dehydration. I remember it was miserable. That whole week I hadn't eaten anything, put anything in my body, and I had stopped taking medicine—and I don't even know what medicines I was on because I wasn't in control. My parents were giving it to me. But I know there was one anti-anxiety medicine and I stopped taking that too. That was really tough. I'd have these—I wouldn't even call them temper tantrums—they were freak-outs. I'd be screaming for hours, rolling around on the ground, and I don't even know why. I just felt so much inside of me that felt so helpless and that had been going on for a long time. Sometimes those episodes would happen, two or three times a day.

So I got sent against my will to Renfrew and I spent three months in inpatient care. One of the biggest things is that you get the opportunity to change. You create a sick identity or an anorexic identity when you're at home. It's very important to be removed from that. At Renfrew we'd have about five groups a day. All kinds of different topics. We had a group called Experiential Group, where we'd do role-plays, which I found to be really helpful. And we also had individual therapy—three times a week—and a family therapy group.

We were each on our own meal plan. You'd look at the menu plan and write out what you wanted. It was very, very hard. I'd spend hours trying to work it out. You weren't required to eat all your food. People would sit at the tables with you and then when you were done, they'd evaluate how much you ate. There's no immediate consequences if you don't eat all of food. That [Renfrew] *was really the turning point for my anorexia.*

Coerced into treatment, Amorn remains healthy. A large U.K. survey found that half of those forced into treatment felt it turned out to be "a good thing" (Newton et al. 1993). In Norway, only 34 percent did (Rosenvinge and Klusmeier 2000).

Conclusion

Our informants were fortunate to recover. Many anorexics do not, perhaps because the "extremely limited amount of research . . . on effective treatments" (Agras et al. 2004: 519) slights "evidence of mating patients to treatments" as Vanderlinden (2010: 164) proposes. Then, too, anorexics resist treatment. Supposedly that is the nature of the disease; however, health care can evoke defiance when the patient becomes an object to treat, not a subject to engage. Listen to Sarah:

> *After our sessions, she* [her nutritionist] *would have a talk with my mom in the lobby in the health center. There was a big gym and you could go to a spa or get X-rays. It was a busy place, and it felt so rude to me that she would talk to my mom in the middle of the lobby. That just pissed me off. I'd have to be sitting there stoically. When she told my mom if I lost any more weight she was going to hospitalize me—she said that right in the lobby—there were people sitting, like, ten feet from us. It just felt like she had no tact.*

Many experts cannot grasp or simply reject the anorexic person's point of view. Then, as Peters (1995: 63) says, "the anorexic's experience is trivialised, as she is labelled mentally ill and deviant. Her self-control, willpower and determination, proof to her of her moral worth and strength of character, are redefined as willful, prideful, stubborn and intransigent behaviours." That evokes resistance.

These recoveries fit our earlier theories and findings. Getting out of anorexia, like getting in, involves complex feedback systems, not simple cause and effect. That justifies our holistic method and biocultural theory. Anorexia is closer to pond ecology than billiard-ball physics.

No one attributes recovery to conquering gender or media oppression—unsurprisingly, as no one gave those as primary causes anyway. Yet it is remarkable how far their experiences diverge from what outsiders expect.

Meanwhile, cures are just as diverse as the causes. Indeed, exactly as Vanderlinden (2010) proposes, the ways out suit the ways in:

- Standing Out: Megan recovers when she hikes the Appalachian Trail, a major accomplishment. A coming-of-age achievement succeeds where a talking cure fails.
- Fitting In: Susanna gets better when she stops trying to fit ballet and starts fitting into modern dance and her own creations. A healthier environment cures her when years of therapy did not.
- Dropping Out: Francesca sinks into anorexia, feeling her parents ignore her needs. She credits her turnaround to getting that attention from counselors and friends.
- Slipping In: Perfecting his running makes Jim anorexic. His turnaround comes from realizing anorexia hurts his running. As he says, performance "*both brought me into it and out of it.*"

Notes

1. A twenty-year longitudinal study found "adult roles such as marriage and parenthood were associated with significant decrease in disordered eating from late adolescence to midlife in women whereas few associations were observed in men" (Keel et al. 2007).

CHAPTER 14

Staying Out
Redoing Life

The object of healing is not elimination of a thing (an illness, a problem, a symptom, a disorder) but transformation of a person, a self that is a bodily being.
—Thomas J. Csordas, "Somatic Modes of Attention"

Knowing anorexia has changed them, our interviewees realize they cannot simply go back to being who they once were. Anorexia revealed a vulnerability that they now need to guard against. No one knows for sure what the misstep was. Hence their bind: to stay healthy they must change—but how? It is not like they are smokers cured of cancer, who know what to change and need only the will to do it. Far worse is that anorexics have abundant will—too much, in fact—but lack useful knowledge.

A culture's knowledge about an illness can be "a resource" to "guide the interpretation and reconstruction of past experience" (Garro 2000: 72). With cancer, it is effective: sufferers get a viable story and a supportive audience. With anorexia, it is a disaster: there is no workable story, no knowing audience—just stereotypes and stigma. What is offered—a useless nature-or-nurture template and an "etiology of blame" (Wax and Cassell 1990)—alienates most anorexics (Beresin et al. 1989: 114). All in all, today's culture is a liability, not a resource.

Yet on the other hand, our informants crafted their own strategies to stay well. None take the cultural prompts—neither media nor gender nor blame matters much. Instead of listening to outsiders, they listen to themselves and come up with healthy practices through trial and error. We will report these, weigh how and whether they work, and then theorize wellness. First, however, we take stock of the challenge.

Assessing the Challenge

The events in our chapter titles, "Getting Out" and "Staying Out," divide logically but not emotionally. Most sufferers come to treatment with mixed feelings and, contrary to tidy schematics, likely do so throughout therapy (Palmer 2006; Waller 2012). Moreover, once medically recovered, they must deal with damaged relationships, the stigma of mental illness, and old inclinations. All of this breeds ambivalence when they need confidence.

Yet there is reason for confidence. Our research says there need be no underlying problem, no fatal flaw or weakness. What happened might well be resolved by growing up. Here the willpower, achieving, physical courage, and social sensibility that brought the disorder on are all potential strengths in recovery and later life. A small qualitative study comparing recovered anorexics to controls found that the "pathologic behaviors of AN resolve into healthy and adaptive behaviors after recovery" (Dellava et al. 2011: 380). Similarly, a large-scale, quantitative life-course study of Swedish twins found that those diagnosed with anorexia "reported lower body mass index, greater physical activity, and better health satisfaction" than others. Apparently "symptoms that were pathologic during acute phases of AN . . . may resolve over time into healthy behaviors . . . that result in better weight control and self-rated health." Supporting their self-assessment, they did not seem to experience the gradual weight gain common in aging, and they had "reduced risk of certain cancers and . . . mortality due to diseases of the circulatory system" (Bulik et al. 2006).

What Works

Asked how they rebuilt healthy lives, our interviewees struck three themes: balance, reversal, and alternative activities. Molly mentions all three in a single statement. Asked what took anorexia's place, she says, "*I guess life in general—friends. And my boyfriend and I were able to work out more. I like triathlons. I can swim, bike and run now. And eating! I enjoy cooking.*" Her first thought, "*life in general,*" expresses balance; her next word, "*friends,*" reverses anorexia's isolation; and then her involvements—working out, triathlons, cooking—are healthy alternatives to anorexia's solitary ascetic activity.

Balance. Anorexia revolves tightly around food and exercise in an obsessive, imbalanced life. Recovery brings—or requires—greater balance. Sarah says, "*I got different friends and that helped a lot. They were so much more balanced and that helped me be more balanced.*" Balance is her watchword. What helps, she says, is

> *just having small amounts all throughout the day, snacking, trying to keep food in my system, trying to keep myself balanced. I think that helped a lot because that led to not*

having guilt about food and more a balanced lifestyle. I could have a big meal and not care.

She also drops anorexia's seriousness, giving up *"being over-dramatic all the time, taking myself far too seriously."* That also describes Jane's recovery:

First semester my roommate would always be like, "I don't know why you take things so seriously." Toward the end of the semester, she saw the transition in me, everyone saw the transition. They were like, "Oh my gosh, you changed so much!" "You don't take things so seriously anymore. You don't pay attention to little details that don't matter."

Jesse's shift also changes what really matters. Asked what replaced anorexia, she answers,

being kind to other people and other beings, and being, you know, a happy person, surrounding myself by people that I liked, things that I liked. That's a much better way to be. That's a better definition of a good person than just being thin.

For Melissa, balance inspires a love of nature:

I used to not even care [about nature] *at all. It was awful—nothing mattered except me. I'd go outside and think, "Why do people think this is pretty? Who cares?" Now, it's like—I don't know. It's replaced my spiritual thing, really. The way I used to connect with God was how I denied myself. Now I connect with God by nature.*

For Francesca, *"hiking and natural places* [have] *always been a joy."* Now this counterbalances her workaholic drive. She has *"reconditioned* [herself] *to take time out for myself and cultivate physical and emotional health outside of work."* Lindsay too now finds *"time for myself."*

Reversals. Whereas balance holds the middle against anorexia's one-sidedness, reversal strategies take the opposite side. One such strategy, staying close to others, counters anorexia's isolating inwardness. According to Janet, *"good stuff is staying busy, having friends, just anything that distracts you."* Megan elaborates:

I definitely know the situation that would be conducive to it coming back. For instance, dorm life is perfect for me. Living constantly with people is helpful. Everything is with your roommate and in the community you live with. That's really helpful for me. There's no chance for me to binge and purge. It doesn't fit into my life.

In keeping busy socially, Janet and Megan contrast with Francesca and Lindsay, who instead make time for themselves. No doubt solutions differ as personalities do, but it is worth noting that their eating disorders differed: whereas Francesca and Lindsay only restricted, Janet's and Megan's restricting took a binge-and-purge turn that keeping social now blocks.

Sarah's solution is reaching out, not social busyness:

> *If I see it coming back, I let my friends know. That way it's not just me—I can have some help and support. Not that my friends have to sit there and watch me—"C'mon now . . ."—but their presence is enough and I appreciate that. I remind myself what it was like and the hell I put my body through.*

Sarah starts with a social solution and ends with a mental one. That consciousness is another reversal strategy. In recognizing that anorexia is *"definitely a way of thinking," "a pattern of thought,"* she says, *"I can see it coming and I can now stop it. I can ration* [reason] *my way out of it."* Jesse expands on how she does that:

> *Any time I get the feeling I'm gaining weight—well it's helpful for me* [to take] *this logical look at where* [I am]. *"So you lose five pounds, you gain five, what fundamental difference is* [that] *going to make in your life? Are your parents going to love you more? Your friends? Are you going to be smarter?" So whenever I was getting upset or having those feelings I've done that. So far I've been successful.*

Does good reasoning counter bad? Or is Jesse trying to reason her way out of bad feelings? Either way, breaking out from the stream of events broadens her focus and imparts a more balanced view of life.

Janet's conscious strategy implicitly recognizes the solution is not just mental. She describes a daily activity (something done physically) that pits reason against the visceral:

> *It's got to be an active thing in your mind every day. When you wake up in the morning and you're getting dressed, you've got to look at yourself. First thought is going to be: "Gross!" But you've got to—it's like an affirmation. You have to tell yourself, "That's wrong." Logically I know I'm not fat. So I have to keep telling myself that, and keep saying, "This is normal, this is good. Normal is fine."*

Janet calls her strategy *"something you do for yourself."* Anorexia consisted in extreme self-denial, but its reversal nurtures the self. Francesca has a well worked-out practice:

> *I had a friend who, when I was in the hospital, would make me make lists of things that made me feel better. She'd be like, "You have to write down thirty-five different*

things, small or big, and you have to put it by your bed." To this day I have a list. That was a counteractive habit that got ingrained in me. Sometimes you just need to sit down and think about the positive stuff instead of getting completely swept away with everything else.

Alternative Activities. We do not have Francesca's list, but her examples of what works for her—photography, journaling, writing letters, sleeping, cooking—are all activities. That is, they are things to do. A third general strategy for staying out of anorexia is to engage in alternative activities. Mary explains the rationale:

You need something else to concentrate your energy. Like before, I focused on food and weight and my appearance. Then my boyfriend came along. I was focused more on him and the relationship and then school and all of that. So I shifted my focus. I had no time to go exercise.

Anorexics' capacity to get lost in activities makes choosing the right involvements especially important. For Megan, it is piano *"because I don't think of anything else when I'm doing it."* Surprisingly, two informants value intense workouts even though vigorous exercise was part of their anorexia. Sheena describes the shift: "[I] *discovered that it was really hard to keep up a strenuous workout if you didn't have any food. So the focus shifted to totally focusing on working out. That's been a huge factor in getting over it* [anorexia]." For Lindsay, the character of exercise has changed:

I started exercising to enjoy it and feel good afterwards, not like I was going to faint and die. For me running now is like sleep. I'm usually really busy and it's like my time for myself. It's when I think about stuff and try to work situations out.

Francesca, one of the few in our sample without athletic involvements (*"I don't really go to the gym. I hate gyms"*), nonetheless finds physical activity helpful:

I walk a lot. When the anxieties over tests come up, when I go on a walk, it realigns my brain. Bike rides also. Two summers ago, when I felt I was slipping into depression because my grandfather had just died, I went out on that bike and it wrenched me out of there really, really well. So I definitely look to physical activity to bolster me back to something better.

Evaluating What Works

In saying what works, our informants could be mistaken. It is guesswork—they have no way to control the variables or know if what works now may later prove harmful. Yet they are not naïve. Take Molly, whose disorder fed on exercise. Is her triathlon training like a recovered alcoholic's hanging out in bars? We think not. Her anorexia's adolescent issues (fitting in, fighting for autonomy) are resolved. True, training could still be a gateway, but if Molly's lifelong athleticism is part of her constitution, she could hardly be herself were she not pushed physically. Insofar as Molly needs and enjoys such challenges, staying healthy means finding healthy activities, not avoiding rigorous training altogether—or so we would say. That assessment is part Molly, part theory, part what the interviews suggest collectively.

Our informants' strategies typically make good biocultural sense in that they stress activities, not just words, and recognize how visceral and social one's health actually is. Sarah captures this when she says she lets her friends know and gets their support. They do not have to talk her out of anorexia—"*their presence is enough.*" In figuring out what works for her, she discovers that health is social, a larger principle that applies across cases.

More broadly, theory endorses our informants' three strategies. Seeking balance counters the perpetual betterment that feeds anorexia's perfectionism and relentless achieving. The more balanced people are, the more they appreciate diverse activities and heed their emotional and self-accepting sides instead of the self-critical executive. While balance opposes anorexia's one-sidedness, reversals like staying connected with friends block anorexia's specific bootstrapping steps. Lastly, alternative activities occupy constitutional inclinations that might otherwise host anorexia. Enjoyable activities that integrate mind and body—playing the piano, enjoying nature, taking walks—work against anorexia's mind-over-body battle. As simple pleasures that marry head and heart, they counter anorexia's puritanical self-denial.

Useful as theory is, what really recommends these solutions is their trial-and-error origins and the diverse sufferers' *independent* arrival at surprisingly similar answers. How did they do it? Clearly some were monitoring mindset and feelings: knowing that self-criticism and malaise incited anorexia, apparently they did whatever raised their mood and made them feel better about themselves.

Listening to feelings is not naïve. Arguably they are a surer barometer than consciousness. Self-critical thoughts may also be an early warning. Given how anorexia bootstraps itself into existence, negative thoughts and feelings are building blocks, not just symptoms. Staying healthy requires dispersal of negativity. People do not *have* anorexia, as if the disease would inevitably express itself one way or another. Rather, they *build* anorexia. The worst approach, then, would be to "tough it out" rather than act to make oneself feel better. Yet we cannot assume that recovered anorexics will act to make themselves happy. Beyond their bent for self-denial, life's choices often pit pursuit of happiness against self-improvement—the play-or-study tradeoff. It is no accident, then, that schooling incites our four relapses.

What Is Missing: Theorizing Wellness

What is missing from these strategies? What-works solutions are just what luck finds and intuition suspects. Though valuable, they are partial and particular. Going deeper requires a theory.

Bioculturalism. Bioculturalism sees each human as an irreducibly social being leading a highly historical life. While our sociality draws us into common values, our historicity makes each person thoroughly unique. Anorexia arises in this matrix, so staying well means understanding one's own biocultural dynamics. Today's ignorance, then, is stunning. Like anyone else, the anorexic person has a constitution but does not realize it, experiences sympathies but cannot explain them, embodies values but does not know them, and feels ascetic urgings but misses their meaning—all Cartesian blind spots.

Biocultural thinking instead requires embracing one's distinctive constitution. Like gender, one's constitution is an enduring but not all-determining fact of life that one can manage in all sorts of ways. So to stay healthy, what constitutional realities must recovered anorexics manage? Three stand out.

First, anorexia wears ruts that recovery does not remove. Take Beth and Mary: restricted eating begins the first bout; then schooling provokes a second. Or consider Francesca: depression initiates starving; then schooling triggers it again. In these instances, where the old pathway serves a new involvement, it is not enough to avoid past practices.

Second, anorexics' constitutionally sympathetic natures connect them closely to surroundings beyond their control. To stay healthy they must learn either to separate their feelings and values from difficult surroundings or to choose healthy environs instead.

Third, recovered anorexics must temper their disposition to performative, ascetic, and virtuous achieving. What sets off anorexia is less the ascetic involvement (exercising, restricting, healthy eating, studying) than pursuing the activity zealously and obsessively.

Managing these constitutional realities gets easier after adolescence. Then these liabilities can be assets. Take sympathy—it opens worlds that antipathy or apathy will never know. Similarly, performative, ascetic, or virtuous drives are how the successful often succeed. And the same capacity for intense involvement that may dispose a person to get lost in anorexia also characterizes happy, purposeful, productive people (Csikszentmihalyi 1990).

An Ecology of Mind. Where Descartes divorces the mind from its milieu, Bateson's ecology of mind weds the two. Mind is not just in the skull or our bodies but is woven into our environs as well. Caught up in an array of feedback loops, human consciousness participates in its surroundings. Incarnating local values as anorexics do is thus perfectly natural. What is pathological, Bateson (2000: 315) would say, is isolating one value to rule the rest—"no part of such an internally interactive system can have unilateral control over the remainder." That pinpoints how the executive self, in asserting total control, pits the anorexic against nature.

Bateson applies his theory to alcoholism. Like an anorexic, an alcoholic separates the mind from its surroundings to let one part, the will, rule over the rest. If your will is strong enough, the thinking goes, you can resist drink. This attitude—dividing "conscious will, or 'self,' [from] the remainder of the personality"—is "an unusually disastrous variant of... Cartesian dualism" (Bateson 2000: 313)—disastrous, because dividing oneself up this way provokes an inner battle that escalates like an arms race: neither side can finally win. An anorexic who stays strong kills the body. But if the will breaks, the anorexic binges into bulimia the way an alcoholic goes on a drunk. Drinking or starving, all such inner games are doomed to violate the natural interdependence of mind with body and all its surroundings.

What is the alternative? Bateson analyzes how Alcoholics Anonymous (AA) defuses the inner competition. In accepting that "there is a power greater than the self," alcoholics rightly recognize an ecological truth about their interdependence with the world. Dethroning the prideful self ends the inner war. Moreover, in supporting each other, AA members build complementary relationships. Noncompetitive relations with others are a model for acting noncompetitively toward oneself.

Could AA principles humble anorexia? They already have: Jill found twelve-step organizations like AA helped; and outside our sample, one Sewanee grad says attending AA to support a loved one cured her anorexia. AA and Bateson's ecology both fit comfortably with biocultural holism. We think AA would not just restore sympathy with one's surroundings: the anorexic's mirroring sensibility suggests that AA's *inter*personal cooperation would also displace an *intra*personal eating struggle. The more a person's inner facets cooperate, the less eating incarnates virtue and the more it respects hunger, pleasure, sociability, and custom.

Spirituality. Garrett's (1998) study of thirty-four Australian anorexics concludes that anorexia is a "distorted spirituality" and recovery completes a rite of passage into a fuller life. However, our sample rejected these phrases. Interviewees did not connect anorexia with spirituality, distorted or otherwise, and a few found the link disturbing. Asked if the two were related, Megan replied, "*I really hope not!*" She valued her spirituality but called anorexia an "*obsession*," rejecting Garrett's fuller-life argument categorically. Did Garrett get anorexia wrong? In her usage, spirituality has a New Age air that reflects its day and perhaps her way of recruiting and interviewing participants. Apparently spirituality's antimodernism captured how her informants broke with anorexia's modernist demand for unending improvement. Our group broke with that same discourse but had no ideological counterculture to validate this opposition. In itself this suggests contrasting recovery styles—the ideological shift Garrett describes, versus and the piecemeal rearranging we found. Our informants had no prepackaged alternative to the modern values and practices that had ensnared them. Getting out left them no place in particular.

Such differences aside, the realities of recovery appear similar. Garrett (1998: 98–99) found the recovered had a new, "three-fold sense of connection." One sense was internal: connecting with oneself meant linking one's many sides "in contrast with the . . . 'split' self during the anorexic period." A second sense was social: developing "personal . . . relationships and also a sense of community." And the third was natural: reconnecting with one's own body "was often experienced as a rediscovery of and participation in nature." All three elements appear in our sample, though not in every case. A fourth element that Garrett found "threaded through the other three" was also "the most controversial—an *awareness of a greater power* than the self" [emphasis in original]. We did not find this, but our protocol did not look for it; anyway, most of our interviewees were religious before anorexia and took such a power for granted.

Overall Garrett systematizes the ideas scattered through our interviews. What we characterize as balance covers Garrett's three sorts of connectedness. Her account also aligns exactly with Bateson's theory: to cure a pathology that wrongly denies connectedness, you reconnect; and putting the anorexic self under a higher power is one way to make that change.

Conclusion

Health, the mantra goes, is an individual responsibility. That axiom misleads. To be sure, staying healthy takes individual initiative. Yet few know the more troubling truth that individualizing health cloaks: our personal well-being rests with others. Humans are social creatures. Our species evolved, develops, and lives in groups. Therefore our health and health-seeking stay close to what our community supports.

What happens when our surroundings are unhealthy? People who have had anorexia face a daily dilemma: they must live within, but not as, a society that still celebrates anorexia's gateways, stigmatizes sufferers, and casts blame loosely. Unlike alcoholics, who can swear off drink, anorexia's escapees cannot deny the virtues that fed their vice. They can, however, hold their old values with new moderation.

To stay well, the eating disordered need to dig beneath the modern mindset. We live in a day that trades in blame but not history. So accidents, much like good intentions gone wrong, carry no weight. Happily, our interviewees are wise enough to avoid recriminations and get on with their lives. Although no one's story simplifies to "only an accident," that is how most recoveries treat anorexia. Our research shows this to be not just emotionally wise but empirically likely. Anorexia is often an accident of adolescence.

Conclusion

Anorexia has many solutions, not one single cure. As we have seen, different approaches work for different people. What is needed, then, is not one pat recipe nor even a dozen. What curing requires is for everyone—sufferer, clinician, loved ones—to understand anorexia's fundamentals well enough to negotiate and renegotiate recovery's involvements. Unlike a disease that biomedicine can vanquish, escaping anorexia's misdirected development requires individualized redevelopment. There is no shortcut, no checklist, but only building healthier involvements. That is no magic bullet, but it is realistic and hopeful.

Negotiating Redevelopment

The NIH workshop mentioned earlier (Agras et al. 2004) is more pessimistic: no treatment works well, and nothing works for sure. Yet it sought a single cure for a single disease—an apt approach for, say, measles, but not for the anorexia we found. The diversity we have documented says that different people with different problems respond to different cures (Vanderlinden 2010). The NIH report, in its one-disease, one-cure thinking, misses this promising possibility.

Is anorexia a disease? That label does and does not fit. To fight cancer, physician and patient ally to vanquish the intruder and restore health. In anorexia, however, patient and pathology all too often ally against physician and treatment, because the syndrome, once established, can pay off practically, emotionally, expressively, or morally. Abruptly eliminating all that would leave a gaping hole. That is no ordinary disease.

Anorexia is less a disease than a way an activity misdirects development. It is built bioculturally over time, just as person and constitution take shape in growing up. As a historical reality, it is emergent—it does not reduce to the biology, culture, and chance that created it. Quite the contrary, this mis-development has an integrity—a resilient life—that strongly resists the reconfiguration of self in healthier ways. Arguably this also characterizes other eating disorders as well as alcoholism, addiction, obsessive-compulsive disorder, and attention deficit hyperactivity disorder. All, it would seem, are bioculturally built mis-developments that misuse our highly evolved human capacity to embody our practices. *Homo sapiens*'s premier adaptation, culture, thus opens us to some tenacious maladaptations.

Mis-development frustrates health care. One reason is epistemological: medicine that divides mind from body finds biocultural hybrids untreatable. Another reason is the way institutions seek to relive their triumphs. Once, in battling infectious disease, biomedicine's single-answer breakthroughs (sanitation, immunization, antiseptics) earned dramatic results and strong social backing. Those glory days are gone. Today's advances are percentage gains, not leaps forward; and today's targets—unhealthy lifestyles—talk back. Anorexia epitomizes the new day.

Tempering Medicalization

Our era makes medicine a cure-all. The public expects health care to solve problems far beyond its effective means and epistemic reach. And like other modern institutions (e.g., law, education, government), medicine can overreach when it should demur. So instead of sticking to what it does well, medicine tackles social, moral, and developmental problems that health care has little means to solve (Nye 2003)—witness anorexia.

Medical intervention saved O'Connor's daughter when nothing else would, but aggressive treatment carries four clear costs. First, intervening can evoke resistance that strengthens the syndrome (chapter 13). Second, medicalizing can breed helplessness, taking control away from the patient, family, and friends (Whitney et al. 2005). Third, a label can be self-fulfilling, encouraging anorexics to live up to popular clichés and clinical criteria (Rich et al. 2004; Vandereycken 2011; Warin 2003b: 113).[1] Fourth, positing a prior trauma sows suspicion, guilt, and blame that can harm patients and their families (Vander Ven and Vander Ven 2003; Whitney et al. 2005).

Weighing these costs is complicated when institutions become trapped in their organizing metaphors and founding assumptions. Medicine's value neutrality, for instance, may not be possible with value-based afflictions like anorexia. Or consider the military metaphor. At least since germ theory emerged, physicians have battled disease as an invading enemy, an analogy that gives physicians command, expects patients to take orders like good soldiers, and urges heroics on everyone. It is effective for some diseases, but it is wrong for anorexia. Some sufferers describe "Ana" as a friend, and the syndrome mixes good with bad. Attacking both in the same way misdirects therapy, discredits the therapist, and squanders an opportunity to disentangle the two.

Normalizing Anorexia

Seeing anorexia as mis-development normalizes it. That does not make the syndrome any less serious—indeed, no mental illness is deadlier (Bulik et al. 2006). Yet it does call for a more moderate response than all-out war, not just because confrontation fails but because negotiating can succeed. To deescalate, consider the following:

- Anorexia can be a vehicle for coming of age. Risk-taking and lifestyle experiments are how many youth grow into adults.
- Elementary anorexia does not point to a serious prior pathology. No doubt some deeply troubled people express their distress through compound anorexia, but essentially the same anorexic syndrome develops in otherwise healthy people who previously led happy, successful lives.
- Anorexia can have relatively trivial origins. Although a serious disease suggests a serious cause, sometimes relatively minor decisions cascade into anorexia.
- Asceticism is not abnormal. To the contrary, it is how many healthy, successful people regulate their lives.
- In anorexia, an activity takes over a person's life. That is not inherently abnormal—it happens quite commonly in sports and work, where it characterizes how many healthy people succeed.
- Like any intensely involving practice, anorexia's bodily momentum frustrates conscious control. In itself that is not a pathology—it is how normal humans live embodied lives.
- Anorexics embody some of today's highest values (achieving, self-denial, self-improvement, autonomy, determination, courage)—all strengths for recovery.

In sum, the character of anorexia does not justify everything the label "disease" evokes. Yet the larger point is not to debate labels but to shed baggage that impedes recovery. Here, normalizing could help.

- Seeing anorexia realistically relieves needless fears, guilt, and blame. Even if some cases are blameworthy, many others are accidents.
- Normalizing anorexia empowers sufferers to participate actively in their own recovery. What they have built they can rebuild.
- Seeing the normalcy within the syndrome helps sufferers redirect their ascetically inclined constitutions into healthier activities.

Unexplained and uncured, anorexia demoralizes health-care professionals by expecting them to cure what biomedicine cannot handle—at present. But like the science at its core, medicine regularly remakes itself. To effect change, everyone—anorexics, their loved ones, medical professionals—could begin by applying the lessons our informants so carefully and graciously taught us.

Notes

1. When the once obscure disease anorexia became widely known, Bruch (1985: 11) found the clinical picture changed, and "several patients deliberately 'tried it out.'" A study of drug- and alcohol-dependent people who cured themselves found refusing the label "addict" or "alcoholic" was key to their success (Granfield and Cloud 1999).

References

Agras, W. Stewart, Harry A. Brandt, Cynthia M. Bulik, Regina Dolan-Sewell, Christopher G. Fairburn, Katherine A. Halmi, David B. Herzog, David C. Jimerson, Allan S. Kaplan, Walter H. Kaye, Daniel le Grange, James Lock, James E. Mitchell, Matthew V. Rodorfer, Linda L. Street, Ruth Striegel-Moore, Kelly M. Vitousek, B. Timothy Walsh, and Denise E. Wilfley. 2004. "Report of the National Institutes of Health Workshop on Overcoming Barriers to Treatment Research in Anorexia Nervosa." *International Journal of Eating Disorders* 35: 509–521.

Aharoni, Ruth, and Marianne M. Hertz. 2012. "Disgust Sensitivity and Anorexia Nervosa." *European Eating Disorders Review* 20: 106–110.

Allegre, P. M. 1955. "Tentative Conclusions." In *Christian Asceticism and Modern Man*. Translated by Walter Mitchell and the Carisbrooke Dominicans, 253–262. London: Blackfriars.

American Psychiatric Association. 1994, *Diagnostic and Statistical Manual of Mental Disorders*. 4th edition. Washington, DC: American Psychiatric Association.

Anderson, Benedict. 1998. *The Spectre of Comparisons: Nationalism, Southeast Asia and the World*. London: Verso.

Armstrong, Este. 1999. "Making Symbols Meaningful: Human Emotions and the Limbic System." In *Biocultural Approaches to the Emotions*, ed. A. L. Hinton, 256–273. New York: Cambridge University Press.

Auerbach, Erich. 1968. *Mimesis: The Representation of Reality in Western Literature*. Translated by Willard R. Trask. Princeton, NJ: Princeton University Press.

Austrian, Sonia G. 2002. "Adolescence." In *Developmental Theories through the Life Cycle*, ed. Sonia G. Austrian, 123–180. New York: Columbia University Press.

Bakhtin, Mikhail. 1968. *Rabelais and His World*. Cambridge, MA: MIT Press.

Banks, Caroline Giles. 1992. "'Culture' in Culture-Bound Syndromes: The Case of Anorexia Nervosa." *Social Science Medicine* 34 (8): 867–884.

———. 1996. "'There Is No Fat in Heaven': Religious Asceticism and the Meaning of Anorexia Nervosa." *Ethos* 24 (1): 107–135.

———. 1997. "The Imaginative Use of Religious Symbols in Subjective Experiences of Anorexia Nervosa." *Psychoanalytic Review* 84 (2): 227–236.

Barkan, Leonard. 1975. *Nature's Work of Art: The Human Body as an Image of the World*. New Haven, CT: Yale University Press.

Bateson, Gregory. 2000. *Steps to an Ecology of Mind*. Chicago: University of Chicago Press.

Bauman, Zygmunt. 1991. *Modernity and Ambivalence*. Ithaca, NY: Cornell University Press.
———. 1997. *Postmodernity and Its Discontents*. New York: New York University Press.
Baumeister, Roy F. 1997. "The Self and Society: Changes, Problems, and Opportunities." In *Self and Identity: Fundamental Issues*, ed. R. D. Ashmore and L. Jussim, 191–217. New York: Oxford University Press.
Baxter, Helen. 2001. "Religion and Eating Disorders." *European Eating Disorders Review* 9: 137–139.
Beausoleil, Natalie. 1994. "Makeup in Everyday Life: An Inquiry into the Practices of Urban American Women of Diverse Backgrounds." In *Many Mirrors: Body Image and Social Relations*, ed. Nicole Sault, 33–57. New Brunswick, NJ: Rutgers University Press.
Becker, Anne E. 1995. *Body, Self and Society: The View from Fiji*. Philadelphia: University of Pennsylvania Press.
———. 2007. "Culture and Eating Disorders Classification." *International Journal of Eating Disorders* 40: S111–S116.
Becker, Anne E., Pamela Keel, Eileen P. Anderson-Fye, and Jennifer J. Thomas. 2004. "Genes and/or Jeans? Genetic and Socio-Cultural Contributions to Risk for Eating Disorders." *Journal of Addictive Diseases* 23 (3): 81–103.
Becker, Anne E., Jennifer J. Thomas, and Kathleen M. Pike. 2009. "Should Non-Fat-Phobia Anorexia Nervosa Be Included in DSM-V?" *International Journal of Eating Disorders* 42 (7): 620–635.
Becker, Gay. 1997. *Disrupted Lives: How People Create Meaning in a Chaotic World*. Berkeley: University of California Press.
Becker, Marshall H. 1986. "The Tyranny of Health Promotion." *Public Health Review* 14: 15–25.
Bellah, Robert N., Richard Madsen, William M. Sullivan, Ann Swidler, and Steven M. Tipton. 1985. *Habits of the Heart: Individualism and Commitment in American Life*. Berkeley: University of California Press.
Beresin, Eugene V., Christopher Gordon, and David B. Herzog. 1989. "The Process of Recovering from Anorexia Nervosa." *Journal of the American Academy of Psychoanalysis* 17 (1): 103–130.
Bledstein, Burton J. 1976. *The Culture of Professionalism: The Middle Class and the Development of Higher Education in America*. New York: W. W. Norton.
Blonder, Lee Xanakis. 1999. "Brain and Emotion Relations in Culturally Diverse Populations." In *Biocultural Approaches to the Emotions*, ed. A. L. Hinton, 274–296. New York: Cambridge University Press.
Bolster, David, and Anna de Lange. 2002. *Fasting: A Fresh Look at an Old Discipline*. Cambridge: Grove Books Limited.
Bordo, Susan. 1997. "Anorexia Nervosa: Psychopathology as the Crystallization of Culture." In *Food and Culture, A Reader*, ed. Carole Counihan and Penny Van Esterik, 226–250. New York: Routledge.
Bourdieu, Pierre. 1990. *The Logic of Practice*. Translated by Richard Nice. Stanford, CA: Stanford University Press.
Bratman, Steven. 2000. *Health Food Junkies: Overcoming the Obsession with Healthful Eating*. New York: Broadway Books.

Braun, Devra L., Suzanne R. Sunday, Amy Huang, and Katherine A. Halmi. 1999. "More Males Seek Treatment for Eating Disorders." *International Journal of Eating Disorders* 25: 415–424.

Brennan, Teresa. 2004. *The Transmission of Affect*. Ithaca: Cornell University Press.

Bronson, Martha B. 2000. *Self-Regulation in Early Childhood: Nature and Nurture*. New York: Guilford Press.

Bruch, Hilde. 1962. "Perceptual and Conceptual Disturbances in Anorexia Nervosa." *Psychosomatic Medicine* 24 (2): 187–194.

———. 1979. *The Golden Cage: The Enigma of Anorexia*. New York: Vintage Books.

———. 1985. "Four Decades of Eating Disorders" In *Handbook for the Psychotherapy of Anorexia Nervosa and Bulimia*, ed. D. M. Garner and P. E. Garfinkel, 7–18. New York: Guilford Press.

Brumberg, Joan Jacobs. 1997. *The Body Project: An Intimate History of American Girls*. New York: Random House.

———. 2000. *Fasting Girls: The History of Anorexia Nervosa*. Revised edition. New York: Vintage Books.

Budd, Michael Anton. 1997. *The Sculpture Machine: Physical Culture and Body Politics in the Age of Empire*. New York: New York University Press.

Bulik, Cynthia M., Patrick F. Sullivan, Federica Tozzi, Helena Furberg, Paul Lichtenstein, and Nancy L. Pedersen. 2006. "Prevalence, Heritability and Prospective Risk Factors for Anorexia Nervosa." *Archives of General Psychiatry* 63: 303–312.

Bushell, William C. 1995. "Psychophysiological and Comparative Analysis of Ascetico-Meditational Discipline: Toward a New Theory of Asceticism." In *Asceticism*, ed. Vincent L. Wimbush and Richard Valantasis, 553–575. New York: Oxford University Press.

Bynum, Caroline Walker. 1987. *Holy Feast and Holy Fast: The Religious Significance of Food to Medieval Women*. Berkeley: University of California Press.

Campbell, Colin. 1987. *The Romantic Ethic and the Spirit of Consumerism*. New York: Basil Blackwell.

Campbella, Iain C., Jonathan Mill, Rudolf Uher, and Ulrike Schmidt. 2011. "Eating Disorders, Gene-Environment Interactions and Epigenetics." *Neuroscience and Biobehavioral Reviews* 35: 784–793.

Carrither, Michael. 1996. "Person." In *Encyclopedia of Social and Cultural Anthropology*, ed. Alan Barnard and Jonathan Spencer. London: Routledge.

Carter, Frances A., Jennifer Jordan, Virginia V.W. McIntosh, Suzanne E. Luty, Janice M. McKenzie, Christopher M.A. Frampton, Cynthia M. Bulik, and Peter R. Joyce. 2011. "The Long-Term Efficacy of Three Psychotherapies for Anorexia Nervosa: A Randomized, Controlled Trial." *International Journal of Eating Disorders* 44: 647–654.

Casper, Regina C. 1990. "Personality Features of Women with Good Outcome from Restricting Anorexia Nervosa." *Psychosomatic Medicine* 52 (1): 56–170.

Cassell, Joan. 1991. *Expected Miracles: Surgeons at Work*. Philadelphia: Temple University Press.

Chambliss, Daniel F. 1988. *Champions: The Making of Olympic Swimmers*. New York: William Morrow.

Clark, Candace. 1997. *Misery and Company: Sympathy in Everyday Life*. Chicago: University of Chicago Press.

Clarke, T. K., A. R. D. Weiss, and W. H. Berrettini. 2012. "The Genetics of Anorexia Nervosa." *Clinical Pharmacology and Therapeutics* 91 (2): 181–188.
Claude-Pierre, Peggy. 1997. *The Secret Language of Eating Disorders: The Revolutionary New Approach to Understanding and Curing Anorexia and Bulimia.* New York: Random House.
Clinton, David. 2010. "Towards an Ecology of Eating Disorders: Creating Sustainability through the Integration of Scientific Research and Clinical Practice." *European Eating Disorders Review* 18: 1–9.
Cognet, L. 1955. "Christian Asceticism in France from the XVIth Century to the XVIIIth Century." In *Christian Asceticism and Modern Man*. Translated by Walter Mitchell and the Carisbrooke Dominicans, 51–70. London: Blackfriars.
Coles, Robert. 1989. *The Call of Stories: Teaching and the Moral Imagination.* Boston, MA: Houghton Mifflin.
Collier, D. A., and J. L. Treasure. 2004. "The Aetiology of Eating Disorders." *British Journal of Psychiatry* 285: 363–365.
Colton, Anna, and Nancy Pistrang. 2004. "Adolescents' Experiences of Inpatient Treatment for Anorexia Nervosa." *European Eating Disorders Review* 12: 307–316.
Counihan, Carole. 1999. *The Anthropology of Food and Body: Gender, Meaning, and Power.* New York: Routledge.
Crago, Marjorie, and Catherine M. Shisslak. 2003. "Ethnic Differences in Dieting, Binge Eating and Purging Behaviors Among American Females: A Review." *Eating Disorders* 11: 289–304.
Crane, Diana. 2000. *Fashion and Its Social Agendas: Class, Gender, and Identity in Clothing.* Chicago: University of Chicago Press.
Csikszentmihalyi, Mihaly. 1990. *Flow: The Psychology of Optimal Experience.* New York: Harper and Row.
Csikszentmihalyi, Mihaly, and Reed Larson. 1984. *Being Adolescent: Conflict and Growth in the Teenage Years.* New York: Basic Books.
Csikszentmihalyi, Mihaly, and Eugene Rochberg-Halton. 1981. *The Meaning of Things: Domestic Symbols and the Self.* Cambridge: Cambridge University Press.
Csordas, Thomas J. 1993. "Somatic Modes of Attention." *Cultural Anthropology* 8 (2): 135–156.
———. 1994. *The Sacred Self: A Cultural Phenomenology of Charismatic Healing.* Berkeley: University of California Press.
Damasio, Antonio R. 1994. *Descartes' Error: Emotion, Reason, and the Human Brain.* New York: Penguin Books.
Danziger Kurt. 1997. "The Historical Formation of Selves." In *Self and Identity: Fundamental Issues*, ed. R. D. Ashmore and L. Jussim, 137–159. New York: Oxford University Press.
Darcy, Alison M., Angela Celio Doyle, James Lock, Rebecka Peebles, Peter Doyle, and Daniel Le Grange. 2012. "The Eating Disorders Examination in Adolescent Males with Anorexia Nervosa: How Does It Compare to Adolescent Females?" *International Journal of Eating Disorders* 45 (1): 110–114.
Davies, Helen, Ulrike Schmidt, Daniel Stahl, and Kate Tchanturia. 2011. "Evoked Facial Emotional Expression and Emotional Experience in People with Anorexia Nervosa." *International Journal of Eating Disorders* 44 (6): 531–539.

Davis, Caroline. 1997. "Eating Disorders and Hyperactivity: A Psychobiological Perspective." *Canadian Journal of Psychiatry* 42 (2): 168–174.
Davis, Caroline, and Gordon Claridge. 1998. "The Eating Disorders as Addiction: A Psychobiological Perspective." *Addictive Behaviors* 23 (4): 463–475.
Dellava, Jocilyn E., Robert M. Hamer, Akansha Kanodia, Mae Lynn Reyes-Rodriquez, and Cynthia M. Bulik. 2011. "Diet and Physical Activity in Women Recovered from Anorexia Nervosa: A Pilot Study." *International Journal of Eating Disorders* 44 (4): 376–382.
D'Emilio, John, and Estelle B. Freedman. 1997. *Intimate Matters: A History of Sexuality in America*. 2nd edition. Chicago: University of Chicago Press.
de Waal, Frans. 2001. *The Ape and the Sushi Master: Cultural Reflections by a Primatologist*. New York: Basic Books.
Dias, Karen. 2003. "The Ana Sanctuary: Women's Pro-anorexia Narratives in Cyberspace." *Journal of International Women's Studies* 4 (2): 31–45.
Douglas, Ann. 1977. *The Feminization of American Culture*. New York: Avon Books.
Douglas, Mary. 1973. *Natural Symbols: Explorations in Cosmology*. New York: Vintage Books.
Dugan, Kathleen M. 1995. "Fasting for Life: The Place of Fasting in the Christian Tradition." *Journal of the Academy Religion* 63 (3): 539–548.
Dumont, Louis. 1970. "Religion, Politics and Society in the Individualistic Universe." The Henry Myers Lecture. *Proceedings of the Royal Anthropological Institute* no. 1970: 31–41.
———. 1986. *Essays on Individualism: Modern Ideology in Anthropological Perspective*. Chicago: University of Chicago Press.
Durrenberger, E. Paul. 1996. "Economic Anthropology." In *Encyclopedia of Cultural Anthropology*, ed. David Levinson and Melvin Ember, 365–371. New York: Henry Holt.
Dyreson, Mark. 1997. "Regulating the Body and the Body Politic: American Sport, Bourgeois Culture, and the Language of Progress, 1880–1920." In *The New American Sport History: Recent Approaches and Perspectives*, ed. S. W. Pope, 121–144. Urbana: University of Illinois Press.
Eckert, Penelope. 1989. *Jocks and Burnouts: Social Categories and Identity in the High School*. New York: Teachers College Press.
Ehrenreich, Barbara. 1989. *Fear of Falling: The Inner Life of the Middle Class*. New York: Pantheon Books.
Erikson, Erik H. 1964. *Insight and Responsibility: Lectures on the Ethical Implications of Psychoanalytic Insight*. New York: W. W. Norton and Co.
———. 1971. "Youth and the Life Cycle." In *Adolescent Behavior and Society: A Book of Readings*, ed. R. E. Muuss, 253–264. New York: Random House.
Fairburn, C. G., Z. Cooper, H. A. Doll, and S. L. Welch. 1999. "Risk Factors for Anorexia Nervosa: Three Integrated Case-control Comparisons." *Archive of General Psychiatry* 56: 468–476.
Falk, Pasi. 1994. *The Consuming Body*. London: Sage.
Feingold, Alan, and Ronald Mazzella. 1998. "Gender Differences in Body Image Are Increasing." *Psychological Science* 9 (3): 190–195.
Field, Tiffany. 2001. *Touch*. Cambridge, MA: MIT Press.
Flood, Gavin. 2004. *The Ascetic Self: Subjectivity, Memory and Tradition*. Cambridge: Cambridge University Press.

Foucault, Michel. 1970. *The Order of Things: An Archaeology of the Human Sciences*. New York: Vintage Books.
———. 1990. *The Use of Pleasure: The History of Sexuality*, vol. 2. New York: Vintage Books.
Frank, Arthur W. 1995. *The Wounded Storyteller: Body, Illness and Ethics*. Chicago: University of Chicago.
Frank, Geyla. 1979. "Finding the Common Denominator: A Phenomenological Critique of Life History Method." *Ethos* 7 (1): 68–94.
Gabaccia, Donna R. 1998. *We Are What We Eat: Ethnic Food and the Making of Americans*. Cambridge, MA: Harvard University Press.
Garner, David M. 1997. "Psychoeducational Principles in Treatment." In *Handbook of Treatment for Eating Disorder*, ed. D. M. Garner and P. E. Garfinkel, 145–177. 2nd edition. New York: Guilford Press.
Garrett, Catherine. 1998. *Beyond Anorexia: Narrative, Spirituality and Recovery*. Cambridge: Cambridge University Press.
Garro, Linda C. 2000. "Cultural Knowledge as Resource in Illness Narratives: Remembering through Accounts of Illness." In *Narrative and the Cultural Construction of Illness and Healing*, ed. Cheryl Mattingly and Linda C. Garro, 70–87. Berkeley: University of California Press.
Garro, Linda C., and Cheryl Mattingly. 2000. "Narrative as Construct and Construction." In *Narrative and the Cultural Construction of Illness and Healing*, ed. Cheryl Mattingly and Linda C. Garro, 1–49. Berkeley: University of California Press.
Geertz, Clifford. 1973. *The Interpretation of Cultures: Selected Essays*. New York: Basic Books.
———. 1997. "Learning with Bruner." *New York Review of Books* 44 (6): 23.
———. 2000. *Available Light: Anthropological Reflections on Philosophical Topics*. Princeton, NJ: Princeton University Press.
Giddens, Anthony. 1991. *Modernity and Self-Identity: Self and Society in the Late Modern Age*. Stanford, CA: Stanford University Press.
Gillberg, C., and M. Råstam. 1998. "The Etiology of Anorexia Nervosa." In *Neurobiology in the Treatment of Eating Disorders*, ed. H. Hoek, J. Treasure, and M. Katzman, 127–141. West Sussex, UK: John Wiley and Sons.
Gillick, Muriel R. 1984. "Health Promotion, Jogging, and the Pursuit of the Moral Life." *Journal of Health Politics, Policy and Law* 9 (3): 369–387.
Gilligan, Carol. 1982. *In a Different Voice: Psychological Theory and Women's Development*. Cambridge, MA: Harvard University Press.
Giordano, Simona. 2005. *Understanding Eating Disorders: Conceptual and Ethical Issues in the Treatment of Anorexia and Bulimia Nervosa*. Oxford: Oxford University Press.
Girard, René. 1996. "Eating Disorders and Mimetic Desire." *Contagion: Journal of Violence, Mimesis, and Culture* 3: 1–20.
Glassner, Barry. 1990. "Fit for Postmodern Selfhood." In *Symbolic Interaction and Cultural Studies*, ed. Howard S. Becker and Michael M. McCall, 215–243. Chicago: University of Chicago Press.
Goffman, Erving. 1967. *Interaction Ritual: Essays on Face-to-Face Behavior*. Garden City, NY: Anchor Books.
Goldblatt, P. B., M. E. Moore, and A. J. Stunkard. 1965. "Social Factors in Obesity." *Journal of the American Medical Association* 192 (12): 1039–1042.

Goldschmidt, Walter. 2006. *The Bridge to Humanity: How Affect Hunger Trumps the Selfish Gene*. New York: Oxford University Press.
Good, Byron J. 2010. "Emil Kraepelin on Pathologies of the Will." In *Toward an Anthropology of the Will*, ed. Keith M. Murphy and C. Jason Throop, 158–175. Stanford, CA: Stanford University Press.
Goode, William J. 1978. *The Celebration of Heroes: Prestige as a Social Control System*. Berkeley: University of California Press.
Gooldin, Sigal. 2008. "Being Anorexic: Hunger, Subjectivity, and Embodied Morality." *Medical Anthropology Quarterly* 22 (3): 274–296.
Gowers, Simon G., Andrew Clark, Chris Roberts, Alison Griffiths, Vanessa Edwards, Claudine Bryan, Nicola Smethurst, Sarah Byford, and Barbara Barrett. 2007. "Clinical Effectiveness of Treatments for Anorexia Nervosa in Adolescents: Randomised Controlled Trial." *British Journal of Psychiatry* 191: 427–435.
Graber, Julia A., and Jeanne Brooks-Gunn. 1996. "Transitions and Turning Points: Navigating the Passage from Childhood through Adolescence." *Developmental Psychology* 32 (4): 768–776.
Granfield, Robert, and William Cloud. 1999. *Coming Clean: Overcoming Addiction without Treatment*. New York: New York University Press.
Green, Harvey. 1988. *Fit for America: Health, Fitness, Sport and American Society*. Baltimore, MD: Johns Hopkins University Press.
———. 1989. "Introduction." In *Fitness in American Culture: Images of Health, Sport, and the Body, 1830–1940*, ed. Kathryn Grover, 3–17. Amherst: University of Massachusetts Press.
Gremillion, Helen. 2003. *Feeding Anorexia: Gender and Power at a Treatment Center*. Durham, NC: Duke University Press.
Griffith, R. Marie. 2004. *Born Again Bodies: Flesh and Spirit in American Christianity*. Berkeley: University of California Press.
Habermas, Jürgen. 1975. *Legitimation Crisis*. Boston, MA: Beacon Press.
Hardman, O. 1924. *The Ideal of Asceticism: An Essay in the Comparative Study of Religion*. London: Society for Promoting Christian Knowledge.
Harpham, Geoffrey Galt. 1987. *The Ascetic Imperative in Culture and Criticism*. Chicago: University of Chicago Press.
Haworth-Hoeppner, Susan. 1999. "Medical Discourse on Body Image: Reconceptualizing the Differences between Women with and without Eating Disorders." In *Interpreting Weight: The Social Management of Fatness and Thinness*, ed. Jeffery Sobal and Donna Mauer, 89–111. New York: Aldine de Gruyter.
Hewitt, John P. 1989. *Dilemmas of the American Self*. Philadelphia: Temple University Press.
Higham, John. 1955. *Strangers in the Land: Patterns of American Nativism, 1860–1925*. New Brunswick, NJ: Rutgers University Press.
———. 2001. *Hanging Together: Unity and Diversity in American Culture*. Edited by Carl J. Guaraneri. New Haven, CT: Yale University Press.
Hinton, Alexander Laban. 1999. "Introduction: Developing a Biocultural Approach to the Emotions." In *Biocultural Approaches to the Emotions*, ed. A. L. Hinton, 1–37. New York: Cambridge University Press.
Hof, Sonja van't, and Malcolm Nicolson. 1996. "The Rise and Fall of a Fact: The Increase in Anorexia Nervosa." *Sociology of Health and Illness* 18 (5): 581–608.

Holland, Catherine A. 2001. *The Body Politic: Foundings, Citizenship, and Difference in the American Political Imagination.* New York: Routledge.
Holland, Dorothy C., and Margaret A. Eisenhart. 1990. *Educated in Romance: Women, Achievement, and College Culture.* Chicago: University of Chicago Press.
Hornbacher, Marya. 1999. *Wasted: A Memoir of Anorexia and Bulimia.* New York: HarperPerennial.
Howell, Signe. 1997. "Introduction." In *The Ethnography of Moralities*, ed. Signe Howell, 1–22. London: Routledge.
Hsu, L. K. George. 1996. "Epidemiology of the Eating Disorders." *The Psychiatric Clinics of North America* 19 (4): 681–700.
Hsu, L. K. George, and Theresa A. Sobkiewicz. 1991. "Body Image Disturbance: Time to Abandon the Concept for Eating Disorders?" *International Journal of Eating Disorders* 10 (1): 15–30.
Hunt, Alan. 1999. *Governing Morals: A Social History of Moral Regulation.* New York: Cambridge University Press.
Jackson, Michael. 1989. *Paths Towards a Clearing: Radical Empiricism and Ethnographic Inquiry.* Bloomington: Indiana University Press.
James, William. 2002. *Varieties of Religious Experience: A Study in Human Nature.* Centenary edition. London: Routledge.
Jenkins, Jana, and Jane Ogden. 2012. "Becoming 'Whole' Again: A Qualitative Study of Women's Views of Recovering From Anorexia Nervosa." *European Eating Disorders Review* 20: e23–e31.
Jordan, Jennifer, Peter R. Joyce, Frances A. Carter, Jacqueline Horn, Virginia V.W. McIntosh, Suzanne E. Luty, Janice M. McKenzie, Christopher M.A. Frampton, Roger T. Mulder, and Cynthia M. Bulik. 2008. "Specific and Nonspecific Comorbidity in Anorexia Nervosa." *International Journal of Eating Disorders* 41: 47–56.
Katzman, Melanie A., and Sing Lee. 1997. "Beyond Body Image: The Integration of Feminist and Transcultural Theories in the Understanding of Self Starvation." *International Journal of Eating Disorders* 22: 385–394.
Keel, Pamela K., Mark G. Baxter, Todd F. Heatherton, and Thomas E. Joiner, Jr. 2007. "A 20-Year Longitudinal Study of Body Weight, Dieting, and Eating Disorder Symptoms." *Journal of Abnormal Psychology* 116 (2): 422–432.
Kern, Stephen. 1983. *The Culture of Time and Space, 1880–1918.* Cambridge, MA: Harvard University Press.
Keyes, Katherine M., Bridget F. Grant, and Deborah S. Hasin. 2008. "Evidence for a Closing Gender Gap in Alcohol Use, Abuse, and Dependence in the United States Population." *Drug and Alcohol Dependence* 93: 21–29.
Keys, Ancel Benjamin, and the Laboratory of Physiological Hygiene, University of Minnesota. 1950. *The Biology of Human Starvation.* Minneapolis: University of Minnesota Press.
Khandelwal, S. K. Pratap Sharan, and Shekhar Saxena. 1995. "Eating Disorders: An Indian Perspective." *International Journal of Social Psychiatry* 41 (2): 132–146.
King, Barbara J., and Stuart G. Shanker. 2003. "How Can We Know the Dancer from the Dance? The Dynamic Nature of African Great Ape Social Communication." *Anthropological Theory* 3 (1): 5–26.

Kirmayer, Laurence J. 1992. "The Body's Insistence on Meaning: Metaphor as Presentation and Representation in Illness Experience." *Medical Anthropology Quarterly*, n.s., 6: 323–346.
Kleinman, Arthur. 1986. *Social Origins of Distress and Disease: Depression, Neurasthenia, and Pain in Modern China*. New Haven, CT: Yale University Press.
Lakoff, George, and Mark Johnson. 1999. *Philosophy in the Flesh: The Embodied Mind and its Challenge to Western Thought*. New York: Basic Books.
Lamont, Michèle. 1992. *Money, Morals, and Manners: The Culture of the French and American Upper-Middle Class*. Chicago: University of Chicago Press.
Lawrence, Marilyn. 1979. "Anorexia Nervosa: The Control Paradox." *Women's Studies International Quarterly* 2: 93–101.
Lears, T. J. Jackson. 1981. *No Place of Grace: Antimodernism and the Transformation of American Culture 1880–1920*. New York: Pantheon Books.
Lee, S., P. Ho, and L. K. G. Hsu. 1993. "Fat Phobic and Non-Fat Phobic Anorexia Nervosa: A Comparative Study of 70 Chinese Patients in Hong Kong." *Psychological Medicine* 23: 999–1017.
Lester, Rebecca J. 1995. "Embodied Voices: Women's Food Asceticism and the Negotiation of Identity." *Ethos* 23 (2): 187–222.
———. 1997. "The (Dis)embodied Self in Anorexia Nervosa." *Social Science and Medicine* 44 (4): 479–489.
———. 1999. "Let Go and Let God: Religion and the Politics of Surrender in Overeaters Anonymous." In *Interpreting Weight: The Social Management of Fatness and Thinness*, ed. Jeffery Sobal and Donna Maurere, 139–164. New York: Aldine de Gruyter.
———. 2001. "Like a Natural Woman: Celibacy and the Embodied Self in Anorexia Nervosa." In *Celibacy, Culture, and Society: The Anthropology of Sexual Abstinence*, ed. Elisa J. Sobo and Sandra Bell, 197–213. Madison: University of Wisconsin Press.
———. 2005. *Jesus in Our Wombs: Embodying Modernity in a Mexican Convent*. Berkeley: University of California Press.
———. 2007. "Critical Therapeutics: Cultural Politics and Clinical Reality in Two Eating Disorder Treatment Centers." *Medical Anthropology Quarterly* 21 (4): 369–387.
———. 2011. "How Do I Code for Black Fingernail Polish? Finding the Missing Adolescent in Managed Mental Health Care." *Ethos* 39 (4): 481–496.
Lévi-Strauss, Claude. 1966. *The Savage Mind*. Chicago: University of Chicago Press.
Lincoln, Bruce. 1986a. "Human Body: Myths and Symbolism." In *Encyclopedia of Religion*, ed. M. Eliade, vol. 6, 499–505. New York: Macmillan.
———. 1986b. *Myth, Cosmos, and Society: Indo-European Themes of Creation and Destruction*. Cambridge, MA: Harvard University Press.
Linde, Charlotte. 1993. *Life Stories: The Creation of Coherence*. New York: Oxford University Press.
Lindt, Gillian. 1995. "Asceticism in Sociological Perspective." In *Asceticism*, ed. Vincent L. Wimbush and Richard Valantasis, 593–596. New York: Oxford University Press.
Lock, Margaret. 1997. "Decentering the Natural Body: Making Difference Matter." *Configurations* 5 (2): 267–292.
———. 1998. "Menopause: Lessons from Anthropology." *Psychosomatic Medicine* 60: 410–419.

Lucas, A. R., C. M. Beard, W. M. O'Fallon, and L. T. Kurland. 1991. "50 Year Trends in the Incidence of Anorexia Nervosa in Rochester, Minn.: A Population-Based Study." *American Journal of Psychiatry* 148 (7): 917–922.

Luhrmann, T. M. 2000. *Of Two Minds: The Growing Disorder in American Psychiatry*. New York: Alfred A. Knopf.

Lupton, Deborah. 1996. *Food, the Body and the Self*. London: Sage.

Lyon, Margot L. 1999. "Emotion and Embodiment: The Respiratory Mediation of Somatic and Social Processes." In *Biocultural Approaches to the Emotions*, ed. A. L. Hinton, 182–212. New York: Cambridge University Press.

MacDonald, Maryann. 2000. "Bewildered, Blamed and Broken-Hearted: Parents' Views of Anorexia Nervosa." In *Anorexia Nervosa and Related Eating Disorders in Childhood and Adolescence*, ed. Bryan Lask and Rachel Bryant-Waugh, 11–24. 2nd edition. East Sussex, UK: Psychology Press.

Marmorstein, Arthur. 1968. *Essays in Anthropomorphism*. New York: Ktav Publishing.

Marrazzi, Mary Ann, and Elliott D. Luby. 1989. "Anorexia Nervosa as an Auto-Addiction: Clinical and Basic Studies." In *The Psychology of Human Eating Disorders*, ed. Linda H. Schneider, Steven J. Cooper and Katherine A. Halmi. *Annals of New York Academy of Science* 575: 545–547.

Martin, Emily. 1994. *Tracking Immunity in American Culture: From the Days of Polio to the Age of AIDS*. Boston, MA: Beacon Press.

Mattingly, Cheryl. 2010. "Moral Willing as Narrative Re-envisioning." In *Toward an Anthropology of the Will*, ed. Keith M. Murphy and C. Jason Throop, 50–68. Stanford, CA: Stanford University Press.

McDonald, Kevin. 1999. *Struggles for Subjectivity: Identity, Action and Youth Experience*. Cambridge: Cambridge University Press.

McNamara, Sarah. 2000. *Stress in Young People: What's New and What Can We Do*. New York: Continuum.

McRobbie, Angela. 1991. *Feminism and Youth Culture: From Jackie to Just Seventeen*. Cambridge: Unwin Hyman.

Mennell, Stephen, Anne Murcott, and Anneke H. van Otterloo. 1992. *The Sociology of Food: Eating, Diet, and Culture*. Newbury Park, CA: Sage.

Merchant, Carolyn. 1980. *The Death of Nature: Women, Ecology and the Scientific Revolution*. San Francisco: Harper and Row.

Merleau-Ponty, Maurice. 1964. "The Child's Relations with Others." Translated by William Cobb. In *The Primacy of Perception and Other Essays on Phenomenological Psychology, the Philosophy of Art, History and Politics*, ed. James M. Edie, 96–155. Evanston, IL: Northwestern University Press.

Meyer, Caroline, Lorin Taranis, Huw Goodwin, and Emma Haycraft. 2011. "Compulsive Exercise and Eating Disorders." *European Eating Disorders Review* 19: 174–189.

Miles, Margaret R. 1995. "Religion and Food: The Case of Eating Disorders." *Journal of the Academy Religion* 63 (3): 549–564.

Milos, Gabriella, Anja Spindler, Ulrich Schnyder, and Christopher G. Fairburn. 2005. "Instability of Eating Disorder Diagnoses: Prospective Study." *The British Journal of Psychiatry* 187: 573–578.

Mintz, Sidney. 1993. "The Changing Roles of Food in the Study of Consumption." In *Consumption and the World of Goods*, ed. John Brewer and Roy Porter, 261–273. London: Routledge.
Mitchell, Walter, and the Carisbrooke Dominicans. 1955. "Foreword." *Christian Asceticism and Modern Man*. London: Blackfriars.
Modell, Arnold H. 2003. *Imagination and the Meaningful Brain*. Cambridge, MA: MIT Press.
Mogul, S. Louis. 1980. "Asceticism in Adolescence and Anorexia Nervosa." *The Psychoanalytic Study of the Child* 35: 155–175.
Mol, Annemarie. 2002. *The Body Multiple: Ontology in Medical Practice*. Durham, NC: Duke University Press.
Morris, David B. 1998. *Illness and Culture in the Postmodern Age*. Berkeley: University of California Press.
Mrozek, Donald J. 1983. *Sport and American Mentality, 1880–1910*. Knoxville: University of Tennessee Press.
National Center for Health Statistics. 1997. *National Health Interview Survey*. http://www.cdc.gov/nchs/products/pubs/pubd/hestats/3and4/overweight.htm.
Neubauer, John. 1992. *The Fin-de-Siècle Culture of Adolescence*. New Haven, CT: Yale University Press.
Newton, Tim, Paul Robinson, and Patricia Hartley. 1993. "Treating for Eating Disorders in the United Kingdom, Part II: Experiences of Treatment: A Survey of Members of the Eating Disorders Association." *European Eating Disorders Review* 1 (1): 1–21.
Nichter, Mimi. 2000. *Fat Talk: What Girls and Their Parents Say about Dieting*. Cambridge, MA: Harvard University Press.
Nissenbaum, Stephen. 1980. *Sex, Diet, and Debility in Jacksonian America: Sylvester Graham and Health Reform*. Westport, CT: Greenwood Press.
Nordbø, Ragnfrid H. S., Ester M. S. Espeset, Kjersti S. Gulliksen, Finn Skårderud, Josie Geller, and Arne Holte. 2012. "Reluctance to Recover in Anorexia Nervosa." *European Eating Disorders Review* 20: 60–67.
Nye, Robert A. 2003. "The Evolution of the Concept of Medicalization in the Late Twentieth Century." *Journal of History of the Behavioral Sciences* 39 (2): 115–129.
O'Connor, Richard A. 2000. "Is Anorexia a Post-Modern Asceticism? Dialogue." *Anthropology News* (February): 7–8.
O'Connor, Richard A., and Penny Van Esterik. 2008. "De-medicalizing Anorexia: A New Cultural Brokering." *Anthropology Today* 24 (5): 6–9.
———. 2012. "Breastfeeding as Custom Not Culture: Cutting Meaning Down to Size." *Anthropology Today* 28 (5): 13–16, 24–25.
Offord, Abaigh, Hannah Turner, and Myra Cooper. 2006. "Adolescent Inpatient Treatment for Anorexia Nervosa: A Qualitative Study Exploring Young Adults' Retrospective Views of Treatment and Discharge." *European Eating Disorders Review* 14: 377–387.
O'Neill, John. 1985. *Five Bodies: The Human Shape of Modern Society*. Ithaca, NY: Cornell University Press.
Oxford English Dictionary. 1989. 2nd edition. New York: Oxford University Press.
Palmer, R. L. 1993. "Weight Concern Should Not be a Necessary Criterion for Eating Disorders: A Polemic." *International Journal of Eating Disorders* 14: 459–465.

———. 2006. "Come the Revolution: Revisiting the Management of Anorexia Nervosa." *Advances in Psychiatric Treatment* 12: 5–12.

Park, Roberta J. 1989. "Healthy, Moral, and Strong: Educational Views of Exercise and Athletics in Nineteenth-Century America." In *Fitness in American Culture: Images of Health, Sport, and the Body, 1830–1940*, ed. Kathryn Grover, 123–168. Amherst: University of Massachusetts Press.

Parks, Sharon. 2000. *Big Questions, Worthy Dreams: Mentoring Young Adults in their Search for Meaning, Purpose, and Faith*. San Francisco: Jossey-Bass.

Peters, Nonja. 1995. "The Ascetic Anorexic." *Social Analysis* 37: 44–66.

Pike, Kathleen, and Amy Borovoy. 2004. "The Role of Eating Disorders in Japan: Issues of Culture and Limitations of the Model of 'Westernization.'" *Culture, Medicine and Psychiatry* 28: 493–531.

Pope, S. W. 1997. "Introduction: American Sport History: Toward a New Paradigm." In *The New American Sport History: Recent Approaches and Perspectives*, ed. S. W. Pope, 1–30. Urbana: University of Illinois Press.

Rampling, David. 1985. "Ascetic Ideals and Anorexia Nervosa." *Journal of Psychiatric Research* 19 (2/3): 89–94.

Reynolds Lyon, Peter C. 1981. *On the Evolution of Human Behavior: The Argument from Animals to Man*. Berkeley: University of California Press.

Rich, Emma, Rachel Holroyd, and John Evans. 2004. "'Hungry To Be Noticed': Young Women, Anorexia and Schooling." In *Body Knowledge and Control: Studies in the Sociology of Physical Education and Health*, ed. John Evans, Brian Davies, and Jan Wright, 173–190. London: Routledge.

Rosenvinge, J. H., and Anna Kuhlefelt Klusmeier. 2000. "Treatment for Eating Disorders from a Patient Satisfaction Perspective: A Norwegian Replication of a British Study." *European Eating Disorders Review* 8: 293–300.

Rosling, Agneta M., Pår Sparén, Claes Norring, and Anne-Liis von Knorring. 2011. "Mortality of Eating Disorders: A Follow-up Study of Treatment in a Specialist Unit 1974–2000." *International Journal of Eating Disorders* 44 (4): 304–310.

Rubin, Julius H. 1994. *Religious Melancholy and Protestant Experience in America*. New York: Oxford University Press.

Russell, Gerald F. M. 1985. "The Changing Nature of Anorexia Nervosa: An Introduction to the Conference." *Journal of Psychiatric Research* 19 (2–3): 101–109.

Sahlins, Marshall. 1976. *Culture and Practical Reason*. Chicago: University of Chicago Press.

Scheper-Hughes, Nancy, and Margaret M. Lock. 1987. "The Mindful Body: A Prolegomenon to Future Work in Medical Anthropology." *Medical Anthropology Quarterly* 1: 6–41.

Schilder, Paul. 1935. *The Image and Appearance of the Human Body: Studies in the Constructive Energies of the Psyche*. London: K. Paul, Trench, Trubner.

Schlegel, Alice, and Herbert Barry III. 1991. *Adolescence: An Anthropological Inquiry*. New York: Free Press.

Schudson, Michael. 1984. "Women, Cigarettes and Advertising in the 1920s: A Study in the Sociology of Consumption." In *Mass Media between the Wars: Perceptions of Cultural Tension, 1918–1941*, ed. C. L. Covert and J. D. Stevens, 71–83. Syracuse, NY: Syracuse University Press.

Schwartz, Barry. 2004. "The Tyranny of Choice." *Chronicle of Higher Education*, January 23, B6–B8.
Schwartz, Hillel. 1986. *Never Satisfied: A Cultural History of Diets, Fantasies and Fat*. New York: Free Press.
Sennett, Richard. 1977. *The Fall of Public Man*. New York: Alfred A. Knopf.
Shohet, Merav. 2007. "Narrating Anorexia: 'Full' and 'Struggling' Genres of Recovery." *Ethos* 35 (3): 344–382.
Spence, Donald. 1982. *Narrative Truth as Historical Truth*. New York: Norton.
Stearns, Peter N. 1997. *Fat History: Bodies and Beauty in the Modern West*. New York: New York University Press.
———. 1999. *Battleground of Desire: The Struggle for Self-control in Modern America*. New York: New York University Press.
Stinson, Kandi. 2001. *Women and Dieting Culture: Inside a Commercial Weight Loss Group*. New Brunswick, NJ: Rutgers University Press.
Sznaider, Natan. 2001. *The Compassionate Temperament: Care and Cruelty in Modern Society*. Lanham, MD: Rowman and Littlefield.
Szymanski, Albert. 1983. *Class Structure: A Critical Perspective*. New York: Praeger.
Szymanski, Lynda A., and Richard J. Seime. 1997. "A Re-examination of Body Image Distortion: Evidence against a Sensory Explanation." *International Journal of Eating Disorders* 21: 175–180.
Taylor, Charles. 1989. *Sources of the Self: The Making of the Modern Identity*. Cambridge, MA: Harvard University Press.
Throop, C. Jason. 2010. "In the Midst of Action." In *Toward an Anthropology of the Will*, ed. Keith M. Murphy and C. Jason Throop, 28–49. Stanford, CA: Stanford University Press.
Tilley, Christopher. 1999. *Metaphor and Material Culture*. Oxford: Blackwell.
Tocqueville, Alexis de. 1945. *Democracy in America*. New York: Vintage Books.
Toyokawa, Satoshi, Monica Uddin, Karestan C. Koenen, and Sandro Galea. 2012. "How Does the Social Environment 'Get into the Mind'? Epigenetics at the Intersection of Social and Psychiatric Epidemiology." *Social Science and Medicine* 74: 67–74.
Valantasis, Richard. 1995. "A Theory of the Social Function of Asceticism." In *Asceticism*, ed. Vincent L. Wimbush and Richard Valantasis, 544–552. New York: Oxford University Press.
Valsiner, Jaan. 1997. "Foreword: Interpretive Adventures in the World of the Adolescent." In *The Culture of Adolescent Risk-Taking*, ed. Cynthia Lightfoot, xi–xvi. New York: Guilford Press.
Vandereycken, Walter. 2011. "Can Eating Disorders Become 'Contagious' in Group Therapy and Specialized Inpatient Care?" *European Eating Disorders Review* 19: 289–295.
Vanderlinden, Johan. 2010. "Do Different Psychopathological Pathways into Eating Disorder Necessitate Different Therapeutic Goals and/or Approaches?" *European Eating Disorders Review* 18: 161–164.
Vander Ven, Thomas, and Mrikay Vander Ven. 2003. "Exploring Patterns of Mother-Blaming in Anorexia Scholarship: A Study in the Sociology of Knowledge." *Human Studies* 26: 97–119.
Van Ness, Peter H. 1995. "Asceticism in Philosophical and Cultural-Critical Perspective." In *Asceticism*, ed. Vincent L. Wimbush and Richard Valantasis, 589–593. New York: Oxford University Press.

Vogüé, Adalbert de. 1989. *To Love Fasting: The Monastic Experience.* Petersham, MA: Saint Bede's Publications.

Wagner, David. 1997. *The New Temperance: The American Obsession with Sin and Vice.* Boulder, CO: Westview.

Waller, Glenn. 2012. "The Myths of Motivation: Time for a Fresh Look at Some Received Wisdom in the Eating Disorders?" *International Journal of Eating Disorders* 45 (1): 1–16.

Ward, Carol. 2003. "The Evolution of Human Origins." *American Anthropologist* 105 (1): 77–88.

Warin, Megan. 2003a. "Be-coming Clean: The Logic of Hygiene in Anorexia." *Sites: Journal of Social Anthropology and Cultural Studies*, n.s., 1 (1): 109–132.

———. 2003b. "Miasmatic Calories and Saturating Fats: Fear of Contamination in Anorexia." *Culture, Medicine and Psychiatry* 27: 77–93.

———. 2005. "Transformations of Intimacy and Sociality in Anorexia: Bedrooms in Public Institutions." *Body and Society* 11 (3): 97–113.

———. 2006. "Reconfiguring Relatedness in Anorexia." *Anthropology and Medicine* 13 (1): 41–54.

———. 2010. *Abject Relations: Everyday Worlds of Anorexia.* New Brunswick, NJ: Rutgers University Press.

Wax, Murray L., and Joan Cassell. 1990. "The Looking Glass Self: Introductory Notes on Anorexia Nervosa." *Mid-American Review of Sociology* 14 (1–2): 135–143.

Way, Karen. 1995. "Never Too Rich . . . Or Too Thin: The Role of Stigma in the Social Construction of Anorexia Nervosa." In *Eating Agendas: Food and Nutrition as Social Problems*, ed. Donna Maurer and Jeffery Sobal, 91–113. Hawthorne, NY: Aldine de Gruyter.

Weber, Max. 1958. *The Protestant Ethic and the Spirit of Capitalism.* New York: Charles Scribner's Sons.

———. 1964. The Sociology of Religion. Translated by Ephraim Fischoff. Boston, MA: Beacon Press.

Webster, J. J., and R. L. Palmer. 2000. "The Childhood and Family Background of Women with Clinical Eating Disorders: A Comparison with Women with Major Depression and Women without Psychiatric Disorder." *Psychological Medicine* 30: 53–60.

Whitney, Jenna, Joanna Murray, Kay Gavan, Gill Todd, Wendy Whitaker, and Janet Treasure. 2005. "Experience of Caring for Someone with Anorexia Nervosa: Qualitative Study." *British Journal of Psychiatry* 187: 444–449.

Whorton, James C. 1982. *Crusaders for Fitness: The History of American Health Reformers.* Princeton, NJ: Princeton University Press.

———. 1989. "Eating to Win: Popular Concepts of Diet, Strength, and Energy in the Early Twentieth Century." In *Fitness in American Culture: Images of Health, Sport, and the Body, 1830–1940*, ed. Kathryn Grover, 86–122. Amherst: University of Massachusetts Press.

Wikan, Unni. 2000. "With Life in One's Lap: The Story of an Eye/I (or Two)." In *Narrative and the Cultural Construction of Illness and Healing*, ed. Cheryl Mattingly and Linda C. Garro, 212–236. Berkeley: University of California Press.

Wildes, Jennifer E., Rebecca M. Ringham, and Marsha D. Marcus. 2010. "Emotion Avoidance in Patients with Anorexia Nervosa: Initial Test of a Functional Model." *International Journal of Eating Disorders* 43: 398–404.

Wilson, G. Terence, Carlos M. Grilo, and Kelly M. Vitousek. 2007. "Psychological Treatment of Eating Disorders." *American Psychologist* 62 (3): 199–216.

Wimbush, Vincent L., and Richard Valantasis. 1995. "Introduction." In *Asceticism*, ed. Vincent L. Wimbush and Richard Valantasis, xix–xxxiii. New York: Oxford University Press.

Winkler, Mary G. 1994. "Afterword." In *The Good Body: Asceticism in Contemporary Culture*, ed. Mary G. Winkler and Letha B. Cole, 232–238. New Haven, CT: Yale University Press.

Wittgenstein, Ludwig. 1953. *Philosophical Investigations*. Oxford: Blackwell.

Wolfe, Alan. 2003. *The Transformation of American Religion: How We Actually Live Our Faith*. New York: Free Press.

Wonderlich, Stephen A., Lisa R. Lilenfeld, Lawrence P. Riso, Scott Engel, and James E. Mitchell. 2005. "Personality and Anorexia Nervosa." *International Journal of Eating Disorders* 37: S68–S71.

Woodside, D. Blake, Paul E. Garfinkel, Elizabeth Lin, Paula Goering, Allan S. Kaplan, David S. Goldbloom, and Sidney H. Kennedy. 2001. "Comparisons of Men with Full or Partial Eating Disorders, Men Without Eating Disorders, and Women With Eating Disorders in the Community." *American Journal of Psychiatry* 158 (4): 570–574.

Woodside, D. Blake, David M. Garner, Wendi Rockert, and Paul E. Garfinkel. 1990. "Eating Disorders in Males: Insights from a Clinical and Psychometric Comparison with Female Patients." In *Males with Eating Disorders*, ed. Arnold E. Andersen, 100–115. New York: Brunner/Mazel.

Worthman, Carol M. 1993. "Biocultural Interactions in Human Development." In *Juvenile Primates: Life History, Development, and Behavior*, ed. Michael E. Pereira and Lynn A. Fairbanks, 339–358. New York: Oxford University Press.

———. 1999. "Emotions: You Can Feel the Difference." In *Biocultural Approaches to the Emotions*, ed. A. L. Hinton, 41–74. New York: Cambridge University Press.

Zihlman, Adrienne L., and Debra R. Bolter. 2004. "Mammalian and Primate Roots of Human Sociality." In *The Origins and Nature of Sociality*, ed. R. W. Sussman and A. R. Chapman, 23–52. New York: Aldine De Gruyter.

Index

Each interviewee has an entry below by pseudonym. Their stories and statements are located in the text but not indexed individually by content.

accident. *See* explaining anorexia
achieving. *See* explaining anorexia
activity disorder, 7, 11, 15, 32, 106, 187
activity in anorexia, 1, 3, 4, 7, 9–12, 15, 21, 25, 29–33, 35–37, 60–61, 77, 87n4, 88–110, 112–17, 134, 136, 168, 174–75, 186–87, 191, 199–200, 206, 208–9, 211, 214, 216
addictive behavior, 18, 28n9, 84, 105
adolescence, 4, 7, 8, 11–12, 19–20, 22–24, 26, 32, 34–36, 51, 64, 67, 84–86, 107, 117, 119–52, 155, 158, 180, 190, 193, 204n, 210–11, 213
 and risk-taking, 125, 131, 216
 and romanticism, 125, 133n
 See also coming of age; identity; life cycle
Amorn, 20–22, 83, 91–92, 94, 96–102, 104–5, 108–9, 116, 125, 147–48, 196, 202–3
 story of, 19–20
 See also interviewees
anorexic viewpoint, 18, 27, 37, 136, 142, 177, 189, 204. *See also* experiencing anorexia; story as unit of analysis
anthropology, 10, 52
 advantages of, 4–5
 approach of, 23, 25, 27n2, 32, 35, 57–58, 113
 inadequacies of, 1, 4
 See also ethnography; holism

appearance, 11, 33, 70, 112, 152, 157, 173, 176–86
 adolescent, 180–81
 eating disorders and, 55, 176, 185
 modernity and, 33, 176, 181, 184
 See also explaining anorexia
Aristotelian empiricism, 3, 112
ascetic disposition, 72–74, 86, 168, 211
asceticism, 4, 6–7, 11, 12n3, 14, 26, 61–62, 72–74, 90, 108, 109n4, 139, 178–80, 186, 216
 as coping with life, 64, 92, 113, 115, 135, 146–47, 149, 168
 as exploring the self, 51, 116, 149
 modern, 30–36, 134, 155, 162, 166n4
 monastic, 24–25, 28n10, 149–51
 as remaking the person, 116–17
 See also explaining anorexia
athletics, 8–9, 11, 24, 33, 41, 43, 48–51, 60–61, 69, 71–73, 75, 77–78, 86, 104, 126, 130–31, 140, 163, 165, 179–80, 183, 209–10. *See also* explaining anorexia

balance. *See* staying healthy after anorexia
Bateson, Gregory, 2, 9–10, 56, 211–13
beauty, 22, 27n5, 33, 36–37, 37n2, 39, 52, 55, 70, 80, 176–80, 182–83, 185–86. *See also* appearance; gender
Becca, 1, 9, 62, 70–72, 77, 79, 84, 96–97, 139, 180, 195, 200–201

story of, 67–69
See also interviewees
Becker, Marshall, 160
Beth, 79, 84, 92, 94–95, 101–5, 179, 195, 201–2, 211
story of, 70–71
See also interviewees
bioculturalism, 5–6, 10–12, 15, 21, 36, 52, 54–66, 108, 169, 190, 204, 210–12, 214–15
hybrid, 3, 7, 33, 57, 60–61, 86, 215
ontogeny, 57–58, 65 (*see also* constitution)
ontology, 58–60, 65
phylogeny, 56–57, 65, 132
biomedicine. *See* medicine
body, 1, 2, 7, 11, 19–21, 24–25, 31, 33–34, 39, 44–46, 51–52, 54–56, 58–61, 65, 68, 71–73, 75–77, 79, 81, 89–91, 98, 100, 102–3, 106, 115, 117, 130, 132, 134, 139, 145, 149, 155–56, 160, 163–65, 167–75, 203, 208, 213
identity and, 79, 116, 135, 173, 185–86
image, 17, 22, 28n5, 31–32, 55, 97–98, 113, 136, 176–86 (*see also* gender)
as metaphor, 34, 62–63, 116, 152, 157, 162–64, 167, 170–75
Bordo, Susan, 20, 83
Bourdieu, Pierre, 11, 36
breastfeeding, 11–12
Bruch, Hilde, 17, 26, 28n5, 37n1, 40, 67, 71, 74, 77, 113, 121, 177–78, 217n
Brumberg, Joan Jacobs, 173
bulimia, 27n3, 32, 42, 45–46, 78, 132, 138, 141, 151, 176, 185–86, 199, 212

Cartesian dualism, 3, 9, 75, 167, 170–72, 174, 175n, 212
inadequacies of, 9, 55–56, 64, 169, 173–74
reworking, 54–56
Claude-Pierre, Peggy, 102, 175
clinical inference, 25–26, 111–12, 114
clinic as ideal type, 3–5, 25–26. *See also* lab as ideal type
coming of age, 112, 119, 123, 134–52, 170, 191, 193, 204, 216

rite of passage, 119, 123, 134, 146, 148, 151, 198–200, 212
See also adolescence; identity
comorbidities, 30, 32, 115. *See also* diagnostic criteria
competition. *See* explaining anorexia
consolidation, 22, 90, 101–3, 106, 116, 178
disgust, 64, 89, 94, 100–103, 179
pattern pleasure, 103, 109n4
process pleasure, 102–3, 109n4
taste change, 22, 101, 103
See also features of anorexia
constitution, 3, 7, 21, 23, 26, 50, 58–59, 61, 67–87, 108, 168, 175, 187, 190, 195, 210–11, 214, 216
contextualizing anorexia, 4–5, 11, 17, 20, 27, 27n2, 29–33, 35, 37, 112–14, 117, 185, 187
control, 2–3, 7–8, 11–12, 19–26, 32–36, 39, 44–47, 55, 62–64, 71–72, 79–83, 89, 91–93, 99–100, 104–5, 115, 117, 122, 126, 131–32, 136, 147–52, 156, 158–60, 163–64, 166n4, 167–75, 185–86, 190, 203–4, 211–12, 216
anorexia-created controlling, 83–84
control-created anorexia, 84–86
Csikszentmihalyi, Mihaly and Reed Larson, 121
Csordas, Thomas, 11, 205
culture and anorexia, 1, 4–6, 8, 10–11, 13n5, 18, 21–23, 26, 33, 35–37, 54–56, 60, 63, 76–77, 106–7, 113–14, 116, 125, 132, 152–186, 198–99. *See also* bioculturalism; explaining anorexia
curing. *See* recovery; treatment

deception. *See* features of anorexia
Descartes. *See* Cartesian Dualism
development. *See* bioculturalism; constitution; mis-development
developmental disorder. *See* mis-development
diagnostic criteria, 31, 101
comorbidities, 30, 32, 115
inadequacies of, 1, 31
dieting, 4, 7–8, 10–11, 15, 18, 22, 25, 37, 60–61, 85, 99, 137–39, 152, 157–58,

164, 166n2, 185–86, 190. *See also* gateways to anorexia; healthy eating; restricted eating
discipline. *See* features of anorexia
disposition. *See* ascetic disposition; constitution; performative disposition; virtuous disposition
distorting anorexia, 3–5, 22, 27n2, 30–31. *See also* Cartesian dualism
diversity in anorexia, 9–10, 12, 23, 26–27, 28n6, 31, 36, 40–52, 74, 87n1, 92, 99, 105–6, 108, 114, 117, 191, 204, 214
dualism. *See* Cartesian dualism

eating. *See* healthy eating; morality: eating and; restricted eating; virtuous eating
Eckert, Penelope, 128
ecology of mind. *See* Bateson, Gregory; staying healthy after anorexia
elementary anorexia, 110–18, 216
Elizabeth, 50–52, 64, 77, 139, 146–47, 168, 194, 198–200
  story of, 49–50
  See also interviewees
emergence, 5–7, 11, 12n2, 52, 56, 65
  and anorexia, 6–7, 9, 64, 106, 115, 214
  See also holism
environmental curing, 189, 198–200. *See also* recovery
epigenetics, 21, 58, 61, 64–65, 66n1. *See also* constitution
Erikson, Erik H., 7, 26, 135
ethnography, 90, 105
  and explaining anorexia, 10, 106–7, 108n1, 110–15, 118
exercise disorder, 32–33, 186, 210
exhilaration. *See* features of anorexia
experiencing anorexia, 3, 10–11, 12n3, 18, 22–23, 28n9, 31, 36, 40, 51, 58–59, 62, 90–105, 107, 116, 118, 147, 167–68, 171, 175, 178–79, 186, 191–92, 204–5, 211
explaining anorexia,
  as accidental, 1–2, 11, 39, 60, 64–65, 113–15, 117–18, 125, 213, 216
  as achieving, 42, 70–71, 106, 114, 122, 126, 131–32, 135–36, 139, 141–42,

145–46, 165, 166n4, 175, 190, 193, 202, 204, 206, 210–11, 216
  as an activity (*see* activity in anorexia)
  as bootstrapping, 12, 63, 116, 210
  by competition, 11, 28n10, 43, 74, 100, 109n5, 131, 137–38, 145–46, 212
  empirically, 3, 10, 71, 74, 86, 90, 105, 111–12, 114, 213
  endogenously, 114
  exogenously, 114
  historically, 32, 56, 60, 65, 67, 211, 213–14
  by ritual, 26, 64, 83–84, 95, 97, 99, 116, 146, 148–49, 170
  See also asceticism; athletics; bioculturalism; culture and anorexia

fathers of anorexics. *See* parents of anorexics
features of anorexia, 22, 90–107, 175, 179–81
  cross-culturally, 106
  deception, 22, 40, 45, 103–4, 106–7
  defined, 90
  discipline, 22, 92–94, 101, 105–6, 116, 175
  disgust (*see* consolidation)
  exhilaration, 22, 25–26, 51, 90–92, 105, 107, 111, 116, 175
  feedback, 22, 90, 97–99, 106, 108, 116
  goading, 90, 99–101, 108, 116, 179
  isolation, 90, 94–97, 107, 109n3, 113, 175
  parsing, 105–7
  pleasure (*see* consolidation)
  surrender, 22, 104–5
  taste change (*see* consolidation)
  See also appearance; consolidation; experiencing anorexia; mirror gazing
feedback. *See* features of anorexia
fitness. *See* health and fitness movements
Foucault, Michel, 35
frames for knowing, 17, 20–27, 28n6, 30, 33, 111, 115, 181. *See also* asceticism; clinical inference; story as unit of analysis
Francesca, 18, 28n7, 52, 64, 72–73, 75, 77, 91, 93–96, 98–99, 102–3, 105, 109n6, 116, 125, 134, 137, 142, 147, 193, 201, 204, 207–9, 211

story of, 47–48
  See also interviewees
Frank, Arthur W., 75
Fred, 74, 90–91, 95, 98, 100–101, 116, 131, 146, 179, 181
  story of, 129–30
  See also interviewees

Garrett, Catherine, 25, 177, 212–13
gateways to anorexia, 49, 145–46, 153, 213
  logic of, 61
  metaphors of, 60–61
  practices of, 9, 60, 165, 210
Geertz, Clifford, 25
gender, 9, 21, 27n5, 33, 46–47, 55, 64, 75, 106, 110, 127–28, 139, 158, 163–65, 170, 173, 179, 182–83, 185–86, 204–5, 211. *See also* male anorexia
Giordano, Simona, 8
goading. *See* features of anorexia
Goffman, Erving, 118n
Goldschmidt, Walter, 10
Gooldin, Sigal, 92
Graham, Sylvester, 162
Griffith, R. Marie, 166n2

health and fitness movements, 155, 162, 165, 166n4, 172–74. *See also* healthy eating; modernity; morality: eating and; vigorous living; virtuous eating
healthy eating, 7, 9, 11–12, 15, 22–23, 55, 60–61, 64, 67–69, 71, 78, 131, 155–57, 165, 211. *See also* morality: eating and; restricted eating; virtuous eating
hermeneutics, 10–11, 12n2
historical explanation, 10–11, 56, 65, 161, 170–71, 211, 214
holism, 4–5, 9–11, 12n2, 17, 20, 27, 29, 56, 160, 173, 204, 212. *See also* emergence

identity, 7–8, 13n4, 19–23, 35–36, 41, 47, 51, 61, 64, 68–69, 79, 118, 123, 125–29, 131–32, 135–37, 142–45, 161, 173, 176, 180, 184–86, 190, 192–93, 203
immigrant threat, 164–65

intervention curing, 200–203. *See also* recovery
interviewees, 4, 6, 8, 10, 17–18, 22, 24, 26, 27n3, 29–30, 33, 38–40, 51–52, 60, 71–72, 74, 86n1, 108n1, 131, 146, 205.
  See also individual names
interviewing, 1, 4–5, 17–18, 20, 27, 27n2, 90, 147
Isabel, 62, 89–90, 94, 100–102, 104, 180–81, 199–200
  story of, 88–89
  See also interviewees
isolating anorexia, 4–5. *See also* Platonism; reductionism
isolation. *See* features of anorexia

Jane, 72, 95, 99, 101, 139, 191, 193, 207
  story of, 137–39
  See also interviewees
Janet, 97, 100, 103–4, 141–42, 179, 180, 193, 207–8
  story of, 140–41
  See also interviewees
Jesse, 73, 86, 95, 97, 100, 180, 191, 195–96, 201, 207–8
  story of, 84–86
  See also interviewees
Jill, 157, 167–68, 179, 196, 212
  story of, 149–51
  See also interviewees
Jim, 40, 49–50, 52, 73, 77, 93, 96–98, 100, 102, 104, 151, 179, 192, 195, 204
  story of, 48–49
  See also interviewees

lab as ideal type, 4–5, 26. *See also* clinic as ideal type
Larson, Reed and Mihaly Csikszentmihalyi, 121
Lester, Rebecca J., 35, 106–7, 117
Lévi-Strauss, Claude, 10
life cycle, 5, 12, 20–21, 119, 123–24, 127–28
lifeworld, 21
Lindsay, 73–74, 83, 86, 92, 94, 96, 103, 105, 131, 137, 139, 156, 179, 192–95, 207–9

story of, 79–82
See also interviewees
Lynn, 43, 48, 51–52, 71–72, 74, 77, 91–93, 95, 99–100, 102–3, 124–25, 181, 183, 193, 202
story of, 41–43
See also interviewees

male anorexia, 9, 27n5, 30, 33, 37n2, 111, 177. *See also* gender
Mary, 98, 101, 168–69, 175, 209, 211
story of, 144–45
See also interviewees
Mattingly, Cheryl, 13n4
medicalization, 10, 193, 215. *See also* normalizing anorexia
medicine, 3, 5, 31–32, 39, 51, 65, 117–18, 190, 215–16
approach of, 2–4, 9, 12, 15, 25–26, 29, 37, 55, 118n, 214
inadequacies of, 1–3, 17, 20, 26, 37, 215
Megan, 39–40, 43, 49–50, 52, 71–72, 74, 77, 91–93, 97–98, 134, 145, 148, 156, 158, 180–81, 193, 199–200, 204, 207–9, 212
story of, 41
See also interviewees
Melissa, 51, 75, 91–92, 98–100, 102, 104, 117, 124, 137, 144–45, 156, 179–80, 192, 207
story of, 142–44
See also interviewees
Merleau-Ponty, Maurice, 11
metaphor, 20, 59–60, 79–82, 151, 168, 170–72, 175, 215
as gateway, 60–61
implication of, 35, 61–63, 92, 152, 167–68, 172, 175, 175n
as sensibility, 34–35, 92, 168 (*see also* oneness: person/world)
Mintz, Sidney, 161
mirror gazing, 179–80. *See also* features of anorexia
mis-development, 7–9, 11–12, 18, 36–37, 61–65, 119, 214–16

misdirected development. *See* mis-development
modernity, 7–9, 12, 26, 30–35, 54, 60–61, 110, 123–24, 131, 137, 146, 165, 170–72, 175, 175n, 190, 212–13
control and, 34–36, 124, 126, 131, 152, 169–70
cultural crisis of, 122, 155, 161–64, 176, 184
fragmenting and, 29, 37, 55, 131
as an imperative, 125, 169–70
progressive middle class and, 33–34, 155, 161–62
Mogul, S. Louis, 4, 25, 135, 139
Molly, 52, 64, 73–74, 77, 92, 94, 99, 101–2, 104, 117, 179, 193, 195–96, 202, 206, 210
story of, 43–44
See also interviewees
monasticism. *See* asceticism
moral impetus, 3, 7, 10–11, 21, 25, 139–40. *See also* religious impetus
morality, 57, 65, 84, 117, 127, 131–32, 139, 146, 179
eating and, 4, 7–8, 10, 25, 63, 69, 93–94, 155–66, 186 (*see also* virtuous eating)
identity and, 8, 13n4, 23, 35, 131, 152, 161, 173–74
social class and, 8, 163–64, 166n3
status and, 35, 157, 159, 161, 173–74
mothers of anorexics. *See* parents of anorexics
motives for anorexia, 9, 12, 21–23, 37n2, 39–40, 43–52, 53n2, 77, 80, 107, 114, 116, 124, 142, 191–92, 204. *See also* moral impetus; religious impetus; types of anorexia

Natalie, 51, 74, 77, 79, 81, 83–84, 86, 90–91, 97–98, 100–101, 116, 137, 156, 191–92, 198–200
story of, 75–76
See also interviewees
negative mind, 102, 196, 210
negotiating, 10–12, 59
disciplines, 2–3

epistemology, 2, 9–10
recovery, 189, 214–16
redevelopment, 214–15
new middle class. *See* progressive middle class
normalizing anorexia, 216–17

oneness, 51, 58
  language of, 170–71
  mind/body, 3, 10, 55–56
  person/world, 34–35, 62, 167, 169, 171–75
ontogeny. *See* bioculturalism
ontological origin of anorexia, 60–61
ontology. *See* bioculturalism
overachieving. *See* explaining anorexia as achieving

parents of anorexics, 1, 40, 43–47, 49, 67–73, 81, 84–85, 88, 98, 104, 113, 127, 137–40, 142, 144–45, 147–48, 150–51, 155, 180, 195–96, 200–203, 208
  father, 9, 43–44, 47–49, 70, 73, 76, 78–79, 84, 129, 131, 137, 139–40, 143, 145, 147, 149–50, 156, 181, 196, 200–201
  mother, 9, 27n3, 41–45, 47–50, 58, 67–70, 73–74, 76–78, 81–82, 84–85, 88, 92–93, 96, 104, 113, 129, 137–45, 147, 149–50, 156, 181, 193–98, 200–204
performative disposition, 71–72, 74, 86, 168, 211
Peters, Nonja, 115, 204
phenomenology, 11, 107
phylogeny. *See* bioculturalism
Platonism, 3, 26, 54, 112, 118n. *See also* explaining anorexia
postmodernity, 123, 126–27, 131
  and eating disorders, 132, 185–86
progressive middle class, 33, 155, 159, 161, 164, 166n3. *See also* modernity: cultural crisis of

recovery, 6, 18, 36, 40, 47, 51–52, 60, 75, 135, 148, 153, 165, 187, 189–217
  bootstrapping, 195–97, 210

divided self in, 100, 195–96
environmental, 189, 198–200
heroic, 194–97
intervention, 2, 6–7, 40, 51, 90, 106, 187, 193, 200–203, 215 (*see also* negotiating)
See also treatment
reductionism, 3–4, 6, 20, 29, 112
relationship, anorexia as a, 1, 10
religious impetus, 10, 24–25, 28n8, 91, 107, 125, 146–51, 157–58, 160. *See also* moral impetus
resistance to treatment. *See* treatment
restricted eating, 5, 8, 12, 19, 32, 39, 62, 79–80, 86, 115, 159, 161, 167, 193, 198, 211. *See also* dieting; healthy eating; morality: eating and; virtuous eating
ritual explains anorexia. *See* explaining anorexia
romanticism. *See* adolescence
Rubin, Julius H., 162
Russell, Gerald F. M., 178

sample, 8, 26, 29–30, 32, 35, 51, 71–72, 105–6, 114, 117, 137, 178, 185, 190, 209, 212–13. *See also* interviewees
Sarah, 28n7, 48, 53n1, 75, 77, 92, 95–99, 102–4, 147, 168–69, 179, 194–95, 204, 206–8, 210
  story of, 46–47
  See also interviewees
Schwartz, Hillel, 163
second wind. *See* treatment
self-disgust. *See* negative mind
Sheena, 74, 79, 84, 99, 156, 180–81, 192, 199–200, 209
  story of, 78–79
  See also interviewees
social class. *See* morality; progressive middle class; WASP eating
somatic expressiveness, 75–79, 86, 87n5
spirituality. *See* staying healthy after anorexia
stand-alone facts, 4, 22, 28n6
starving research, 25, 95, 114–15
status. *See* body; eating; modernity; morality
staying healthy after anorexia, 205–13
  evaluating strategies of, 209–10

theorizing wellness, 211–13
Stearns, Peter N., 163–64
story as unit of analysis, 17–18, 20, 22–24, 27, 38–53, 112
  absence of, 38, 75, 107, 205
  ending of, 40
  middle of, 39–40
  See also frames for knowing
surrender. *See* features of anorexia
Susanna, 45–46, 48, 51–52, 71–73, 75, 77, 83, 90, 97, 101–2, 105, 117, 125, 148–49, 157, 191, 195, 199–200, 204
  story of, 44–45
  See also interviewees
sympathy, 11, 33, 37n3, 57–58, 63, 139, 167, 170–72, 175, 212
  implication of, 34, 64, 77–79, 81, 86, 151, 211
  sympathetic attitude, 7, 34–35, 75, 77, 81–83, 86, 87n1, 87n6, 195, 211
  See also morality

Taylor, Charles, 124
technologies of self, 10, 35
therapy. *See* treatment
Throop, C. Jason, 51, 107–8, 109n5
Tocqueville, Alexis de, 123, 170
trauma, absence of, 1, 9, 22, 50, 110, 215
treatment, 2, 29–30, 32, 48, 107, 118, 118n, 189–93, 200–204, 206, 215
  none proven, 189, 214
  resistance to, 111, 193–94, 200–204, 214–15
  second wind in, 115–17
  See also recovery

types of anorexia
  defensive and expressive, 8, 34, 60
  dropping out, 46–48, 51, 53n2, 77, 204
  fitting in, 43–46, 51, 53n2, 77, 114, 142, 204
  incidental and incited, 26, 40
  slipping in, 48–51, 77, 204
  standing out, 40–43, 51, 77, 204
  See also elementary anorexia; motives

unexplained anorexia, 24, 54, 216. *See also* explaining anorexia

Vanderlinden, Johan, 191, 203
vigorous living, 162–63. *See also* modernity: cultural crisis of
virtuous disposition, 74, 86, 168, 211
virtuous eating, 5, 8, 24, 33, 64, 113, 132, 155–66, 170, 175–76, 185. *See also* healthy eating; morality: eating and
virtuous living, 23, 25, 156–65

Warin, Megan, 90, 105–6, 108n1, 109n5
WASP eating, 158, 165, 166n2. *See also* modernity; morality
Weber, Max, 108
wellness. *See* staying healthy after anorexia
will, 2, 6–8, 13n4, 21, 24, 31, 35, 43, 51–52, 55, 62–63, 72, 80, 83, 89, 92, 103, 107–8, 109n6, 116–17, 124–25, 132, 134–35, 138, 145, 159–60, 163–64, 171–72, 175, 201, 203–6, 212

youth. *See* adolescence